FOSSILS

The Oldest Treasures
That Ever Lived

Rudolf Daber

FOSSILS
The Oldest Treasures That Ever Lived

Jochen Helms

Translated from the German by C. S. V. Salt
Revised by Joan Watson

Endpapers:
Medullopitys sclerotica, Namibia, Permian,
radial long section in polarized light.
Magnification: 150×

Page 2:
Illustrations from the book *Petrefactenkunde*
by E. F. von Schlotheim (1820–1823).
The original fossils (types) belonging to the
drawings top middle, left middle and bottom
left are represented firstly as photographs
(see pp. 63, 44, 57).

English Edition © 1985 T.F.H. Publications, Inc., Ltd.

ISBN 0-86622-047-X

© *1983 by Edition Leipzig*
Drawings: Eugenie Tanger, Berlin
Design: Helmut Selle, Leipzig
Manufactured in the German Democratic Republic

Distributed in the UNITED STATES by T.F.H. Publications, Inc., 211 West
Sylvania Avenue, Neptune City, NJ 07753; in CANADA by H & L Pet Supplies
Inc., 27 Kingston Crescent, Kitchener, Ontario N2B 2T6; Rolf C. Hagen Ltd.,
3225 Sartelon Street, Montreal 382 Quebec; in ENGLAND by T.F.H. Publica-
tions Limited, 4 Kier Park, Ascot, Berkshire SL5 7DS; in AUSTRALIA AND
THE SOUTH PACIFIC by T.F.H. (Australia) Pty. Ltd., Box 149, Brookvale
2100 N.S.W., Australia; in NEW ZEALAND by Ross Haines & Son, Ltd., 18
Monmouth Street, Grey Lynn, Auckland 2 New Zealand; in SINGAPORE AND
MALAYSIA by MPH Distributors (S) Pte., Ltd., 601 Sims Drive, # 03/07/21,
Singapore 1438; in the PHILIPPINES by Bio-Research, 5 Lippay Street, San
Lorenzo Village, Makati Rizal; in SOUTH AFRICA by Multipet Pty. Ltd., 30
Turners Avenue, Durban 4001. Published by T.F.H. Publications Inc., Ltd. the
British Crown Colony of Hong Kong.

Contents

The Aim of this Book

There are books about fossils and there are books on knowledge. The number of known fossils is very large and becomes larger with every year. The number of Latin names already seems countless. Works of reference such as the Index of Generic Names of Fossil Plants, 1820–1965 (Washington, 1970), Nomenclator animalium generum et subgenerum (Berlin, 1926–1936), Nomenclator Zoologicus (London, 1939–1940, 1950, 1966) and Fossilium Catalogus I Animalia and II Plantae (The Hague, 1954–1975) provide the specialist with exhaustive information about the multiplicity of known fossils and their classification in fossil and recent animal and plant families. There are also fine and useful books on fossils which are of assistance for the seeking and collecting of fossils and which convey an idea of the beauty of many fossils. The museums, in turn, proudly display the wealth of their exhibitions and collections and the eager eye of the reader and visitor will be entranced by the variety and many individual characteristics of the objects. Yet despite all this there is a series of special fossils so rare that the fossil collector or even the specialist will scarcely ever find them or come into contact with them in the course of his work. Their names and pictures are not emphasized—or only in exceptional cases—in the books and works mentioned above. They are usually if they had not been found many of the concepts in our understanding of the evolution of the creatures and plants which lived millions of years ago would be somewhat different. There would be much of which we had no knowledge at all not even a rough idea. The existence of these special fossils—since the time of Charles Darwin known as missing links or connecting links—has had a great influence on our understanding of early life, evolution and phylogeny and, in some respects, has even led to fundamental knowledge of the specific complexity of the historical sequence of development in general.

It was the wish of the two authors of this book to advance into the silent realm of these strange creatures and to share this experience with the reader. It was not possible to avoid a very personal approach in this since the objects examined here were those which both authors had had to deal with in the course of their work.

Fortunately, some of these great rarities are in the collection of the Museum for Natural History of Berlin (German Democratic Republic). Others came into the hands of the authors as duplicates, loaned by other collections and museums. These descriptions are thus to be seen as a first introduction to this special treasure-chest and an understanding of nature. When we counted the number of illustrations, they more than filled the space allocated for them in the book. We would have liked to include even more specimens in our illustrations and also some from distant countries and museums. In this or that case, it was possible to do this since original slides were at our disposal or had been used when the specimen was not very suitable for photographic reproduction. The authors also wanted the photographs to reflect their views as far as possible and photographs by photographers from other museums often deviated too much from the aim and the emphasis desired. May this book be a beginning and may our photographs and interpretations bring distant objects a little closer to the reader.

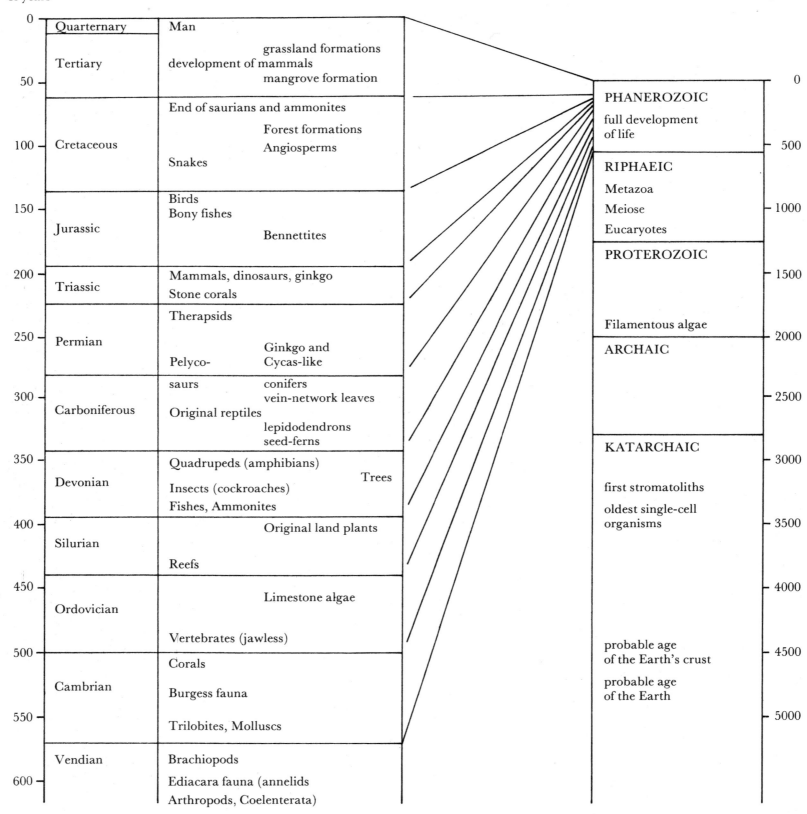

millions
of years

millions
of years

0	Quarternary	Man
	Tertiary	grassland formations
		development of mammals
50		mangrove formation
	Cretaceous	End of saurians and ammonites
100		Forest formations
		Angiosperms
		Snakes
150	Jurassic	Birds
		Bony fishes
		Bennettites
200	Triassic	Mammals, dinosaurs, ginkgo
		Stone corals
250	Permian	Therapsids
		Ginkgo and
		Pelyco- Cycas-like
300	Carboniferous	saurs conifers
		vein-network leaves
		Original reptiles
		lepidodendrons
		seed-ferns
350	Devonian	Quadrupeds (amphibians) Trees
		Insects (cockroaches)
		Fishes, Ammonites
400	Silurian	Original land plants
		Reefs
450	Ordovician	Limestone algae
		Vertebrates (jawless)
500	Cambrian	Corals
		Burgess fauna
550		Trilobites, Molluscs
	Vendian	Brachiopods
600		Ediacara fauna (annelids
		Arthropods, Coelenterata)

0	PHANEROZOIC
	full development of life
500	RIPHAEIC
	Metazoa
1000	Meiose
	Eucaryotes
	PROTEROZOIC
1500	
	Filamentous algae
2000	ARCHAIC
2500	
	KATARCHAIC
3000	
	first stromatoliths
	oldest single-cell organisms
3500	
4000	
4500	probable age of the Earth's crust
	probable age of the Earth
5000	

· 8 ·

It is not enough to note down knowledge in books. Some sciences at least, which are concerned with problems, hypotheses and facts of natural science, compare written notes, verbal descriptions, technical formulae, illustrations, diagrams and tables showing mean and extreme values with an actual piece of nature. This piece was the point of study but the knowledge acquired is still incomplete.

There is knowledge which is derived from frequent and constantly repeated observations and there is knowledge which comes from rare and fortunate finds. The multiplicity of nature puts common evidence side-by-side with items of great rarity. Both are necessary for our understanding. It is consequently not surprising that some of the natural sciences, in the course of their quest for knowledge, have established collections and that in places where these natural sciences proved useful and, for a time, even indispensable for technical and social progress, these collections have developed into institutions with an independent existence. Some of the natural history collections which developed from the search for scientific knowledge have become mineralogical, palaeontological or geological museums or institutes with a museum department at universities, mining academies and national geological surveys. In some countries, institutions of this kind have also been established at the Academy of Sciences or have been advanced and financially supported by trusts and associations for the promotion of science. In parallel with the above-mentioned institutions, which served for training or for the exploration of the natural resources of the country, municipal collections and museums came into existence which were open to the general public for broadening individual horizons of knowledge.

We are no longer in the early days of this development. The technical and scientific progress of society and the intellectual atmosphere of the Age of Enlightenment laid the foundations of the scientific disciplines, of their institutes and museums whose accumulated knowledge and treasures not only excite our admiration but also provide food for thought. It is to this foundation that modern science is constantly adding new knowledge and facts.

Knowledge and Museum

Palaeontological studies have brought charm and variety to the science of the rigid structures of this Earth. Petrified strata show us, preserved in their graves, the flora and fauna of past millennia. We climb upwards in time when, noting the spatial stratification conditions, we penetrate downwards from one stratum to the next. Long-vanished plant and animal life emerges before our eyes.

A. von Humboldt

We sometimes forget that less than two centuries separate us from the establishment of palaeontology as a science.

Nowadays, every schoolchild learns that the birds descended from the reptiles and that they first appeared in the shape of the primitive bird *Archaeopteryx lithographica*. This knowledge, however, is linked to the discovery of a small bird-feather in the limestone quarries of Solnhofen in 1860. This find was not known to Charles Darwin when he wrote his famous book on the *Origin of Species* (1859).

The finding of three almost complete skeletons of primitive birds supplemented the then still hesitant acceptance of a reptile origin of birds (1861, 1877, 1951), whereby the first two finds represented the confirmation of the theory formulated from morphological comparisons.

At a certain stage of supposition and perception, the experimental sciences need experiment and the historical sciences the historical document. It is not chance which leads to the perception and finding of a long-suspected and long-sought link (missing link) in the long chain of knowledge although chance is certainly an element in this. It is the scientific research work, which is constantly needed for the technical progress of society, which allows such finds to be identified, which gives them their value and which anticipates them.

A certain percentage of valuable finds—possibly ten to twenty per cent at the present time—are made by discoverers who are not themselves directly concerned with research but who recognize the value of the discovery which chance has put in their hands and sell it or present it as a valueable gift to a museum or institute.

Sometimes the working process, for example the excavation of limestone, travertine, coal deposits or ore-veins resembles a scientific excavation when the worker concerned (miner, excavator-driver) makes a rare find. He merits our most sincere thanks when, instead of allowing the mining-machine to crush it, he passes it on to those able to identify it. It is probably a special feature of natural history that we owe great advances to such people. This interplay of research and long-awaited chance which does indeed occur was described by one of the great names of geology in the first half of our century, H. Cloos (1885–1951) in a little chapter about himself. H. Cloos was professor and director of the Geological Institute of the University of Breslau between 1919 and 1926 and of Bonn between 1926 and 1951.

The Geologist and the Sea-Lily

In one of the secret valleys which belong to the great river reaching out to the world like snug niches, there stood a rocky wall, high above the road. I laboriously climbed up over undergrowth and boulders to add to my thousand-and-one numbers and measurements a thousand-and-second.

But instead of the expected data from the double accounting system of the formation and transformation of the strata I discovered something which was quite surprising. As if drawn on the sheer schist face, the slim stem of a sea-lily presented itself, crowned with a calyx like a tulip and ending downwards in a coiled spiral as if it had just closed up at the sight of sudden danger and had withdrawn a little from the surface of the water towards the seabed.

What a find! How few fully developed specimens from the great family of the sea-lilies had been found at all so far and all of these were recorded somewhere in books and treatises in words and pictures and the most sober description cannot conceal the joy of their discovery. And scarcely a single one of even these few had been discovered by a real geologist in the rock and had been freed by him from it. In most cases, a chance finder had taken the attractive booty and passed it on to an expert in return for a handsome fee.

And now this delightful calyx, like a bud about to burst into flower, appears suddenly before me, just waiting for me to free with gentle but hesitant hand the already half-separated flake from the mountain which had held it captive since time immemorial and had protectively embraced it until this rare hour.

But stop! Let the flower stand there for a moment more since this peaceful creation stands upright as if in welcome. Or is that the charming deception of chance? Could it not just as well lie at an angle or flat since when it died it must have sunk to the ground and only been set up again by the fold and, with the stratum matrix, turned upwards at precisely this pleasing angle by chance? Yes, that's it. After all our long and laborious studies of the folds, strata and undulations of this mountain and its geosynclinal cradle, we can appreciate the effort necessary for this rare flower to appear before us like a tulip in a stone vase. An entire geosyncline was necessary which, for aeons of the Earth's existence, did nothing but collect and prepare strata. A geological revolution was necessary to force up the collected contents of the stratum cradle and to take it up to the peaks of the mountains. And a fold was necessary which was so powerful that it was able to turn many kilometres of sediment and to knead it like wax and yet so gentle that a lily, as fragile as glass, remained in this turmoil what it was when, in the moment of death, it laid its little head on the downy pillow of the flocculent depths of still water; a fold which was enough to resurrect the flower and to raise it up towards the light in a mummified resemblance of the life which it had once led for a few weeks or years.

Or should we seriously imagine that the sole purpose of all this effort was to give reality to this small but uniquely beautiful event?

No, we should not. And we should not even allow this one flower to stand in the petrified garden of Paradise in which nature placed it. For if we do not pluck it, the winter will break it with the lever of its frosts and the spring will disintegrate the already fragile support of the weak stem and of the burdensome little head into a little pile of brownish-grey fragments and, with clay and rubble, despatch it down the steep hill-side into the valley.

And this is why it was certainly right that I plucked it myself. A cautious pull behind the thin flake of clay and I held the stone and the flower in my two hesitant hands, the flower which had once been a living and feeling creature and was now nothing more than a somewhat unusually formed piece of grey schist which was cool and sandy to the touch and smelt a little musty.

Let us climb down again to the road, taking care not to stumble and let us leave above us the rock which is now like an empty grave without a soul.

We will not try and find out which sea-lily it was that H. Cloos found between 1915 and 1940 or in which collection it now remains. In his book, he left us only the description of the event. This account was reprinted in a journal (1957) together with the picture of a beautiful sea-lily bearing the name of *Acanthocrinus rex*. It was the most splendid sea-lily found so far—found and described long before the story told above. O. Jaekel described it in 1895 as a new species. The specimen itself came from the collection of the Government Geologist Koch and it is likely that such a large and complete specimen of this species has never again been found.

In the course of the work carried out on this specimen, a plaster cast was made and the flower itself exhibited in Berlin, but with bomb-damage and the destructions of war between 1943 and 1945 nothing more is known of its fate. Perhaps it will turn up one day in some collection or other, the loss of its label hiding its identity as it wanders from one drawer to another; or perhaps it is lost for ever. The plaster cast was prepared true-to-nature and allows us to visualize the find in its former beauty.

Thus it is not just a piece of nature which lies in the drawers of the museum. It has become an object of understanding, perhaps even the original of a scientific study. A few sentences, perhaps a chapter, perhaps the conclusions of many generations of researchers, will lie with it, so to speak, in the museum. The old labels underneath note the references to these documents.

Scientific collections and museums are the product of the work of excavation research and classification and they reflect this—the product of mineralogy, palaeozoology, palaeobotany, zoology, botany. The existence in museums of these sciences is somewhat of a secondary matter, a consequence of the profusion of facts which each of them, as an individual science, has to deal with independently.

When most people still had to work 12 to 14 hours a day, it was often only select circles of society which visited these places with the desire to inspect the treasures. When it is

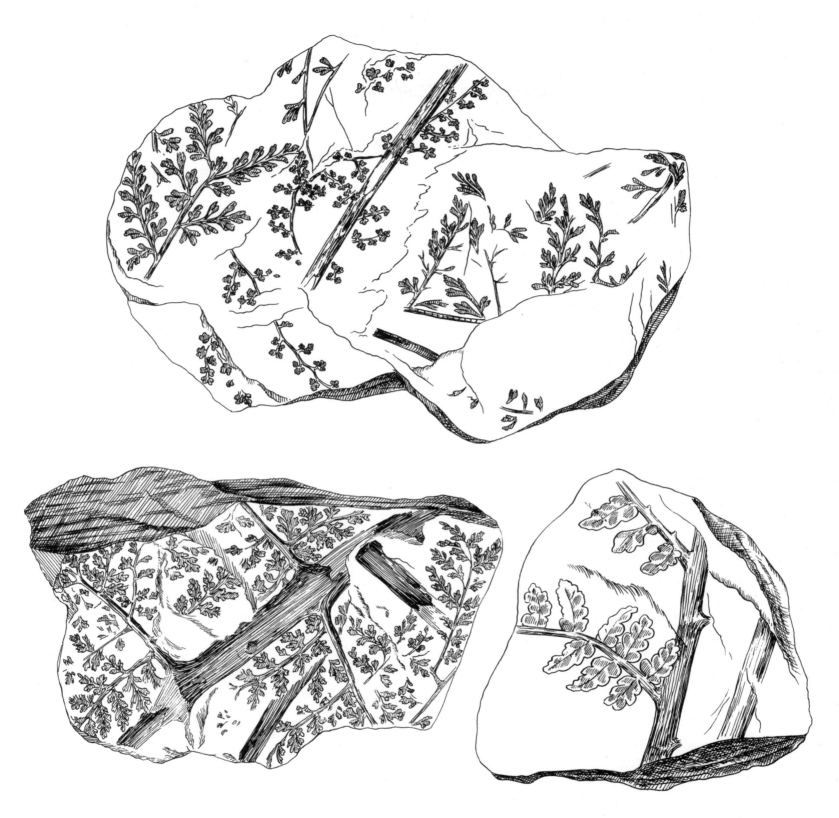

*E. F. von Schlotheim's illustrations of fossil plants
of the Carboniferous period of 1804 and 1820 laid
the foundation stone of scientific palaeobotany.*

said that these places were open to the public 150 to 200 years ago, then this was only in an elite sense.

When human beings were freed from the disproportionate burden of labour, there resulted at the same time a distinct wish on the part of many of them to see the exhibits of museums for themselves.

The wealth of perceived and proven knowledge also led to the establishment of museums for purely educational purposes. Exhibitions of objects which are of importance for a town or a region and correspond to an educational need convey an experience to visitors which widens their horizons and thus remain in their memories.

Natural history museums in the capitals and principal cities of the world which attract two to three hundred thousand visitors annually are no longer a rarity. In the last decade, the number of visitors to such museums has risen by about the double and will doubtlessly continue to rise. At certain times, many museums are full to capacity with visitors and sometimes there are even too many visitors.

The existence of natural history museums is therefore justified in convincing manner from the viewpoint of the desire for social experience and education. But there is a risk that the sources of the production of knowledge which led to the emergence and growth of these places and which put them in the very forefront of knowledge may come to a standstill. We need museums which are a home where sciences can be active! When these sciences leave a museum it becomes a beautiful but uninhabited palace—a palace with glass show-cases but without the boffins in their white coats, armed with magnifying-glass, microscope, instruments and the eternal urge to acquire more knowledge.

On the other hand, nobody will deny the need for a large number of museums in the towns and larger villages, run by an energetic director with an all-round education and assisted by a small band of helpers never tired of preparing exhibitions which are presented in as modern a manner as possible—and visited by many grateful people. But these museums have to rely on the presentations of scientific results which have been assembled elsewhere—models and replicas, plaster-casts and illustrations provide only a secondhand view, as it were—or their own collections, dating from an earlier period are examined by researchers from other establishments for a research project which is brought to fruition in another place.

Both types of natural history museums are part of present-day life. With the first, it can happen that unpublicized treasures lie dormant in the archives and research departments—not yet sufficiently accessible for the public, that scientific work is unintentionally over-emphasized and that the exhibition function is somewhat neglected. With the second category, the exhibitions are presented in such a modern and hygienic manner that they resemble a collection at a fair but the original basis, the scientific problem, is unwittingly neglected.

When we begin to read a book about the treasures in museums, these truths of our time about our museums, should not be left unsaid. It conveys an idea of how the international character of science and the treasures in the museums of each country form a whole. Books, however, unite the knowledge of the treasures of many museums in many countries.

Preceding page :

Brachiosaurus

The Dinosaur Exhibition of Berlin Natural History Museum is the largest in Europe. It consists primarily of saurians from Tendaguru in East Africa and is thus a unique counterpart of the exhibitions of North American saurians in the great museums of the USA. The most impressive exhibit is the skeleton of the largest of all reptiles, Brachiosaurus brancai *Janensch.*

Archaeopteryx

The finding of a single feather in 1860 was the first evidence of birds in the Upper Jurassic. The principal slab is shown here. The feather is preserved in the form of a carbon film. It is thus of a different nature to the feather impressions of the skeletal finds.

The counter-slab of the Berlin specimen of Archaeopteryx *with the imprint of the left wing. When the slab was first split, large splinters were left on the principal slab, especially in the area of the wings and the tail. These have been lifted off, fragment by fragment and glued to the counter part.*

The Berlin specimen of the primitive bird. The unique clarity of the skeleton in conjunction with the natural and aesthetically pleasing arrangement of the tail and feather imprints are such striking evidence of the association of this specimen with the origin of birds that it may be regarded as the most famous of all fossils.

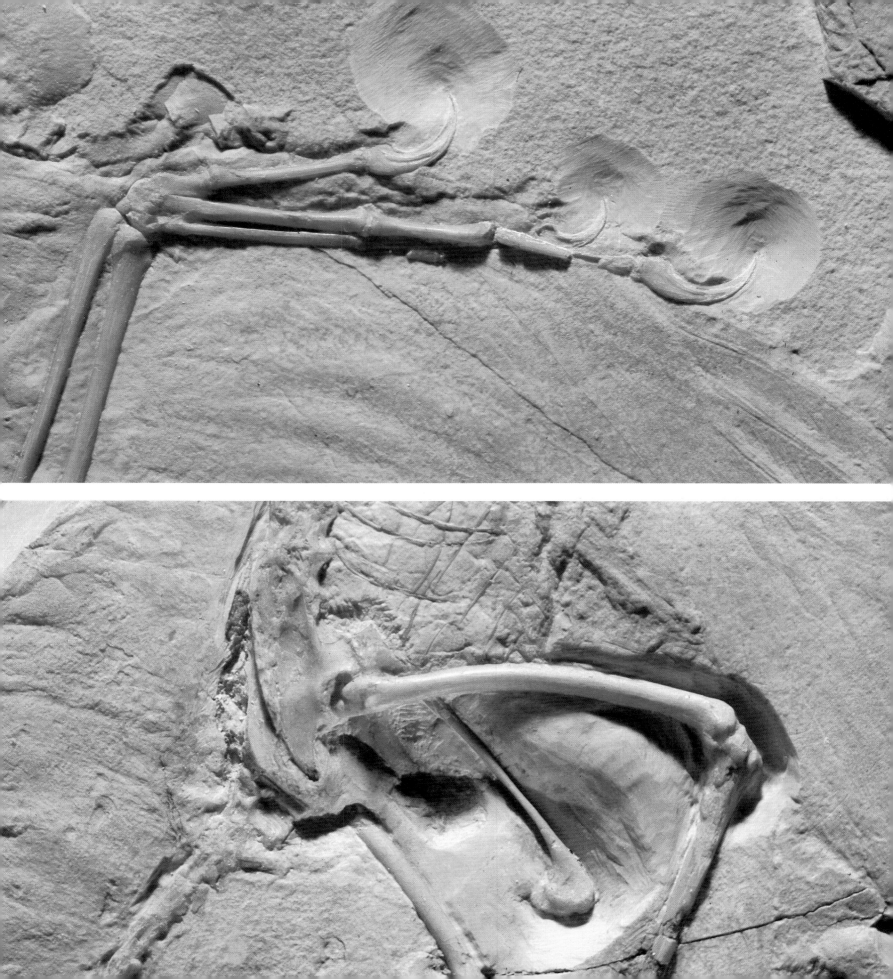

Details of the Berlin specimen

The Berlin specimen of Archaeopteryx is one of the most widely illustrated of all fossils and yet the details of the picture are scarcely known. These photographs were taken in 1978 when the curved and very pointed claws were exposed and the delicate work on the skull was also taken a stage further.

The right hand in comparison with the left hand (p.83) gives an excellent idea of the structure of the hand which consists of three fingers with two, three and four joints and the claws. The second and third fingers were obviously held together by ligaments whereas the first could be moved freely.

At the pelvis (lower left), the pubic bone between the upper thigh-bones can be seen. Its position, resulting from a fracture, was long thought to be the normal position and led to wrong conclusions being drawn about the origin of birds. The squashed skull (top) clearly shows the ring of bone around the eye and the teeth in the two jaws. The rear part of the head has largely been destroyed. See also p.94/95.

Dorygnathus banthensis *Theodori*

This flying saurian was excavated as the fifth of only thirteen specimens in all in the Upper Liassic of Holzmaden (Federal Republic of Germany). It was discovered there in 1915. Since the coast was relatively far away, it was only seldom that flying saurians happened to land in the sludge sediments which form oil shales at the present day. Dorygnathus is one of the long-tailed forms. Striking features include the large skull with the disproportionately large fish-catcher jaw, the long flight-fingers and the tiny feet.

Nothosaurus raabi *Schröder, 1914*

This skeleton, from which the matrix material was removed, is the most complete one of a nothosaur ever found. It comes from the Raab Nothosaur Collection of Rüdersdorf, the various species of which were described by Schröder in 1914. The other remains consist exclusively of skulls. The skeleton was the first evidence of the true length of the neck and showed details of the extremities. During preparation work, the skull easily came away from the limestone matrix so that the top of it also became accessible for examination, as shown in the second picture. There is some damage to the snout area. Orbicularis beds of the lower Muschelkalk, Rüdersdorf near Berlin (German Democratic Republic).

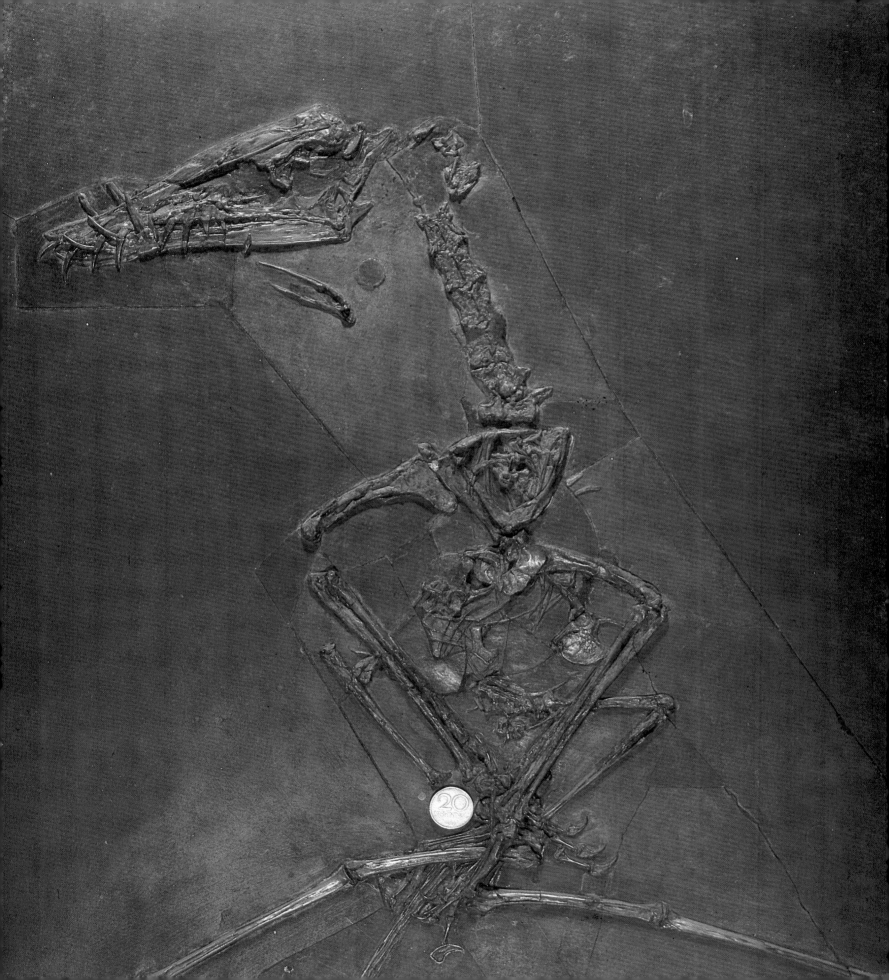

Dicraeosaurus hansemanni *Janensch*

In addition to Brachiosaurus *bones, the remains of four other species of large herbivorous sauropods were found in the material excavated at Tendaguru, including this almost intact skeleton of* Dicraeosaurus, *which is a close relative of the American* Diplodocus. *Dinosaur Hall of the Natural History Museum, Berlin.*

Thin section of coal

E. C. Jeffrey of the Botanical Laboratory of Harvard University, Cambridge, Massachusetts (USA), achieved what had previously appeared improbable but he did it only with pieces of fossilized wood and coal which he had succeeded in softening with the aid of chemical techniques. Jeffrey succeeded in slicing the coal of Zwickau (German Democratic Republic) into thin, translucent sections. The spores (centre of picture) appear yellow, the vitrinite stripes a translucent brown and the fusinite (wood) as black as charcoal, real fossil charcoal. A squashed megaspore appears as a yellow ribbon, likewise the remains of the cuticle of a leaf. The degree of carbonization varies according to the chemical composition, which accounts for the light colouring of the cork substance (cutin, suberin, sporopollenin).
Magnification: approx. 40×

Spheroid oil algae, similar to the recent volvox, are to be found in the algae-clay-sludge coals (bogheads) of the southern continents. This is a thin section of Australian coal, prepared by E. C. Jeffrey. The once spheroid forms have become flat but their delicate structure can still be recognized.
Magnification: approx. 50×

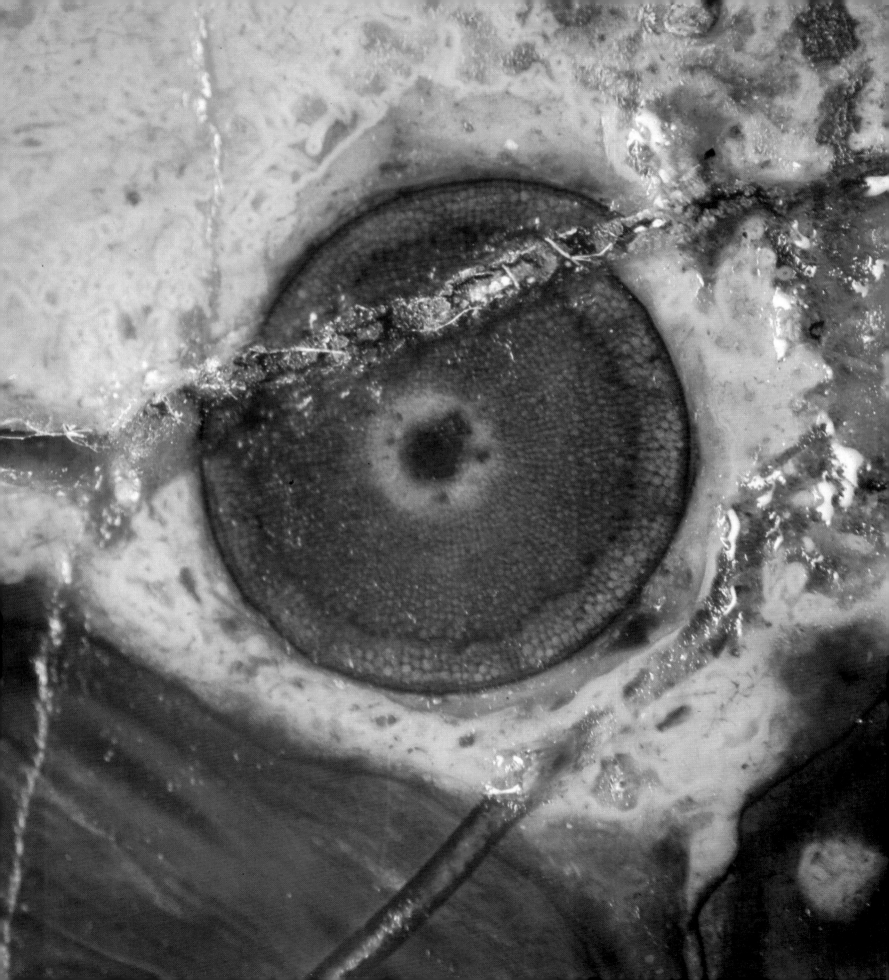

Rhynie chert

Ground cross-section of a Rhynia *stem (magnification: 25×). The chert at Rhynie near Aberdeen in Scotland is about 370 million years old (Middle Devonian or upper Lower Devonian). Cross-sections of stems of* Rhynia *and other plants from the early days of the first invasion of the land show exquisite details. In the centre there is the woody tissue, which served for the conduction of water, surrounded by light-coloured tissue which was surely capable of conducting the sap (an early form of the phloem). The Rhynie chert fossils studied by Kidston and Lang were the subject of a famous series of papers published in the Transactions of the Royal Society of Edinburgh. For natural history museums, this chert is a precious jewel.*

Medullosa stellata

Ground section of a stem of Medullosa stellata *(2:1). The silicified stems of Karl-Marx-Stadt (German Democratic Republic) are about 270 million years old (lower New Red Sandstone).* Neuropteris *and* Alethopteris *foliage formed part of* Medullosa *plants. The wood of the outer zone of the stem, which thickened in the secondary stage, and an extensive pith inside the stem can be recognized here. Numerous star-shaped woody strands have been formed in this pith. Such polystelic structure with numerous woody strands at the centre must have been of great importance for a hundred million years (see* Pietzschia *and* Lyginodendron*).*

Psaronius *roots*

*The root mantle of the tree fern (*Psaronius*) of the lower New Red Sandstone is often magnificently preserved in a mineralized, silicified form. The stems were frequently enclosed by a thick mantle of aerial roots. This specimen (4:1) comes from the lower New Red Sandstone of Karl-Marx-Stadt (German Democratic Republic).*

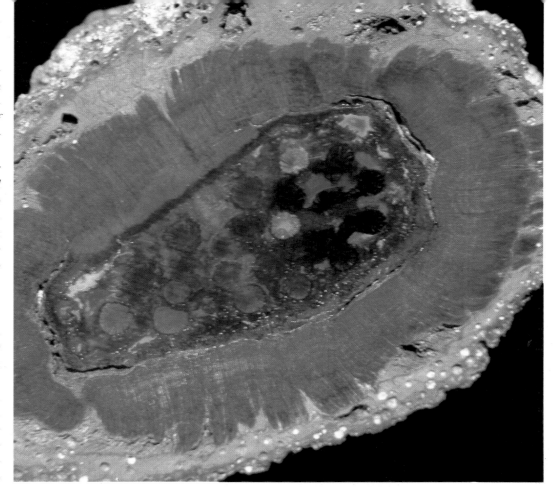

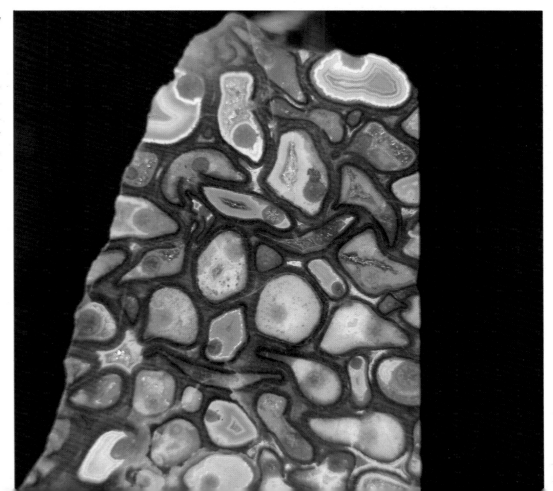

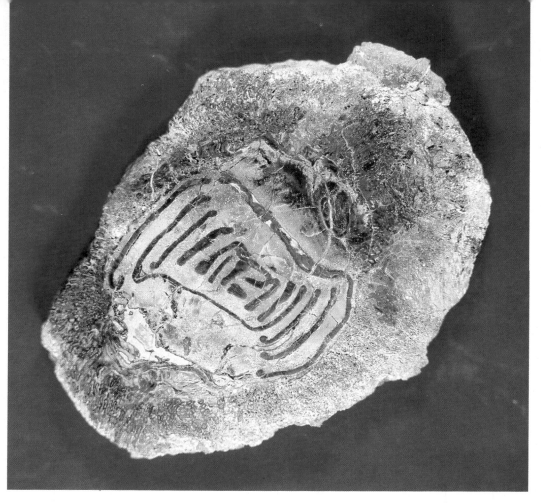

Psaronius simplex

Ground cross-section of a fern stem which had had two rows of leaves (Psaronius simplex) *from the lower New Red Sandstone of Karl-Marx-Stadt. Fern stems with two rows of frond stigmas* (Megaphyton) *have also been preserved in the carbonized form. These stems had leaves such as* Pecopteris plumosa.

Pecopteris plumosa

A typical fern, frequently found in the Upper Carboniferous (Namurian B to Westphalian D) of Central Europe. This species of fern with the characteristic pinnae (Aphlebiae) *at the axis are classified with the family Schizaeaceae. This original specimen was found in a coalmine at Saarbrücken (Federal Republic of Germany).*

Alethopteris davreuxi *and* Jacaranda mimosifolia

Many of the seed-ferns of the then tropical Upper Carboniferous period of Central Europe were small-leaved, such as the leaf from the Saar Basin illustrated here. Present-day plants of the tropics are often small-leaved, too, such as the Jacaranda mimosifolia *shown next to it. It is said that this small-leaved feature is to protect the surface of the leaf from being scorched by the fierce sunshine. Thus leaf forms may be found in modern flora which sometimes repeat the shapes of the past.*

Lyginopteris larischi

An original pictured in many international textbooks and manuals to illustrate seed-ferns (Pteridosperms): Lyginopteris larischi *from the lowermost Upper Carboniferous (upper Namurian A) in Europe and North America. In the Palaeozoic Europe and North America formed a cohesive continent with one and the same flora (the Euramerican flora).*

When at the beginning of this century the seed-ferns were recognized and many species were identified, H. Potonié chose this frond as typical (1891).

Palmatopteris furcata

This classic find of a seed-fern frond from the Upper Carboniferous (Westphalian B) of Upper Silesia (Poland) shows the displacement of the forked frond structure by a penduling overtopping of now one frond side and then the other. Perhaps this was the path which led from the leaf of the Carboniferous period, the bifurcated frond, to the leaf of modern times.

Paripteris gigantea

A piece of frond from a seed-fern of the Upper Carboniferous period (Namurian B to Westphalian C, D). The points of special interest here are the double nature of the terminal pinnae and the intercalated pinnae at the frond axis (Rhachis).

Features have suddenly appeared here which were not to be seen in the immediate predecessors. Is this a partial revival of old features? Is this how new developments come about?

Following page:

Ginkgo *leaves*

A branch, a long shoot bearing smaller shoots already several years old and green leaves, of the modern Ginkgo biloba L. (brown, natural damage on leaf). Next to it the oldest proven ancestor of Ginkgo (280 to 230 million years old) found in the Permian copper schist at Mansfeld. The specimen at lower left is approximately equivalent to the original of the species illustrated in 1828 by Adolphe Brongniart. The other specimens demonstrate the great variation of the first Ginkgo-type leaf. Since it was not identical with the modern Ginkgo genus, this forerunner is known in palaeobotany as Sphenobaiera digitata *(rgt)* Florin. *From what Carboniferous plants could* Sphenobaiera digitata *have come—from the mysterious, theoretically predicted progymnosperms or from parallel groups to the Pteridosperms?*

gigantea STBG.
Unt. Westphal
OTONIÉ (1891)
Y (1959)

Baiera digitata
Wolfschacht
1934

Baiera
Wolfschacht
1928

XI. 19.

XI. 3.

Baiera
Wolfschacht
1932.

XI. 15.

Baiera
fündig
MaxKöhler
1938.

Wolfschacht

XI. 14.

As far as museums are concerned, two different approaches have emerged. The first of this sees them as centres of science; institutions of activity dedicated to research and scientific englightenment. Since sciences such as mineralogy, palaeontology, zoology and botany are concerned with many objects (at the present time there are about 380,000 plant species, more than a million animal species and about 9,000 kinds of minerals), this work of research and scientific enlightenment is associated with the establishment of large collections. Since some minerals, some fossil animal and plant species and also many present-day animal and plant species are very rare or seldom recovered as perfect examples, it is also a question of the possession of unique pieces of evidence, of precious jewels of natural history such as, for example, the primitive bird *Archaeopteryx lithographica*. These treasures and the message associated with them can and should be shown in an appropriate and worthy form. Aesthetic considerations and a corresponding standard of preparation and presentation are certainly an important part of every exhibition and nor should the architecture of the building be forgotten.

The second approach is based more on the possession and display of rare and precious objects and owes nothing to research. This means that the aesthetic display of the possessions of the museum is the sole aim. When the production of such a display predominates, the real scientific value of the object can become a matter of secondary importance. It is replaced by a replica and a large museum show-case is filled to such an extent with eye-catching pictorial material, text and illumination equipment that the visitor no longer sees and appreciates the precious exhibit—a piece of Pre-Cambrian coal, a bone from a Palaeozoic vertebrate, a fossil leaf of the Carboniferous period—as an original and unique object. The visitor is entertained, stimulated, excited and informed but no longer confronted with original objects. There are modern museum exhibitions of this kind but this latter variant already existed centuries ago in the form of curiosity cabinets in gentlemen's residences. They were intended for a small circle of selected personalities, providing

Natural History Museums and their Treasures Science as an Experience

For the present level of education is the result of the past and, especially in science, one always stands on the shoulders of the other. We only contribute individual bricks of the edifices whose completion is not yet possible; thus, from the genetic viewpoint, the first incomplete achievement is as valuable as the last and complete one since without the one the other would not be possible.

H. R. Goeppert

education, entertainment and complementing their knowledge of the world. There are a few places where such cabinets from the 18th century are still preserved in their original form—in the German Democratic Republic, for example, at Waldenburg and at the Martin Luther University, Halle. They are still to be found in the country houses in England.

The authors of this book subscribe to the first view of what a natural history museum should be which asserts that scientific research creates museum collections and museum exhibitions. It is therefore our opinion that one should be informed by all methods of acquiring knowledge, whether this is by exhibitions or by books such as this one.

As members of expeditions to distant lands and inaccessible desert and steppe areas, scientists strive for knowledge from geological explorations.

The exchange of new findings is one of the purposes of international scientific congresses and groups of specialists make excursions to famous sites for the same purpose. For example, valuable finds came into the possession of the Berlin Museum following excursions organized by the International Botanical Congress (1959 Canada, 1964 Scotland), the International Geological Congress (1960 Denmark, Sweden, Norway, Finland, 1964 India) and through joint work in stratigraphic sub-commissions.

Professors and staff-members, together with their students, made valuable finds which had to be laboriously chiselled from the rock in the course of these excursions.

Some scientific institutes and museums have carried on excavations over a period of years in certain opencast lignite mines and have systematically worked through the sites to recover their finds.

Geological drillings have led to the discovery of valuable finds at widely varying depths. Very deep drillings reach depths of 5,000 to 9,000 metres but the diameter of the drill-core obtained is then so small that precious finds are rare.

Valuable finds are also made underground in mines and often, on the tips as well. From time to time, these finds are documented for the specialist in the publications on the proceeding of geological services, geological institutes and regional geological authorities.

In the past, when excavation technology was still at a low level of development and all work was done manually, finds of very great value were made in stone-quarries, such as those at Solnhofen and Holzmaden (Federal Republic of Germany), for instance. Is it now almost impossible for such finds to be made? Many of the small stone-quarries which supplied so many fossils have been closed and in others the removal of material with heavy excavating machinery of advanced design takes place so rapidly that the potential sites which are exposed with such speed are overlooked and eliminated by the actual quarrying process. The responsibility for this has become a more serious matter. Finds which could also be made in industrial Europe are perhaps crushed by modern excavating machinery and processed as raw material.

When a find is made, it is then the skill of the scientist or technician which enables this find to be freed as far as possible from the rock.

These are finds whose value is immediately apparent, on account of their size (dinosaur skeleton), their beauty and completeness (the primitive bird *Archaeopteryx*, the flying reptile *Pterodactylus*, etc.) or by the preciousness of their material (e.g., amber inclusions, copper-schist fish preserved in native silver, silicified fragments of plants). In many cases, however, the worth of a find only becomes apparent after scientific preparation. Objects which at first sight appear very ordinary prove to be significant and possibly even unique after closer examination. It might be a coaly something-or-other which you have in front of you, a piece of clay bearing the brittle remainder of a leaf which could easily break off if carelessly wiped over with a cloth. A microscopic maceration preparation reveals its value but this is scarcely apparent to the outsider. The explanatory drawing and the attached photomicrograph draw attention to that which is not immediately obvious. A jewel for a museum, an object unique in the knowledge it imparts, but not worth exhibiting!

The assets of the national museums of every country grew in proportion to the increase in scientific understanding. The variety of sciences, types of production and branches of art are reflected in the diversity of the kinds of museums—to quote a sentence heard at the 11th General Conference of the International Council of Museums (ICOM) in 1977. Even if many a natural science collection is somewhat older than the date of birth of the scientific discipline in question, the natural history museums are, by and large, institutions of the Age of Enlightenment, an era which began with Denis Diderot's *Encyclopédie* in 21 volumes (1751–1772) and, with Immanuel Kant in 1774, formulated the demand that "man should be mature enough to understand his own nature and that of his environment with the aid of the methods of science".

With the self-confidence of its citizens and increasing public ownership there increased as well the feeling of responsibility for the museum treasures of one's own land. Thus, in many countries, all the scientific treasures preserved in museum collections are state museum assets. For many years now, many countries have appropriate laws on this subject. It is interesting to read the remarks of the delegates from the various countries at the general conferences of the ICOM. Some countries have a great network of museums of great variety and possess exceptional experience in this field showing particularly close links between their museums and the various sciences, industries and arts.

In the last ten years, a growing interest in museums has been noted in all countries, the number of visitors to the museums in the individual countries having doubled in general. There may be many reasons for this but it is perhaps appropriate to quote the philosopher Georg Wilhelm Friedrich Hegel (1770 to 1831) who once described the museum as a collection in which social experience is crystallized and reflected in such a manner that the path to understanding it is shortened. Clearly the unique specimens in museum collections are attracting the interest of modern people. May they find ways and means of displaying their great stores of treasures and, where possible, of encouraging people to collaborate, collect and observe and to preserve sites and nature conservation areas.

A particularly good and internationally well-known example of the acceptance of joint responsibility is the collaboration, which has already been maintained for more than 55 years, of the Geiseltal Museum of the Martin Luther University (Halle/German Democratic Republic) with the opencast lignite mines in the Halle-Merseburg district. Here, in narrowly delineated excavation cones and in fossil beds 48 million years old mummies and skeletons of mammals, reptiles, birds, amphibians and fish have been found, including the remains of primitive horses, lemurs, insectivores, snakes, crocodiles, turtles, shimmering beetles, cell-nuclei of a frog epidermis, green leaves, marks left by bacteria in insect tracheas and so on. The great excavating machines carefully avoid the scientific sites which they have just exposed and made accessible to the scientists. The monuments of Nature from the Eocene lignite period, a profound insight into natural history, are now exhibited, in the form of numerous finds, in the Geiseltal Museum in Halle. Even though many of the finds are not particularly attractive in appearance—lignite does not display a beautiful range of colours— they were nevertheless recovered.

A particularly bad example and one which has already been the subject of several discussions at international congresses is the Messel oil-shale mine at Darmstadt (Federal Republic of Germany). The finds in the oil shale are of about the same age as the Geiseltal coal and have been a source of scientific knowledge for more than a century. The special festure of this unique 50 million years ago natural museum, is that an oil-bearing algalshale coal (dysodile) has embedded all the remains of fossil creatures and plants in a particularly durable manner. The deposit is totally enclosed by geological faults and is located in a trench. In recent years (1976), there have been projects to convert this former oil-shale pit into a refuse-dump and, by filling it up, to make it inaccessible for ever for visitors, researchers and nature-lovers. The protests of scientific societies and institutes, international congresses and action groups were given a great deal of publicity in the daily press.

Of course, there are many examples worth

mentioning of both these attitudes. By their existence, they emphasize that modern large-scale industrial production of the present day affords us profound and unique glimpses of the distant past of our planet, glimpses made possible only by deep mines, geological drilling and by tunnel, canal and highway projects. At the same time, however, they underline the great responsibility borne by the present generation in the event that such finds are encountered. Unique natural objects, often linked in a unique manner with possibilities for the acquisition of knowledge, are like the natural resources of the past: they were either utilized or wasted. They will not be found again for generations—and perhaps even never again.

How could it happen that knowledge of natural history remained almost at a standstill for about 1,500 years?

It seems incomprehensible since everything was on the move, at least in some very small degree. Even the Middle Ages had its great thinkers, commerce, cities, crusades, dynasties, great edifices of an impressive architectural standard. Yet there was no significant progress in the consideration, quest and perception of a long pre-history of Nature, the living world?

It is as if the field of creative imagination had remained restricted for many centuries, only a moment after it had been entered by the far-seeing Greek philosophers before Socrates (470–399 B.C.) with their accurate and unprejudiced observations.

The First Perceptions

At about the same time—500 B.C.—similar perceptions, based on the observation of nature, were also formulated in India and China. Perhaps this was a particularly fruitful time for the development of human knowledge, a time in which innumerable observations of nature were made by a partly nomadic, partly settled mankind, some members of which had begun to till the land; humanity was experiencing commerce, the great migrations and, in ancient Europe, slavery, was creating the city-states and magnificent works of art of Asia Minor and Greece and was now expressing itself with new words, eloquent expressions and the first poetic works.

As far as we know, it was Theophrastus (372–287 B.C.), a pupil of Aristotle, who collected all the knowledge of nature in Ancient Greece and recorded it in 18 volumes of which, unfortunately, only fragments survived. This work, in fragmented quotations, also contains the thoughts of the early Greek natural philosophers and thus dates back to the time six to eight centuries before Christ. To be sure, the philosophers of that time were, above all, attentive observers of Nature and this is the background to a quotation concerning Xenophanes of Kolophon (570–480 B.C.):

"Xenophanes believes that a mixing of the earth with the sea is taking place and that the

The Beginnings of Knowledge and Understanding

The logical continuity of science is only a pious wish; the progress of knowledge is erratic and irrational. Ideas die not because they are wrong but because they find no substance and are reborn and become capable of development when the substance is available.

S. von Bubnoff

former will be dissolved by the moist elements in the course of time. He asserts he has evidence of this because mussels have been found in the middle of the interior and on mountains and he says that in Syracuse, in the stone-quarries, impressions of fish and seals have been found but in Pharos the impression of an anchovy in the channel of the rock and on Malta impressions of all possible sea-creatures . . ."

The fossilized remains of leaves in rocks were also known and, finally coal was known and used, the Greek name for this being *anthrax*. Theophrastus notes for us the oldest written evidence on the use of coal:

"Of the brittle stones, there are some which, when placed in the fire, become like lit coals and remain so for a long time. Those which are found in the mines in the area of Bena are of this kind . . . They catch fire when glowing charcoal is thrown on them and burn strongly as long as they are made to do so by blowing. Afterwards, they go out but can be rekindled again. In this manner, they last for a very long time. But their smell is unpleasant. On the foothills of Erinea already mentioned, a stone is to be found which is the same as that which is encountered in the region of Bena. When it is burnt, it emits a resin smell and leaves a substance behind which is something like cold earth. Those stones which are called coal and are obtained for domestic use are like earth. They burn and catch alight like charcoal. They are found in Liguria where amber is also mined and at Elis on the mountains across which one goes to Olympia. The smiths use them."

The Very First Collections

However, the date of the first knowingly made fossil finds must be considered as being very much earlier. What is believed to be the earliest unquestioned collection of fossils, assembled by a nature-living and reflective man of the La Tène period and left for us to find in an urn, merits our special interest. The keeping of this or that fossil object long before this fossil-collector of the later pre-Roman Iron Age (5th–1st c. B.C.) and the reasons for it may now no longer be clear—perhaps it seemed unusual, or it was a keepsake, a toy or an ornament. But what other conclusion can be drawn from this collection of fossil snails, mussels and scaphopods and two recent snail-shells than that this person—a contemporary of Plato and Aristotle—had devoted thought to the subject?

The urn in question was excavated in 1898 at Gross-Wirschleben, not far from Bernburg on the Saale River. In addition to the ashes of the dead man, it contained 39 examples of various Oligocene (35 million years old, Tertiary period) snails, nine examples of Oligocene mussels, nine examples of Oligocene scaphopods and two recent snail-shells, obviously for comparison.

At that time, the Bernburg area was on the edge of the socio-economically advanced societies of the Mediterranean region but was nevertheless influenced by them due to trade routes. It was also at this time that first quasi-urban settlements appeared in central Europe. Ornamental and luxury articles were imported from the Mediterranean region so perhaps philosophical thoughts also found their way to Bernburg.

Oligocene strata crop up not far from Bernburg. The type-locality of Latdorf, well known to geologists and palaeontologists, is in the vicinity. And yet the fossil-collector of Gross-Wirschleben must have acquired his collection only by special circumstances since exposures of fossil-bearing Oligocene clay, which is the evidence of sea-transgressions in the Mid-Oligocene, are a day's journey away from the place where he was buried. We can only have a vague idea of where and how he found or acquired his collection of fossils—perhaps on a sandbank of the Elbe near an Oligocene exposure, perhaps in a fossil-bearing cleft, as also found later in stone-quarries at Bernburg. At any rate, he must have cherished this collection of fossils otherwise it would not have been placed with him in his last place of rest.

The noteworthy feature of this collection is its variety. Only one or two examples were kept of each species. The examples which always were and still are common are represented in this collection only by individual specimens, just like those that are rarer. As is well known,

the merit of Aristotle (384–322 B.C.) was that he concentrated his thinking and vision on the perception of the world in general. We cannot help but suspect that the fossil-collector of Bernburg must also have pondered over the fossil molluscs. That these include both snails and mussels is clear but what led him to consider the scaphopods as belonging to them? Had he heard of the Scaphopoda which are still to be found in the Mediterranean—or was it because they had been found at the same fossil site? In 1902, O. Merkel (Bernburg) examined this collection and published a short report (1904). Since then, not much attention has been paid to this incredible find. With our picture (on the back page of the jacket) and list of the fossil names (from the list by O. Merkel 1904), we would like to document once again this evidence of two and a half thousand years of cultural and scientific history.

There is still other ancient evidence worth mentioning: namely objects which were placed in Stone Age graves, such as a Lias ammonite or a *Glycymeris* shell, but whether these 75,000- to 100,000-year old finds were merely curiosities or even ornaments—the *Glycymeris* perhaps even a make-up shell— is a matter of conjecture.

About a century ago, at Marzabotto in the vicinity of Bologna (Italy), a 4,3000-year old Etruscan temple was uncovered and in this temple there was the petrified trunk of a *Cycadeoidea*, a Lower Cretaceous bennettitalean stem with embedded blossoms. This is the historically oldest plant find ever made.

It was thus rather the end of a period of observation and sometimes of collection, too, in human development which the Ancient Greek philosophers put into words than as a new beginning in natural history activity with the evaluation of fossils. And so the writings which now appeared in the following one and a half thousand years did not progress very much further than the concepts of early Greek natural philosophy first worked out in the time before Socrates. It is not known if collections were put together, museums established or mines opened which might have led directly to new knowledge about the mineral deposits in the ground and about the history of nature. In the Middle Ages, knowledge of

mining, of the places where minerals were to be found and how these could be extracted was often wrapped in secrecy. Thus, after long centuries of oblivion had followed the original acquisition of knowledge of theory, the Renaissance became the age of rebirth of such knowledge of natural history, even though it was still only in theoretical form at first.

Mining has certainly always been the source of experience and ideas concerning mineral veins, rocks and strata, has provided mineral and fossil finds and time and again has encouraged the formulation of concepts concerning these finds in the thoughts of people. But when did these thoughts take on the shape of logical theory? Black, bituminous jet from the Liassic strata of England, Spain and Central Europe was already known to the people of 20,000 years ago. Small ornaments, and later buttons, were carved from this jet. Flint mining with shafts and adits was carried on in Holland and Poland thousands of years before Christ. The mining of coal in Central Europe and China dates back to the 10th century. In the works of Albertus Magnus (1193–1280), there are quotations from Aristotle and Theophrastus and also the first new thoughts on observations of living plants (390 species are mentioned). There are also remarks on mining but the progressive thinking of that time has nothing to say about fossils and natural history.

The Renaissance—the Age of the Intellectual Giants

When, in Italy, men came across petrified fish and shells, which was inevitable of course when working limestone for the construction of churches or fortifications, it was admittedly realized that these were the remains of what had once been living creatures (G. Boccaccio, 1313–1375) but it was thought that they had merely been swept up by the Flood (Ristoro d'Arezzo, 1282). Here only Leonardo da Vinci (1452–1519) was more profound in his observations and recorded his thoughts on the subject as follows:

— These are the remains of sea-creatures

which had once lived where they were found today.

— The sea was thus at one time to be found where the mountains now are in which these petrified remains occur.

— The mud brought down by rivers penetrated the shells of the dead creatures on the sea-bed and turned them into stone.

— The Flood could not have washed up these remains since they would then be found in a single stratum and not in numerous layers of rock both at the foot and on the peak of the mountains.

— Certain sharp teeth in the strata (known as Glossopetrae) are petrified shark-teeth, the marks left by worms are other indications of life.

— The numerous finds of fossils of very different kinds, such as shells, crabs, leaves, seaweed, etc., could not possibly be due to the influence of the stars or other mysterious forces.

To us today, these thoughts of Leonardo da Vinci seem relatively modern. This great artist, mathematician, engineer and biologist was obviously a "giant in thinking, energy and character, in versatility and scholarliness" in respect of the first geological and palaeontological observations and concepts. Unfortunately, his first thoughts on geology, were understood only much later.

The first illustrations—small and undistinguished woodcuts of not very identifiable fossils—appeared in the middle of the 16th century: Christophorus Encelius in his "De re metallica . . .", published in 1551, describes a series of details worth reading.

For example: De Gagate—schwartz bornstein—fit ex nigra naphta aut bitumíne, cum stillat nel fluit in mare (jet—black amber—consists of black naphta or bitumen, as found in the sea).

Encelius, with this opinion expressed in mediaeval Latin, was indeed correct, although it was only in our century that this was confirmed by microscopic investigations (W. Gothan: On the origin of jet. 1908). Jet is wood which is subsequently penetrated to the point of saturation by bitumen.

Gagates: gelb bornstein, bernstein
            schwartz lapis Thracins
            schwartz aageststeyn
            steynkole species gagatis;
            Lapis ex naphta seu bitume.

Somewhat later in the text, Encelius notes: "Naphta und Steynkolen von multis locis in Germania, in Saxonia sowie thorff" (naphtha and pit-coal from many places in Germany, in Saxony and peat). Finally, Encelius includes two woodcuts, but these are unfortunately not typical index fossils in the more modern sense. One is possibly a mussel-shell from the Tertiary Period which might be compared with

The historically oldest illustrations of fossils

1551

Encelius shows a fossil mollusc and a fossil snail but does not make any comment on them; Gesner used this illustration a few years later for his own book.

1558

Gesner shows a fossil shark's tooth, a so-called Glossopetra next to a modern shark to make it clear

the Lower Oligocene *Cardita* while the other may be a snail but it is not in a very clear state of preservation which makes precise identification difficult since tubiculous worms also have similar forms, e.g., the *Serpula* shell.

A few years later, C. Gesner referred to precisely these illustrations, even reprinting them and adding other illustrations, including the picture of just such a tooth as had been interpreted as a shark's tooth by Leonardo da Vinci which he placed next to a drawing of a present-day shark, thus relating a fossil to a living creature (1558) (see accompanying drawing). In 1565, he showed pictures of ammonites and belemnites but only considered the former to be molluscs. There are excellent illustrations of echinoids in Gesner's book.

A few decades after this work, J. Bauhinus showed illustrations of ammonites from the Swabian Jurassic but did not identify them as the remains of living creatures, considering them to be only freaks of nature (1599). It is difficult for us today to understand how it was possible for Gesner, Bauhin and many other authors of that time to consider their clear illustrations, or at least some of them, as no more than freaks of nature. Edward Lhwyd (1660–1709) showed very clear illustrations of Carboniferous seed-ferns of the genus *Neuropteris* in a book published in 1699. He was the curator of the Ashmolean Museum at Oxford and was responsible for the hypothesis, much discussed at the time, that Carboniferous fossil plants and fossil insects had germinated from seeds and sperm which had penetrated the rock, as stone creatures, which had never seen the light of day!

The 18th Century

There is still many an author worth mentioning from the centuries between the Renaissance and the beginning of the great age of coalmining (roughly from 1780 to the present day): N. Steno (1638–1686), W. G. Leibniz (1646–1716), J. J. Scheuchzer (1672–1733). Above all, these authors have given us pictures and comparisons of fossil finds with living creatures of the present time. A particularly comprehensive and lavishly illustrated work was published in 1768 by G. W. Knorr and J. E. I. Walch. Their outstanding colour illustrations clearly demonstrated the organic nature of fossils. But also sites such as the well-known coal deposits of Manebach and Kammerberg in the Thuringian Forest (German Democratic Republic) provided a stimulus for the documentation of the fossils found there. In his "Memorabilia Saxonia subterranea" of 1709, G. F. Mylius described the fossilized remains of plants at Manebach. This encouraged Goethe in 1776 to pay a visit to Manebach where he went down a mine and saw the coal and the fossil plants *in situ*.

Progress in the knowledge and understand-

1669

that these Glossopetra finds must have come from prehistoric sharks.

Lhwyd shows fossil plants from the Coal Measures (seed-ferns of the genus Neuropteris*), calling them lithophytes and considers them to be contemporary*

plants which germinated in the dark, underground, and grew between the layers of the rock.

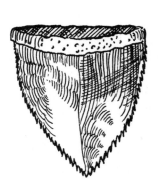

ing of fossils followed two lines of approach in the 18th century: pictorial representation such as the splendid work in four volumes of G. W. Knorr and J. E. I. Walch, and the perception of the epochs of natural history in the form of a theory of the development of the Earth, such as published by I. Kant and G. L. L. de Buffon.

Whereas Buffon in 1743/1778 still assumed that the age of the Earth was about 75,000 years, Kant (1775) was already calculating in terms of millions of years—"and entire mountain ranges of millions of centuries".

It was only some decades after the publication of these works that it was reluctantly and slowly realized that fossils, as marks of time in the history of nature—could also be useful for mining, for the construction of roads and canals.

Goethe, that man of universal interests, made the following note in 1782: Abbé Soulavie made an interesting remark. In the highest limestone mountains, which at the same time are the lowest in the Midi of France, fossilized sea-creatures are to be found which no longer exist in living form at the present time. The rock formation which is lower and lies on the previous one contains remainders of them but, at the same time, also of those species which endure. The third row of rock formations which, in turn, lies on the second, contains only fossils of creatures which still live in the Mediterranean. The question is, and this will soon have to be investigated, whether this is the same here, too. Has anyone of the fossil collectors considered the matter from this viewpoint perhaps and written something about it? I scarcely believe it. With every day, I am increasingly of the opinion that we will indeed continue along the path of Buffon but we will have to move away from the epochs that he lays down. The matter, so it appears to me, is becoming more and more complicated."

The line of approach of the second half of the 18th century, documented by illustrations, only needed to be conscientiously continued for the accumulation of knowledge of fossil finds. However, the stimulus of a definite aim, such as its evident usefulness for a great purpose, was lacking. As long as the finds were

considered to be identical with modern living creatures this purpose was not apparent. At the moment, however, when it became clear that fossils were the remains of extinct creatures, totally unknown remains of previous life, there was a very great increase in the urge to publish illustrations and descriptions. This problem of perception could only be tackled in a scientific manner by comparative morphology and anatomy. Whether Buffon with his epochs of the history of the Earth was right or not, whether it was a question or not of creation or transformation in the crust of the Earth, the science of palaeontology came into being to give scientific names to these fossil creatures.

The Beginnings of Scientific Palaeontology

C. von Linné (1707–1778) gave scientific names not only to modern plants but also to a fossil trilobite. However, scientific palaeontology really begins with G. Cuvier's *Megatherium* skull work (1796) and his subsequent illustration of the lower jaw of a mammoth (1799). He had a fossil *Megatherium* skull from Paraguay at his disposal which he compared with the skulls of modern sloths. For the purpose of comparative anatomical study, these skulls were illustrated on the same scale, i. e., the fossil *Megatherium* skull was greatly reduced in size. His comparison of the fossil lower jaw of a mammoth with that of an Indian elephant was based on a similar procedure. Mammoth skulls had been found since the time of Pliny but had been incorrectly identified, often as the remains of elephants brought by Hannibal to Europe. Cuvier's investigation showed the difference between the lower jaw of the mammoth and the lower jaw of all modern elephants.

The beginning of scientific palaeontology and especially of palaeobotany must be associated with the books of E. F. von Schlotheim (1804, 1820). This investigator was concerned with a description of "strange imprints of herbs and plant fossils" and he consequently published "A contribution on the Flora of the Primitive World" (1804). It seemed to him that because fossils were of stone it was reason-

able that they should be in mineral collections but considered that in a time dominated by the emergent coal-mining and iron-smelting industries this was no longer sufficient. It appeared to him that the opinion that these fossils were to be regarded as undeniable documents of the Flood had led to all further investigations being halted.

We now know about the anti-scientific concept, which lasted at least a century and regarded fossils as relics of the Flood. No less than K. A. Zittel (1875), perhaps the most important palaeontologist of the last century, made the following merciless comment on the subject:

"Scarcely had the idea of the freaks of nature been abandoned than theologizing science now hit on the no less crazy theory of the Flood. Since it was no longer possible to deny the organic origin of fossils, they had to serve at least for the greater glory of the Church and be brought into harmony with the Mosaic story of Creation. It was considered meritorious and was advantageous to share this standpoint and to oppose it involved persecution and danger."

What Schlotheim meant in 1804 and what others, such as Cuvier, implemented through comparative anatomical and morphological studies was the quest for stimulating ideas as the forerunners of knowledge, the identification of new scientific tasks. In his books of 1804 and 1820 and in other works, E. F. von Schlotheim provided a description of his collection of fossil animal and plant remains. For us today, his two books and the associated specimens, preserved in the Natural History Museum of the Humboldt University in Berlin, are precious evidence of the scientific beginnings of knowledge about fossils and their role in the history of nature. It was only in the 1830's that the terms palaeontology and palaeobotany were coined and it was much later before they came into general use.

However, the approach associated at that time with the word philosophy also continued to develop. It was based on wise and far-seeing thoughts on the creation of the Earth and the life on it, on the long history of nature and its epochs. In some respects it was in agreement with the conclusions to be drawn

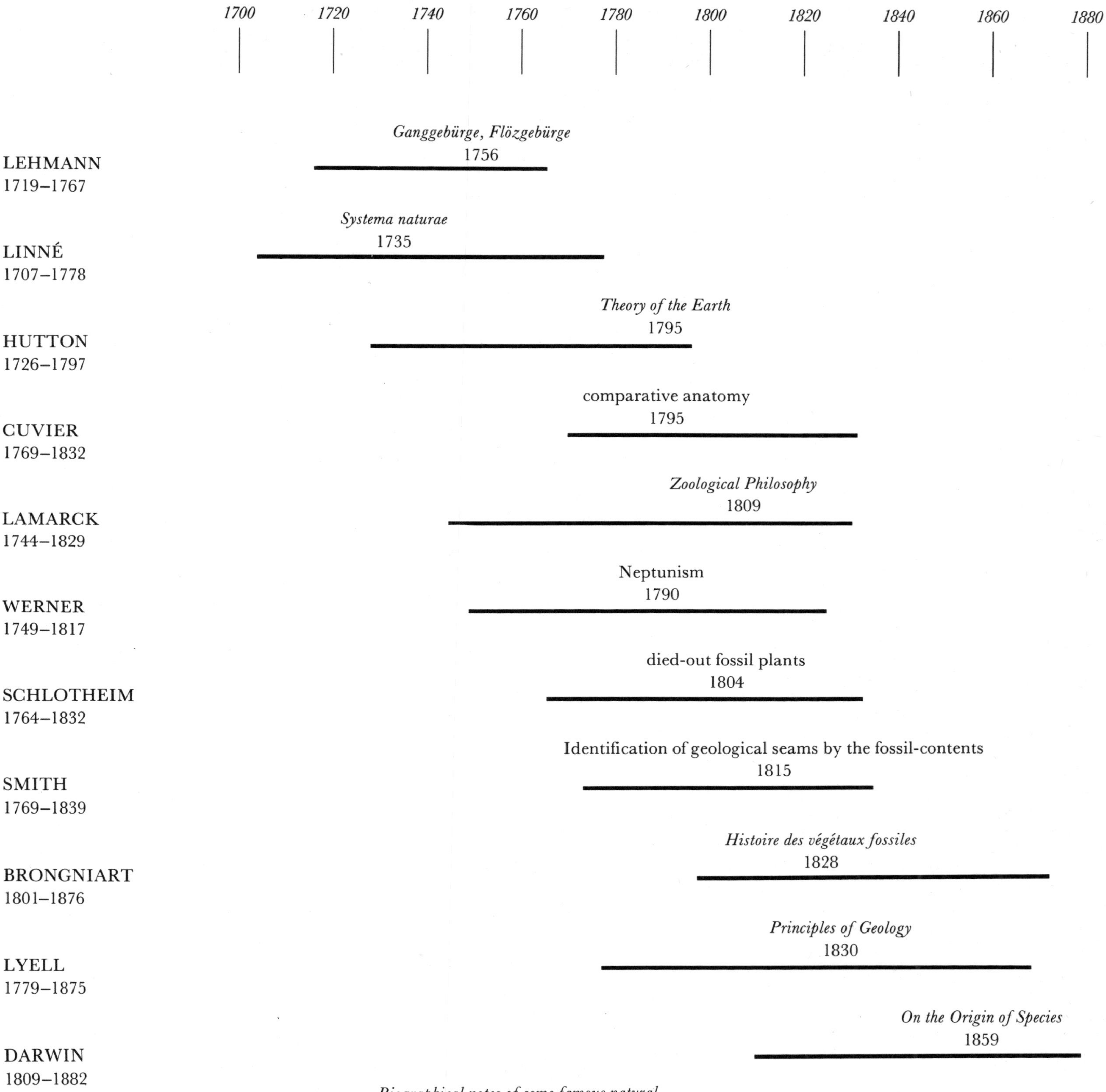

| | | | 1700 | 1720 | 1740 | 1760 | 1780 | 1800 | 1820 | 1840 | 1860 | 1880 |

LEHMANN
1719–1767

Ganggebürge, Flözgebürge
1756

LINNÉ
1707–1778

Systema naturae
1735

HUTTON
1726–1797

Theory of the Earth
1795

CUVIER
1769–1832

comparative anatomy
1795

LAMARCK
1744–1829

Zoological Philosophy
1809

WERNER
1749–1817

Neptunism
1790

SCHLOTHEIM
1764–1832

died-out fossil plants
1804

SMITH
1769–1839

Identification of geological seams by the fossil-contents
1815

BRONGNIART
1801–1876

Histoire des végétaux fossiles
1828

LYELL
1779–1875

Principles of Geology
1830

DARWIN
1809–1882

On the Origin of Species
1859

*Biographical notes of some famous natural
scientists of the 18th and 19th centruries and the date of
their great idea or their famous publications*

from fossil finds while in others it was far in advance of them or totally outstripped the limited knowledge to be derived from them.

Great Theories

The age of the great geological theories began. Jean Lamarck (1809) discussed whether it was possible at all to talk of extinct species since all of them must have devoloped further and came to the conclusion that it can "only be the case among the large animals which inhabit the dry parts of the Earth where man could eliminate the individuals of some species which he did not want to preserve or tame". Lamarck had his doubts on the existence of fossil mussels, brachiopoda and ammonites: "Why should they have become extinct since man was not able to eradicate them?"

Cuvier took a very different view when, at this time, he had to provide an answer to the following question: Is there a history of nature are there extinct creatures, can the strata, which have been increasingly exposed on a large scale and penetrated by mining, be characterized by fossils?

In 1812, Cuvier had this to say: "As an investigator of antiquity of quite a new kind, I had to supplement these witnesses of past transformations of the Earth and at the same time I had to try to decipher their real significance; I had to collect their crumbling fragments and put them together in their original order; to restore from these once more the creatures of an age long since past to which they belonged; to create them anew from their characteristics and conditions, as it were; finally, to compare them with the living creatures of the present world . . . We admire the energy with which the human spirit has measured the movements of the celestial bodies . . . Genius and science have passed beyond the limits of space; some observations have revealed the workings of the Universe. Would it therefore also not contribute to the glory of Man if it were possible to pass beyond the limits of time and, with the aid of some observations, to discover the history of the Earth . . .? To be sure, the astronomers have progressed more rapidly than the naturalists and the

epoch in which the theory of the Earth still is at the present time is roughly equivalent to the time when some philosophers thought that the heavens were a vault of stone and that the Moon was as large as the Peloponnesian peninsula. But . . . Anaxagoras was followed . . . by Copernicus, Kepler, and they prepared the way for Newton; and why should natural history not have its own Newton too, one day?"

Schlotheim was just as realistic when he wrote the following words in 1804: "It is to be wished that even more attention than in the past should be paid to the formations and circumstances in which imprints of plants occur and to which species the latter belong or if they are totally lacking in them in some districts; . . . because we may perhaps be enabled, quite unexpectedly, to make even more accurate determinations of the various formations and even to state their relative age since it could easily happen that we might discover in some only extinct and in others still existing plant species or that in general in the course of this investigation we might obtain even several important indications, among others as to whether we find, in the overlying rock or even in the coal deposits of the older formations, undoubted products of the sea and in general only shell fossils and other fossil bodies not belonging to the family of plants."

Two lines of approach contributed to the development of mining—the theoretical approach by raising major questions while the approach based on the documentation of fossil images provided names for the fossils found in the strata of the mining areas which it classified, compared with others and thus prepared and formulated conclusions on the relative age of the rocks and coal seams of the sedimentary basins. The two methods of acquiring knowledge had to measure their results with the experience gained in mining and finally had to unite. The views associated with them penetrated the mining areas and it is often difficult to say whether mining areas such as the coalmines in England and Scotland, were not the real sources of the two lines of approach. Great use was made of these

sources by travellers imbued with the spirit of enlightenment. They brought the knowledge which had been acquired there to the Mining Academy founded at Freiberg in 1776 and to the Berlin Mining Academy, established in 1770, were it developed into the science of mineralogy, geology and palaeontology.

In his report on his travels in England, the French traveller and rationalist G. Jars (1765) remarks that in Newcastle he met a foreman-driller who was an expert in drilling coal-seams and could give precise details of the thickness of the seam, the nature of the coal, the intrusions of water and so on. G. Jars reports: "Experience has taught him how to judge this correctly, the only thing is that he makes a very great secret of everything and only communicates this information to that person who has paid the expenses of drilling."

In Berlin, J. G. Lehmann (1756) published a book on the successive superimposed layers of rock and drew the first profiles of these strata. William Smith, the English canal engineer, now returned at about the turn of the century (1799) to the concept of fossils which characterize layers, illustrated tables finally being published by him in 1819. More than a century before (written in 1688 and published posthumously in 1705), the English physicist and mathematician R. Hooke (1635–1705) had already considered the possibility of elaborating a chronology from such fossil finds and of thus determining the "intervals of time of the catastrophes and changes which occured". This idea now took shape in William Smith's observations, instructions on the construction of canals and published tables.

Finally, between 1750 and 1820, a fusion of the individual component-parts was achieved: experience gained in mining and everyday life, technical progress and the urge to acquire knowledge, the spirit of enlightenment which still continued to recall something of the atmosphere of the French Revolution (1789). Belief in the Flood theory declined although it reappeared as the Neptunist theory. And so, at the beginning of the 19th century, from the subjects concerned with the art of mining (represented at mining academies) and systems of thought based on natural philosophy (represented at universities), science assumed the position previously occupied by dogmas and fantasy with reference to the nature of minerals, fossils, coal-bearing layers and ore-veins. It became customary, in the course of State visits, for kings, tsars and princes to be taken on tours of the mineral cabinets displaying the mineral wealth of the country.

Interest in natural history was re-awakened in the Age of Enlightenment, the time of the philosophers Kant and Hegel. New and previously unknown facts were brought to light and the era of the elaboration of great theories of development began. People's notions of the Earth's tropical flora of the past grew more concrete and led to first pictorial representations (Goldfuss, 1841–1844, Unger, 1851, Geinitz, 1855) of the Carboniferous forest and to notions of the Tertiary flora. These assumed an affinity between the Tertiary flora of Switzerland (Heer, 1855–1859) and Greenland, Spitsbergen and the Arctic. First conceptions of the Ice Age (Schimper, 1837) were made and rejected again. Charles Darwin began his famous research trip on the Beagle and as early as 1837 considered life to be a bundle of development branches from a common root: he noted in his diary: "My theory could stimulate palaeontology, it would call for the study of instincts, heredity and intellect . . . detailed research into hybridization . . . and the creation of species as well as into the cause of variations so that we could imagine where we come from and where we go."

"It is hard to say when knowledge of any particular natural body began and to whom this knowledge must be ascribed. Is it the one who first raised the body from the mass of the unknown or he who first perceived the special nature and individuality of this body or he who first coined a special name for it? Obviously, one would not opt for the finder nor for he who gave it its name but for the naturalist who first showed how its special characteristic might be recognized and whereby the creature is to be essentially separated and distinguished from all similar ones. But this knowledge only emerges very slowly and gradually and is obscured by many other things which, in the course of time, have to state at which point in time the first discovery of a product of nature is to be sited."

In the Proceedings of the Royal Academy of Sciences at Berlin of 1831, there appeared a paper by the German geologist L. von Buch, this being a lecture which he had read three years previously on the process of fossilization. As an additional note, he described a piece of limestone with numerous small fossils, this being illustrated by a copper plate. The small glacial erratic from Buch's collection had been found on the fields near Güstrow (German Democratic Republic).

Buch, in his late fifties at the time, began to concern himself more and more with palaeontological questions. Palaeontology had become established as a science in France, England, Germany and Sweden and had entered its great systematizing phase. Buch took a special interest in ammonites and in brachiopods, to the understanding of which he contributed a series of basic works. Stimulated by the work of the Englishman J. Sowerby and the Swede J. W. Dalman and by the piece of rock in his collection referred to above, he concerned himself as early as 1828 with the spine-bearing brachiopods *Productus* and *Leptaena*. He was the first to notice the differences in the number, arrangement and form of the spines among the *Productus* species and he was confident that these features would prove to be an important aid to determination.

"It is certain that these tubes will be just as characteristic for the different species of *Leptaena* as the echinoid spines for the *Echinita*."

Only a Slab of Transitional Limestone

What can be more exciting than the continuing discovery of an entirely new creation in almost every layer

von Buch 1843

The characteristics of the *Productus* spines caused Buch to devote a lot of thought to their biological significance but this was no more than an episode on the fringes of his main work. This illustrious geologist was primarily interested in fossils as signs of their time, in the same way that coins interest historians. He saw fossils as marks of identification in the rock layers, able to guide miners or geologists through the confusion of broken, displaced and twisted formations. It was Buch who coined the expression index-fossil (Leitfossil). With this knowledge as a basis, he turned his attention in later years to other groups of fossils with the aim of providing a critical and precise description of them as an important aid for geology. He never regarded fossils in isolation but always sought relationships and conformities with natural laws. Buch saw palaeontology as an historical science when he wrote: ". . . through knowledge of it we obtain not only the history of the Earth but also the history of life." In 1843, when the 5th edition of his geological map of Germany appeared in 24 sheets, he wrote in the introduction to his paper "On *Productus* or *Leptaena*":

"What can be more exciting than the continuing discovery of an entirely new creation in almost every layer which shows us forms through which frequently the inner arrangement, the purpose and, one would like to say, the history of the internal organization of creatures still living becomes comprehensible and visible for the first time! What can be more impressive than when, through observations, we see time and again how a few shells or other organic remains are able to guide us so reliably through the labyrinth of rock strata which are often confused, dispersed, upturned or totally scattered that they can even be used for practical applications. Indeed, even the thinking miner also believes already that for his activities he cannot at all dispense with palaeontology which, thirty years ago, could never have been imagined by anybody and would rightly have been considered absurd."

With less enthusiasm, Buch criticizes in the following lines tendencies which even a century later had still not been overcome:

"The only thing is that no zoologist has yet seriously concerned himself with these forms

Transitional limestone

"*A petrified slab from the fields near Güstrow in Mecklenburg, probably originating from Southern Sweden*" (*Leopold von Buch 1831*). *The slab here, of which this is the first published photograph, is of great interest in respect of the history of science. It is a quarternary Beyrichians erratic, limestone with 'Beyrichienkalk' in the broader sense. Upper Silurian. Area of origin: Central Baltic.*

Animals preserved include snail and mollusc stein-kerns, bryozoan colonies, crinoid remains and shells of ostracoderms, brachiopods and tentaculites.

Page 41: Detail with Protochonetes striatellus, Tentaculites lebiensis, Neobeyrichia buchiana, Frostiella lebiensis, Lioclema *sp. and* Loxonema *cf.* obsoleta.

Top: complete, magnification: 2×

Right: Buch's illustration, 1831
Fig. I the specimen with marginal diagrams;
Fig. II Reconstruction of Leptaena lata.

Fig. I.

Fig. II.

Feelers

Original from the Schlotheim collection with the type examples of Tentaculites scalaris *and* Calymene tentaculata *boulder, Silurian, Beyrichian limestone. The specimen shows why Schlotheim came to the conclusion that tentaculites were the feelers of trilobites. Present state of preparation, shown here for the first time (see p.2).*

Tentaculites scalaris

Original of Zagora 1969. Silurian, Beyrichian limestone, boulder. Zerben near Magdeburg, German Democratic Republic. Steinkern and external mould. Magnification: 8×

Calymene tentaculata

Original of Schrank 1970. Silurian, Beyrichian limestone, "Leba" drilling, 780 metres depth. Poland. Complete example for explanation of the opposite type specimen. Magnification: 8×

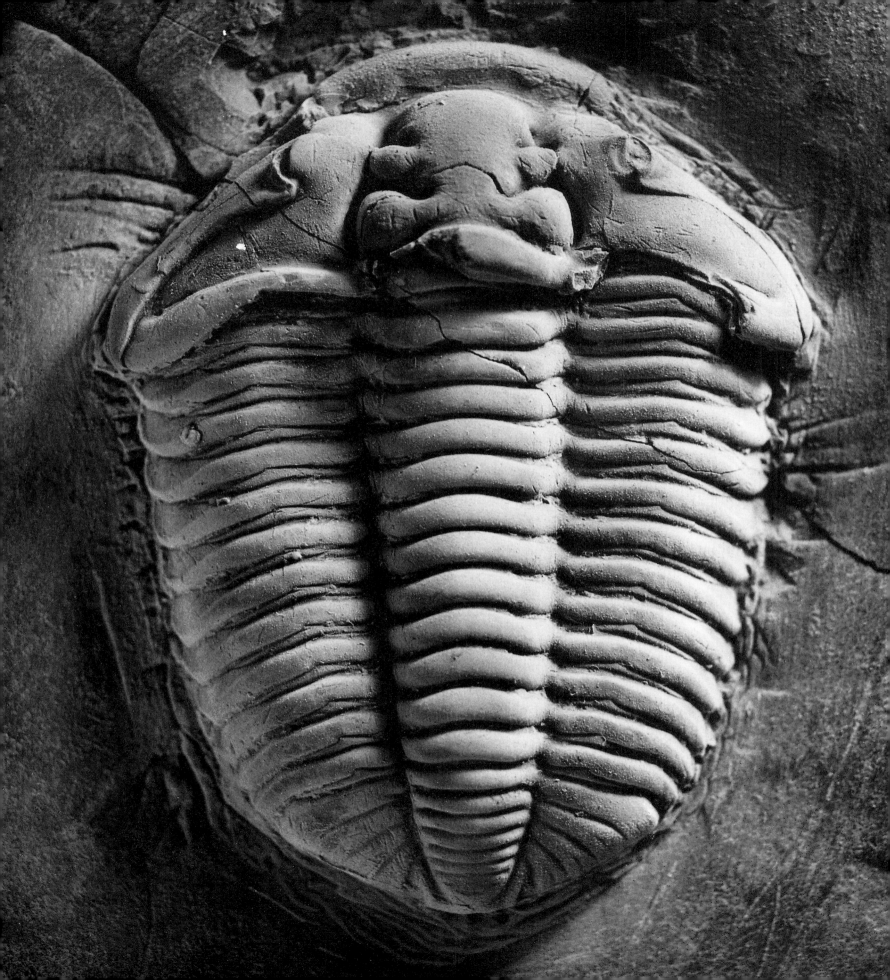

Protochonetes striatellus

Fine-ribbed form. Silurian, Beyrichian limestone, boulder. Wriezen, Frankfort/Oder district (German Democratic Republic). Inside of three pedicle valves. Bifurcated median septum (generic characzeristic). Schlotheim collection. Original specimen from Wriezen (Schlotheim 1820, p. 255) with the type specimens of Terabratulites pecten *Schlotheim 1820. Shown here for the first time. Magnification: 8×*

Large-ribbed form. Silurian, Beyrichian limestone, boulder. Specimen from the Schlotheim collection. According to Schlotheim's original label Terebratulites pecten *var.* gregarius. *Next to it:* Camerotoechia nucula *and* Frostiella plicatula. *Shown here for the first time. Magnification: 4×*

Page 48:
An old mollusc

Mobergella holsti *(Moberg, 1892). Boulder of Lower Cambrian, glauconite sandstone flags. Shell-diameter: 3 mm. The tiny, shallow-cone shells of this species are some of the oldest shell-fossils of Europe and characterize the deepest biozone of the Baltic Cambrian. The phosphatic shells were first thought to be brachiopods and then patellae. Nowadays, they are classified with the monoplacophores, single-shell molluscs. This class was first postulated in 1940 for palaeozoic fossils, an opinion which was convincingly confirmed when in 1952 a recent deep-sea form was discovered (a living fossil,* Neopilina galathea*). The segmented attachment muscle imprints on our shell are signs of an original segmentation of the body.*

since he still retreats with repugnance from palaeontology and the richest and most comprehensive collections of fossils are still to be found not where one would expect them, in zoological collections but, in a most contradictory manner, as part of mineralogy.

Nevertheless, one scarcely has the courage to reproach the zoologist with this lack of attention when one sees with what facility, with what thoughtlessness and with what lack of judgement the geognosts form a species or even a genus from each fragment resembling an organic form and believe they have achieved great fame when they are able to count the quantity of the newly named species in their hundreds!''

Palaeontology, as a science between two stools, has long suffered from the lack of mutual sympathy between geology and biology although even G. Cuvier showed the right way in his works. However, we have to return to the erratic of Güstrow.

The small slab shown in 1831 as transitional limestone came, with the Buch collection, to the palaeontological collection of the Berlin University in 1854. It was at that time, in the hands of E. Beyrich, that this collection developed into the systematically arranged collection which still exists, in expanded form, at the Natural History Museum of the Humboldt University. The slab was preserved but it was quite forgotten that it had been the original of an illustration by Buch since neither Buch nor Beyrich mentioned this fact on their labels.

The rediscovery of this piece of Silurian limestone led to the present remarks. At the time it was first described it was designated transitional limestone since it was only in 1834 that the term Silurian was introduced by C. Lapworth in England for such strata.

Nowadays, an object which is known to originate from the collection of L. von Buch is an item of great value for the history of science. When, however, such an object proves to be a long-lost original, this is quite an exciting matter. Buch interpreted the fossils on the slab in a way which appears curious to us. He regarded tentaculites as spiny valves and Beyrichiae as brood of brachiopods. Apart from this, it is particularly fascinating to look

at a familiar faunal spectrum, such as that of the Beyrichian limestone, through the eyes of Buch. Fixed on a piece of rock, a small collection of fossils remained intact for 150 years with no possibility of fossils and labels being mixed up.

Buch recorded the visible fossils of the boulder in his drawing, put numbers to them and listed their names in a key. The rock was drawn lifesize but important details at the edges were portrayed on a larger scale. We have placed Buch's drawing in facsimile form next to a photograph of the rock. This is what Buch had to say about it:

"Among the many blocks which cover the Baltic lowlands, pieces of limestone and sandstone may often be found which consist more of the remains of animals than of the principal substance itself.''

Buch, a native of the Uckermark, must have been referring here to erratics of Beyrichian limestone, as well as others of Upper Jurassic and Tertiary age. He then says of the fossil remains: ". . . their diversity in a small area is so great that these peculiarities of form, the character of the shells . . . can often be studied on a small part of the hand.''

"Fig. 1 . . . shows the outline of such a one, with the designation of some of the most remarkable forms. There are several heart-shaped bivalves, extended in lenght, probably venericardiae; steinkerns of a univalve shell-fish with six whorls, without doubt a *Turritella*; a branchy, very delicate and clear millepora; encrinite vertebra with points and lines, sometimes connected, sometimes separate, down to an incredible smallness; traces of a large *Modiolus*; a small *Trochus*; some small patellae; several spirifers and finally shells in an excellent state of preservation of a new and as yet undescribed *Leptaena (Producta)*, in all stages of size and growth, from the first egg to the largest possible form. The young brood lies between the larger shells [. . .] in an indescribable quantity.''

This description by Buch throws a clear light on the state of palaeontological knowledge 150 years ago. At that time, it was living species and especially genera which provided in many cases the only clue for the determination of fossil forms (*Turritella, Trochus, Patella,*

Millepora, etc.) or it was Tertiary genera *(Venericardia)* which gave the lead. At the beginning, generic names were still chosen which recall similar living genera but then the independence of fossil genera which were observed was reflected to an increasing extent in the names they were given.

E. F. von Schlotheim, the founder of palaeobotany, introduced the binary nomenclature, pioneered by Linné, to Germany for fossils as well. He still formed the generic names with the aid of the -ites suffix from the familiar names of recent forms, e.g., *Terebratula—Terebratulites, Echinus—Echinites, Nucula—Nuculites.* If we take a look at the supplementary note by Buch, it will be seen that there are a few changes in determinations as compared with his work of 1831. It is certain that these corrections were made only a little later. They show that it was not long before Buch abandoned his ideas concerning *Leptaena lata.* In addition to *Leptaena lata,* there are now also the names *Tentaculites ornatus* and *Agnostus pisiformis.* These were a reference to those fossils which he had previously considered as spines and offspring of *Leptaena lata.* As far as the tentaculitids are concerned, a better classification was not possible. Only in recent years has it been possible to identify and classify an increasing number of species from the profusion of the tentaculites. The examples on the block (Nos. 2, 4, 5, 6) belong to *Odessites lebiensis* (Zagora, 1972). They were determined by the author of the species. In the case of *Agnostus pisiformis,* however, this was an incorrect determination to which reference will be made later. The offspring proved to be an innumerable quantity of ostracods and Beyrich's label already indicates this.

The form listed as *Avicula rectangularis* on Buch's note is not shown in the drawing. This is clearly the steinkern of a shell at the left edge which can now be identified as *Ptychopteria modiolopsis* Roemer. *Cucullella ovata* was previously mentioned as *Venericardia* (No. 19) but is probably a *Nuculites* species. Only the outline is indicated of what was thought to be a *Modiolus.* The steinkerns of snails are referred to as *Murchisonia cingulata* Hisinger. Shellfish and snails are very rarely found preserved with their shells in Beyrichian limestone and are thus not easy to study but a fortunate find which was recently made shows once again the delicate slit-band of the species.

It is not clear which forms were considered by Buch to be *Trochus* and spirifers. The "small patellae" refer to the cup-like shells of the hingeless brachiopod *Craniops antiqua* (Schlotheim, 1813). The millepore (No. 20) is called *Calamopora fibrosa* in the key to the drawing and *Aulopora* on the label. At that time, the genera *Calamopora* and *Aulopora* had just been described by Goldfuss (1829). And yet this is not a coral colony but a bryozoan colony with a multitude of twigs, probably a *Lioclema* species. This kind of confusion between certain Palaeozoic Bryozoa and tabulate corals continued for a long time even after the clarification of the problem. In both groups, an exact determination of the species is only possible after the preparation of sections with various orientations. The brachiopod *Leptaena lata* (Nos. 1, 3) is, in fact, designated at the present time as *Protochonetes striatellus*. This species will now be examined in more detail.

The enlarged reconstruction of the brachiopod shell is immediately apparent from Buch's illustration. Anyone who has come into contact as a collector with Beyrichian limestone will immediately notice something curious about this reconstruction. Buch has put *Tentaculites* as valves on a *Chonetes* pedicle valve, precisely at those points where, in real life, there had been the much more delicate *Chonetes* spines. Although we are still not completely sure about the exact systematic position of *Tentaculites* within the group of the molluscs, it is nevertheless known that they were certainly not brachiopod spines—an assumption which Buch himself was very quick to abandon—nor were they the tentacles of trilobites, as considered possible by E.F. v. Schlotheim in 1820.

What was the background to this reconstruction of *Leptaena lata*? From the many rocks of the transitional limestone period which had been collected, it was already known at that time that tubulites, with their slender pointed cones, were found in the same places as the delicately ribbed shells. They were picked up in the fields of Mecklenburg and Pomerania and also in Gotland. And the theory had long

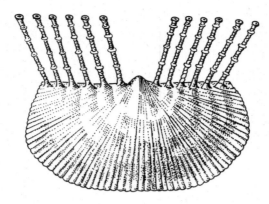

Reconstruction of Leptaena lata *according to L. von Buch 1831*

been advanced as well that the loose stones of Northern Germany must have come from the corresponding kinds of bedrock in Sweden (Von Ahrenswald, 1775). The tubulites had thus already attracted the attention of the conchologists and Buch was aware of various opinions on the subject. Nevertheless, none of these interpretations—which will be examined later—really convinced him.

A glance at the enlarged marginal figures 5 and 9 reveals—to our astonishment—that the *Chonetes* spines in these details are depicted with coils like *Tentaculites*. Is this the key to this remarkable reconstruction? What has Buch seen? The examination of the original slab did indeed reveal delicate annular lines on the spines but these have been reproduced in the drawing in an exaggerated manner.

The annular lines follow each other at the same, slightly irregular spacings as the concentric growth lines on the *Chonetes* shell and are thus to be interpreted as a growth structure. Macroscopically, the picture may remotely recall the conditions in the erased tentaculite tips but when examined under the microscope there is nothing which remains of the supposed conformity. The apparent similarity of the *Chonetes* spines with the calcite steinkerns of the delicate tentaculite tips puzzled Buch which was why he wrote: "It can scarcely be doubted that they are not to be determined in the same way since very similar rings are to be seen on Nos. 5 and 9 and even on No. 3." On the other hand, Buch stressed the disproportion in the sizes but did not regard this as a serious objection. "The valves, which are to be seen individually on the slab in Fig. 1, are very large in relation to those which are to be observed still attached to the shells and a shell of such a size as would be necessary for these valves is not to be found." He also remarked: "Furthermore, those still in position have almost always lost their outer shell but in the case of the larger ones it is well preserved in a respectable length." The clear differences in the state of preservation of the shell in the case of the tentaculites on the one hand and the *Chonetes*, together with their spines, on the other was thus obviously explained by the presence or absence of an outer shell of the valves. Perhaps the optical instruments then available did not yet permit observations of the accuracy required or theoretical wishful thinking was a temporary obstruction on the path to truth. As is evident from his label, Buch was very quick to abandon his incorrect interpretation of the tentaculites as brachiopod spines, probably being convinced by better finds and arguments.

As already indicated, the coiled tentaculites attracted the attention of collectors and conchologists at a very early stage. E.J. Walch in 1775 was the first to describe the strange tubulites and compared them to scaphopods. He was thus closer to the truth than many later observers since this group of animals, which was already extinct in the Devonian, certainly belonged to the molluscs, this being apparent from the shell structure.

Schlotheim (1820) gave the "so peculiar a family" the name of tentaculitids and described and illustrated the two species of *T. scalaris* and *T. annulatus*. He too was naturally intrigued by the question of the systematic position of this group of fossils. Schlotheim listed all four possibilities. Under *Tentaculites annulatus* we find the reference to pieces from the Harz Devonian with this remark:

"It seems most likely to me that these are perhaps parts of the crown of *Encrinites epithonius*, about which only completely preserved examples can provide us with information."

Somewhat later, this comparison with the cirri of sea-lilies was considered apt by Goldfuss, too.

Under *Tentaculites scalaris*, however, he had this to say:

"They were thought by Schröter to be segmented tooth-shells, with which they are not related at all, while others suspect that they are the detached members of trilobites which were situated on the well-known protusions of the head shields and acted as antennae. Perhaps the coming period will soon bring further enlightenment."

Schlotheim expressed similar remarks about the description of the trilobite head under *Trilobites tentaculatus*:

"It is very likely that the fossils lying in various directions next to the same which are of a strange step-like arrangement and similar to tooth-shells and are described in the Appen-

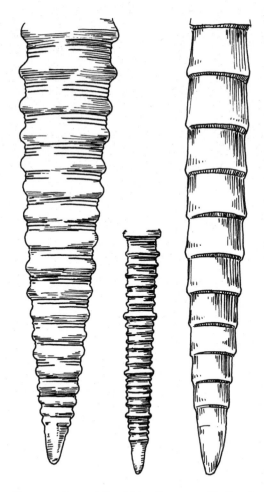

Tentaculites *of Beyrichian limestone. Shell and steinkern of the large* Tentaculites scalaris *and shell specimen of* Tentaculites lebiensis. (7×)

dix belong to these trilobites and were perhaps located like feelers on the side-lobes."

It is from this opinion that the generic name *Tentaculites* is derived. In comparison with the hypothesis formulated by Buch, it must be pointed out that the two researchers based their conclusions on different species of *Tentaculites*. *O. Lebiensis* is much more slender and delicate than *T. scalaris*. The type examples of *Tentaculites scalaris* Schlotheim and *Calymene tentaculata* (Schlotheim) lie next to each other on the same piece of Beyrichian limestone. This was found as an erratic at Oberwiederstädt in the district of Halle (German Democratic Republic) and is now in the collection of the Museum for Natural History, Berlin. In recent years, the two holotypes have been dégaged and subjected to a revision. Although the remains of the two types are incomplete, the removal of matrix material has now enabled the major diagnostic features to be revealed. The two examples can be reliably classified in their groups which are now understood much more fully and, as the type specimens, they each characterize their newly revised species as named by Schlotheim. The numerous misinterpretations of the two species formulated in the past are understandable when the old original illustration is compared with the new photograph (see pages 8 and 44).

When account is taken of the state of research in 1820, it is not difficult to understand why, on the basis of such finds, there was an urge to see a basic relationship between tentaculitids and trilobite heads. But, like Buch many years later, Schlotheim soon revised his original interpretation. In this case, too, this is to be inferred from the original label which, interestingly enough, reads as follows:

"*Orthoceratites tentaculatus*—listed in *Die Petrefactenkunde* as a separate species under the name Tentaculith but, according to more recent investigations, belonging to the orthoceratites by virtue of the longitudinal nerve valve."

The reference to this called more recent investigations is unclear but the conclusion we have to draw today is very similar. Recent investigations, using grinding techniques, indicate that the tentaculites, by reason of their septa with siphuncles and their triple-layer wall structure, belong to the cephalopods or at least are closely related to them. W. Blind (1969) considers them to be an early branch of the cephalopods with a series of primitive features. But Larsson (1979), exploring countless tentaculites from Gotland, emphatically denies the theory of the molluscs. Yet it was not long ago at all that the tentaculites were considered as belonging to three different families of creatures, the annelids, the scyphozoa and the molluscs. There is consequently little justification for criticism of the early researchers.

In the Matter of *Striatellus*

Let us return to the starting point of our considerations, to the boulder from Buch's collection. To us today it may seem confusing that the great mountain researcher classified the brachiopod species, which he regarded as being new, as belonging to the genus of *Leptaena* Dalman. However, Dalman's definition of this genus gave it a much wider scope at that time. With the publication of J. W. Dalman's second book on Swedish fossils at the beginning of 1828, the study of brachiopods had just taken an important step forward. A notable and exemplary feature for that time was the clear detail of this monographic work. Dalman provided a diagnosis and description for every genus and species with measurements, comparisons and details of origin. Without doubt, the systematic school of Linné is reflected in the work of the Swedish Dalman.

In his treatise, Dalman identified and named not only *Leptaena* but also other palaeontological genera: *Orthis, Cyrtia, Delthyris, Gypidula* and *Atrypa*. He was thus the first to indicate groups of forms which are of great importance in the present taxonomy of fossil brachiopods. For instance, a superfamily is now designated as Atrypacea and the *Orthis* relations are to be found as name-sources even up to the level of order in the taxonomic hierarchy: *Orthis, Orthidae, Orthacea, Orthina, Orthida*.

As a derivation from the Greek word *leptos*, Dalman named his genus *Leptaena* and, according to our present-day understanding, thus

referred to those forms among the members of the largest brachiopod order, the extinct Strophomenida which, by virtue of their concave brachial valve and their similarly convex pedicle valve, appear so exceptionally thin (Greek: leptos). In relation to the size of the shell, the space available for its inhabitant was very restricted. As a consequence, Dalman was also obliged to include the species of *Productus* described by the Englishman J. Sowerby in his genus.

At the present time, the species of *Leptaena* in the concept of 1831 are considered to belong to three different sub-orders: to the spineless Strophomenidina with the genus *Leptaena* in the present sense and to the spiny Chonetidina and Productidina which evolved separately from the former during the Silurian and at the beginning of the Devonian. Even Buch, who took a particular interest in the spiny productids, was not entirely satisfied with Dalman's *Leptaena* concept and was reluctant to abandon the term *Productus*. He used both names side-by-side. For him, it was the spines which were the decisive feature:

". . . which so far have not received their due attention and which, in my view, nevertheless really constitute the main character for the entire genus of the *Leptaena* or *Producta* . . ."

To begin with, Buch still used the generic name *Leptaena* for species of this group but he soon returned to *Productus*, which he used consistently. Obviously stimulated by Dalman's work, Buch studied this erratic block in more detail and, in the same year, even before the completion of his investigations, expressed his pleasure at the find when discussing erratics from the vicinity of Berlin.

". . . several, quite excellent species of *Productus* . . . have not yet been described, including a very delicate *Leptaena tubifera* which is in my possession and whose edge is ornamented with extremely artistic valves. In reality, however, as I was pleased to discover with no little astonishment only a few days ago, these are a strange and highly developed organ which was probably used by the creature as feet for moving over rocks."

Buch classed this brachiopod shell in Dalman's new *Leptaena* genus but he chose a different species-name *tubifera*—the tube-bearer.

This name is only of historical interest since Buch's observation was only published in 1885, long after his death, in his collected works. Buch's description of the brachiopod was published under the name *Leptaena lata* in 1832 but, like its reconstruction, the name was forgotten, too. The species had already been described as *Orthis striatella* by Dalman in 1828 and, by the international rules on zoological nomenclature, it is the older name which takes precedence. Dalman's description and illustration are clear but in one important point incomplete. There is no reference to the spines at the hinge-line. Dalman should have really classified his species from Gotland as *Leptaena* if he had had shells with the delicate and rarely well preserved spines at his disposal. Buch, on the other hand, did come across such shells. For him, however, the spines were so important that he was unwilling to identify his material with Dalman's species and, under the impression of this special feature, described it as *Leptaena lata*.

Experts refer to this variable species by the name of *Chonetes striatella*. However, bearing in mind the modern generic classification, it must now be correctly designated as *Protochonetes striatellus* (Dalman, 1828) until a modern analysis based on variation statistics finally resolves the problem of whether it is a question of one or more species or sub-species. The typical *P. striatellus* from Gotland and the more recent *P. ludloviensis* from England would have to be included in this examination.

The delicate and finely ribbed shells of *Protochonetes striatellus* are some of the most frequently found fossils of the southern Baltic lowlands with their moraines left by the Ice Age. They are to be found everywhere between the mouth of the Rhine and Neman in the widely dispersed blocks of Beyrichian limestone. It is thus to be expected that even the early collectors of the 18th century were familiar with the species. As early as 1717 by Pastor M. G. A. Helwings, a member of the Royal Scientific Society at Berlin, illustrated the species in his Lithographia Angerburgica as *Pectunculites*. It was confirmed by K. F. Klöden in 1834 that *Leptaena lata* was to be found in all the old collections of the Mark Brandenburg area. He also remarked that:

"It is found in very great quantities in the mountain limestone of Brandenburg and it often seems that entire pieces consist . . . only of it. It is evident that there are two varieties, one with finer and the other with more marked stripes, in the latter the stripes or radiating ridges then being fewer in number."

This statement by Klöden that there were two varieties in this species was subsequently repeated by other authors, and is still valid today. A. Krause in 1877 pointed out that in the handwritten notes left by the scholar E. Boll the two forms are described as separate species "which, incidentally, are usually found in different pieces of rock but with the same fossils of other kinds". Krause discussed the arguments of Boll but did not associate himself with them. Nevertheless, modern experts have reason enough, within the framework of modern fauna analysis of Beyrichian limestone, to concern themselves with this question once again. Even Krause's remarks enable possible conclusions to be drawn as to the younger stratigraphic level of the more coarsely ribbed form.

As early as 1838, A. Quenstedt, who later won fame als the explorer of the Swabian Jurassic (now the territory of the Federal Republic of Germany), pointed out that Schlotheim in Gotha already possessed this species and had described it in 1820 as *Terebratulites pecten*. Following the purchase of Schlotheim's collection for the university collection at Berlin, Quenstedt had catalogued it between 1833 and 1837 and was thus more familiar with it than any other person. In Schlotheim (1820), under *Terebratulites pecten*, there is the following entry:

"Pieces of transitional limestone rock from Sweden and erratic blocks of this limestone from Wriezen on the Oder, exposed and enclosed, with some shells in a very fine state of preservation."

It is also noted that the shells of this species are characterized by delicate, radiating markings, are wider than they are long and only moderately curved "sometimes quite flat with a shallow concave depression in the upper shell".

An examination of the originals revealed that both variations of the erratic-type *Chonetes*

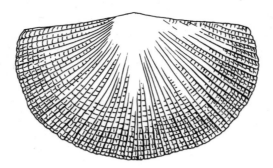

Illustration of Orthis striatella *according to Dalman 1828*

are to be found in Schlotheim's collection. The block from Wriezen (Frankfort/Oder district, German Democratic Republic) is most likely to have been Schlotheim's original. The group of the three best-preserved valves on this specimen is depicted here for the first time (see p. 46). The three pedicle valves, belonging to the finely striated type, display their inner side with the features of the *Protochonetes* genus. The more coarsely ribbed form (see p. 47) is found together with *Camarotoechia nucula* in large numbers on a slab for which Schlotheim gave two alternative site-designations as the probable site. His uncertainty indicates that this block may have come from the old Schröter collection which was taken over by Schlotheim. As a result of Schlotheim's publication, *Terebratulites pecten* is, according to the rules, the oldest species-name which, as demonstrated by the originals, is clearly assigned to the two varieties of the brachiopod shells most frequently found in Nordic erratics. It was adopted by Quenstedt and Goldfuss modified it to *Leptaena pectinata*. For more than a century, however, and for no good reason, it has ceased to be used.

Twelve years after Buch had described *Leptaena lata*, he turned his attention once more to this common species. In his treatise of 1843 "On *Productus* or *Leptaena*", he opted for the use of an even older name. Like Schlotheim in 1820 in the case of *Terebratulites sarcinulatus*, he made use of an illustration and details originating from J. W. von Hüpsch of 1768 and now used the name *Productus sarcinulatus* Hüpsch. In this usage Buch took account of Schlotheim's illustration, Dalman's *Orthis striatella* and his own *Leptaena lata* but disregarded Schlotheim's *Terebratulites pecten*. Not knowing what Schlotheim wished to be understood by *Terebratulites pecten*, since he was obviously unfamiliar with the latter's originals, Buch confused two species of *Chonetes* which had already been correctly distinguished by Schlotheim.

One of these species, *Terebratulites pecten* (= *Orthis striatellus* = *Leptaena lata*), is found in layers of the Upper Silurian while the other, *Terebratulites sarcinulatus*, comes from the rocks of the Devonian. It is evident from his remarks that Buch used the inappropriate term *Productus sarcinulatus* for *Chonetes* in general but was primarily thinking of his old *Leptaena lata*, i.e. the Silurian species.

"This object, which is very delicate in shape and radiations, is a true index-shell for upper Silurian strata; and it is the more remarkable in that it almost exclusively belongs to these strata . . . And it is practically the only *Productus* which Silurian strata can show."

Terebratulites sarcinulatus Schlotheim (1820) is now considered to be the type-species of the genus *Chonetes* which was put forward by Fischer de Waldheim in 1830. The Lectotype of this species selected from Schlotheim's originals can thus be regarded as the basic model for the approximately 30 genera of the Chonetida. The illustration shown here (see p. 57) is the first complete picture of the specimen with the type. However, the impressions and steinkerns of other brachiopods are far more prominent on this piece of Kahleberg sandstone which comes from Rammelsberg in the Harz mountains. Whoever sees the steinkern of *Euryspirifer paradoxus* cannot help but be reminded of a sea-gull gliding through the air. The species was described and illustrated by Schlotheim in 1813 from a find at the same site. In the meantime, it has proved to be quite an important index-fossil of the Upper Emsian stage in the Lower Devonian between the Harz mountains and Morocco.

Ostracodae

Let us return to that second notable feature in the process of awakening in palaeontology which we came across in connection with *Leptaena lata*. Buch, in 1831, mentioned that there was an astonishing quantity of *Leptaena* brood lying around between the larger shells— "in all degrees of size and growth". We now know that these tiny shells are the characteristic valves of certain palaeozoic ostracods (crustaceans). This realization had not yet been arrived at in 1830 since the modern ostracods known at that time bore hardly any similarity to the relatively large Silurian forms.

The observer of the tiny valves at that time must have noticed not only the considerable variation in size but also the clear, triple division of the larger valves with their more

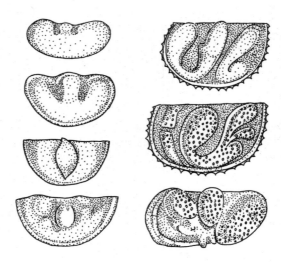

Illustration of the stages of Battus tuberculatus *according to Klöden 1834*

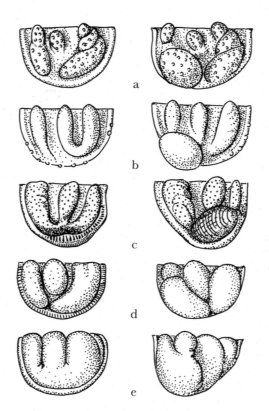

Illustration of the five Beyrichia *species according to Krause 1877. Male specimens on the left, female on the right.*

a Beyrichia tuberculata
b B. buchiana
c B. maccoyiana
d B. salteriana
e B. wilckensiana

marked curvature. The differences in size and shape of the different species, as we now know, were interpreted as the stages of growth of a single species; the triple division, however, stimulated comparisons which led to two noteworthy attempts to establish a systematic classification. Buch's brood thesis was possibly inspired by the brachial valves of *Protochonetes* which display three short radial septa on their inner sides which are continued, in corrugated fashion, into the lamellae of the shell and thus are superficially similar to some of the ostracod valves.

K. F. Klöden rejected this interpretation as early as 1834. He was responsible for the oldest collection of glacial erratics to be scientifically studied which is still in existence today. Klöden's finds came only from Potsdam (German Democratic Republic) and Kreuzberg (West Berlin) for the most part. Klöden was not the first Berliner to collect erratics but he was the first whose conclusions and collection have survived and can be checked. The fossils deposited in collections remain the enduring touchstone of our knowledge. A scientific analysis, accurate though it may be, is always limited to the highest level of knowledge of the time. Truth is relative. We want to see things as they are and yet we only ever see them to the extent that we are capable of seeing them.

In his book, Klöden devoted pages to the specimen with which we are concerned here and depicted it in several drawings on a plate. Under *Battus tuberculatus*, he wrote the following words:

"Up till now, this little creature, which occurs in countless numbers in the transitional limestone of Brandenburg, has almost entirely escaped the attention of our palaeontologists. Only Mr. L. von Buch remembers it . . . but considers it to be no more than the brood of *Leptaena lata*. A more precise investigation has obliged me not to share the view of the excellent researcher and I am forced to classify it with the trilobites and specifically with the *Battus* family."

However, the genus name *Battus* Dalman 1827, now long since forgotten, was inappropriate as a more recent synonym of *Agnostus* Brongniart 1822 from the very start. The distinction between *Battus* and *Leptaena* was justi-

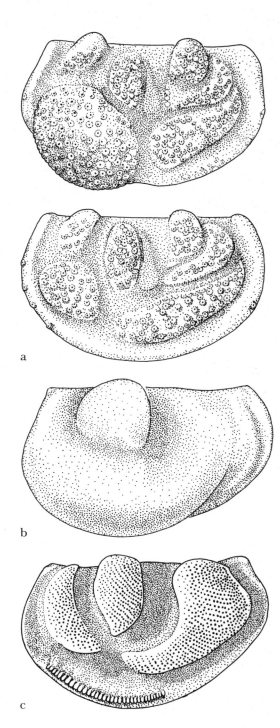

Important ostracods of Beyrichian limestone, partly according to Martinson 1963 and 1973. About 20×. The left forms characterize Beyrichian limestone in the narrower sense, the right forms the older layers of Beyrichian limestone in the broader sense.

a Nodibeyrichia tuberculata (♀ ♂)
b Kloedenia wilckensiana
c Hemsiella *cf.* maccoyiana

fied in great detail by Klöden who pointed out the differences in their shells in respect of colour, gloss and sculpture and in the absence of intermediate forms. In classifying it with the trilobites, he based his opinion on the trilobite-like appearance of the shell and its triple-division, semi-circular shape, similar to that of *Battus pisiformis*. Klöden then regrets that he is unable to say any more about the mysterious creature, "as little as is known up till now about *Battus pisiformis*. It cannot yet be said whether these bodies are the entire animal or only individual head and tail plates, as with the species of the genus *Asaphus*, for instance."

When Klöden compared the ostracods of Beyrichian limestone with *Agnostus pisiformis* from Cambrian bituminous limestone, it must be remembered that he had no personal knowledge of the occurrence in masses of the Cambrian trilobites in glacial erratics but based his conclusions on older descriptions. The obvious differences in comparison with *Agnostus pisiformis* as expressed in the asymmetry of the triple division and in the tubercle ornamentation led him to consider the new form as a new species *Battus tuberculatus*.

If, at this point, we take another look at Buch's unfortunately undated label, we find that it also bears the words *Agnostus pisiformis*. This determination is certainly to be attributed to Klöden's studies. It is only not known for certain whether Buch wrote his label before the publication of *Battus tuberculatus* by Klöden or afterwards, already aware that the smoother ostracods on his glacial erratic from Güstrow did not correspond to the coarsely tuberculated forms of Klöden.

As already remarked, Klöden described *Battus tuberculatus* in very great detail. Thus it is easy for the present-day palaeontologist to confirm some of the alleged growth-stages but to see others as belonging to different species. The species regarded by Klöden as the final stage is the easiest to identify. It is even shown as a complete bivalved shell. Subsequently, the species-name *tuberculate* was only applied to this species. It is the most frequent and characteristic fossil of the type of erratic block discussed here. In 1838, A. Quenstedt called this *Productus* limestone after the brachiopod shells which are likewise often found in masses in it,

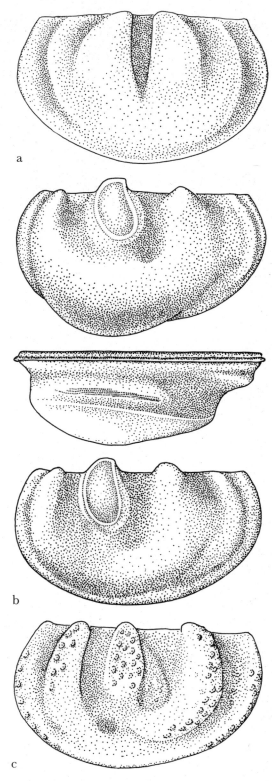

a Londina kiesowi
b Frostiella groenwalliana (♀ *from the side and from underneath* ♂)
c Neobeyrichia buchiana

the designation later being corrected to *Chonetes* limestone. Quenstedt was also the first to express doubt about the trilobite thesis when, with reference to the small fossils, he drew particular attention to their bivalved nature.

A few years later, weighty arguments were put forward against the trilobite thesis. E. Beyrich assigned the species described by Klöden a place among the ostracods. In his honour and immediately after this, the genus *Beyrichia* was simultaneously proposed by two people for different species. In 1846, F. M'Coy described a species from Ireland as *Beyrichia klödeni* while quite independently and at almost the same time E. Boll of Mecklenburg introduced the Klöden-type itself as *Beyrichia tuberculata*. From this, the generic name was later transferred to the type of glacial erratic which it fills in such masses. Today, the two species are classified in separate genera and so the second species described had to be given a new generic name: *Nodibeyrichia tuberculata*.

The designation Beyrichian limestone dates back to G. Kade (1855). He was the first to give a more specific designation to this type of erratic block but in the period which followed the scope of the term was extended to include all similar Silurian boulders containing Beyrichiae so that a more precise definition of the term became necessary. Today, Beyrichian limestone in the narrower sense is defined by the occurrence of the genus *Nodibeyrichia* and of the Kloedeniae associated with it.

It was also in 1855 that a book devoted to Beyrichiae was published by the English ostracod researcher R. Jones, whose name subsequently became well known in this field.

Beyrich had sent him several erratics which had originally been collected in Berlin and Breslau. Specialists still regard the palaeozoic ostracod fauna of Beyrichian blocks as one of the best-preserved on Earth. Jones described several new species at the same time which are still used for the supplementary characterization of Beyrichian limestone even though, in the meantime, there has been a considerable proliferation of genera. However, the old species-names remind us of the palaeontologists of that time: *Neobeyrichia buchiana, Hemsiella maccoyiana, Macrypsilon salteriana, Kloedenia wilckensiana.*

In the course of time, the old familiar species have been joined by many new ones, especially as a result of the intensive research work carried out by A. Martinson and others in the last two decades. It was found that the ostracods allow Beyrichian erratics to be classified in groups. The ostracods, together with other groups of fossils, play an important role for geologists. Thus, classification of Beyrichian limestone in the Silurian has been carried out; the probable place of origin being the sea floor in the middle of the Baltic to the south of Gotland. It was there that the glaciers of the Ice Age must have picked up the rock and transported it southwards. Typical Beyrichian limestone is still only known in the form of glacial erratics, even though rocks of the same age with the same fossils have also been found in the Silurian strata at the southern tip of the Estonian island of Saaremaa and in deep boreholes in the south-eastern coastal area of the Baltic.

Contrary to the old ideas on the subject, the stratigraphic level of Beyrichian limestone in the Silurian of Gotland is not at all obscure. It is younger, in fact, than Beyrichian limestone in the wider sense whose equivalents are known as bedrock with the corresponding fos-

sils from the island of Saaremaa (Oesel) and from Schonen. One can now speak of a Baltic province in the Upper Silurian which can be followed, with the aid of index Beyrichian species, from the Baltic area as far as England and even further to Nova Scotia on the eastern edge of the Canadian shield. Its position in the Silurian was obviously not so far from the Scandinavian shield as it is today. To the East, the Baltic Sea province extended in modified form as far as the Northern Urals and to the South as far as Podolia.

Let us now close the circle of our observations and return to our starting-point, to the erratic from Buch's collection. From the *Leptaena* valves, the path of knowledge led, in the course of 150 years, to *Tentaculites lebiensis*, from the *Leptaena* brood to the determination of the ostracod species *Londinia kiesowi* (Krause), *Frostiella lebiensis* Martinson, *Neobeyrichia buchiana* (Jones) and *Hemsiella* cf. *maccoyiana* (Jones). All these species are now characteristic, in a broad sense, of Beyrichian limestone and for the transitional fauna of the Leba bore-hole (Poland) in the sense of Martinson. Furthermore, a part is also to be found on Saaremaa and in Schonen and, indeed, in the Dowton strata of England which, some years ago, were still regarded as the base of the Devonian. This erratic of uncertain origin was to become a valuable biostratigraphically dated document, bearing the type of a species: *Leptaena lata* Buch, 1831. Even though this species name is now outdated, it nevertheless symbolized a step on the path of knowledge. The piece of transitional limestone has been given a place in the history of science.

Preceding page:

Terebratulites

Chonetes sarcinulatus *(Schlotheim, 1820) and* Euryspirifer paradoxus *(Schlotheim, 1813). Devonian, Upper Emsian, Festenburg beds of Kahleberg sandstone. Communion Quarry on Rammelsberg near Goslar (Federal Republic of Germany). Magnification: 2.5×*
A valuable piece of evidence from the Schlotheim collection containing in the centre the lectotype of Chonetes sarcinulatus *while the winged steinkerns belong to the spirifer species (see p. 2).*

Gryphites

Productus aculeatus *(Schlotheim, 1813). Permian, Lower Zechstein, basal slaty marl, Schmerbach, Thuringian Forest (German Democratic Republic). On the originals for the three illustrations of* Gryphites aculeatus *published by Schlotheim in 1813, only this clearly recognizable specimen could be traced. English material of the species was named* Productus horridus *by Sowerby in 1823. In the centre a fenestella stem.*

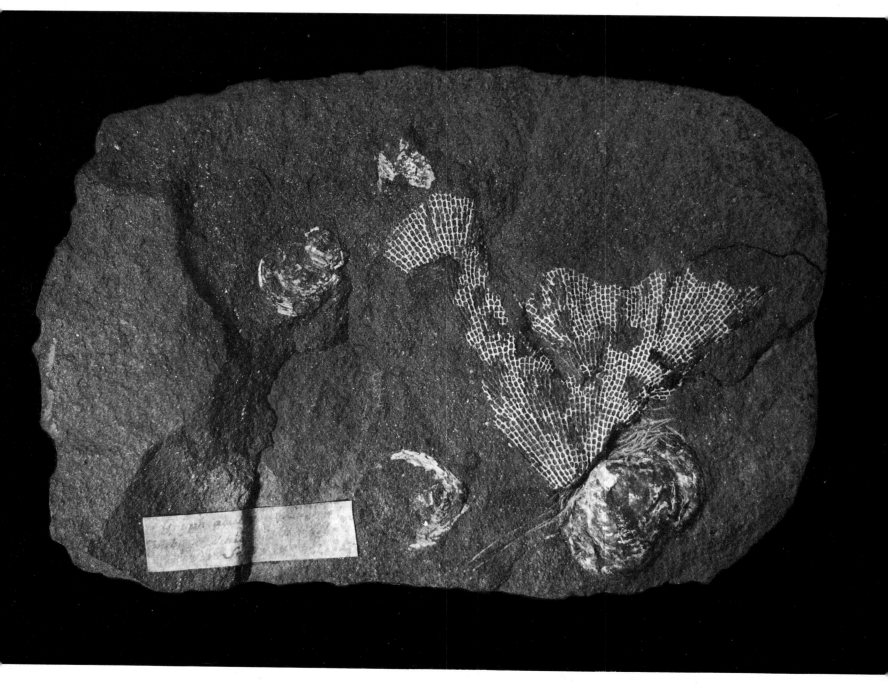

Productus

Echinoconchus punctatus (Sowerby, 1822). Lower Carboniferous, Namurian, Podolsk horizon of the Moscow stage. Podolsk, near Moscow. Magnification: 2.3×

A specimen from Leopold von Buch's collection. Brachial valve which was exposed when the rock between the shell lamellae was split (silky lustre). The concentric strips with short spines are typical of the genus. The spiny productids were some of those fossils which attracted Buch's special interest. For him, they were index shells which were shown from experience in England to occur under coal seams and so helped to guide miners through disturbed strata.

Odontopleura

Odontopleura ovata *Emmrich 1839. Holotype in greenish-grey graptolite rock, Wenlock/Ludlow, Silurian. Kujakowice Dolne (Poland). Magnification: 9×*

Emmrich described these Silurian trilobites and named them as a new species of a new genus in his dissertation of 1839. Today this fossil is the type specimen for an entire family of heavily sculptured and spined trilobites—the Odontopleurids.

At the same time, it demonstrates once more in this chapter how fossils from glacial erratics became starting points for the acquisition of knowledge about entire fossil groups. The spines of the Odontopleurids are thought to be a balancing arrangement. These little trilobites probably propelled themselves with jerky movements of their legs. This example is lacking the characteristic and powerful pair of spines on the occipital ring. On the other hand, the right cheek of the armouring on the head was missing already at the time it became embedded. Following detailed preparation ten years ago, this precious type-example has only been illustrated so far on a small scale and has also been used as a model for the design of a postage stamp.

"Tentaculite battlefield"

Tentaculites ornatus *Sowerby,* Howellella angustiplicata *Kozlowski (folded valves) and* Mutationella podolica *Kozlowski (ribbed valves). Lower Devonian, Chortkov horizon. Kasperowoje on the Zeret, near the junction with the Dniester. Podolia (USSR). Magnification: 2.5×*

This specimen shows that tentaculites, in contrast to their occurrence in Beyrichian limestone, can also form rock, too, in many places. They are seen here in a burial community with brachiopod shells. At the time of sedimentation, the movement of the water was slight, as indicated by the largely stable position of the shells (curved upward position of the brachiopods, clearly orientated position of the tentaculites at right angles to the movement of the water with reciprocal obstruction).

In recent years, tentaculites have proved to be good index fossils. However, even famous occurrences have not yet been re-examined with modern techniques nor have the results been published in monographs. The species here is still entered in the fossil lists as Tentaculites ornatus *Sowerby.*

The two brachiopod species on the fossil slab from the same site was first described by Kozlowski in 1929.

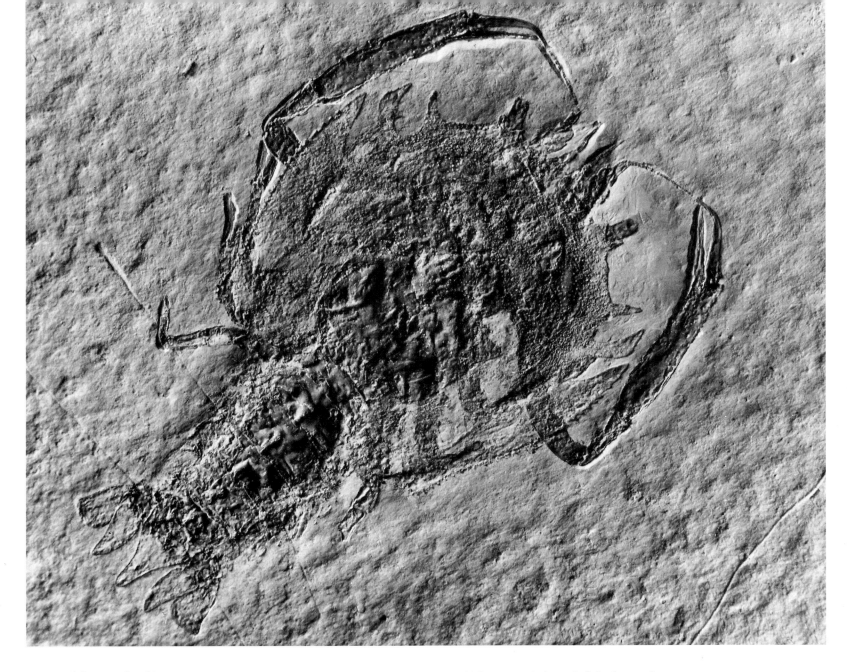

Original from Colombia

Neodeshaysites karsteni *(Marcou, 1875)*—Ammonites acostae *(Karsten, 1856). A piece of the Karsten collection with types. Lower Cretaceous. Lower Marl. Tocaima, but probably Apulo la Mesa near Bogota (Colombia).*

Like A. von Humboldt, C. Degenhardt and L. von Buch before him, H. Karsten made a great contribution to knowledge of the geology of Colombia and Venezuela in the middle of the last century. Like Buch, he also described very many of the fossils found there. In particular, it was the beautiful ammonite fauna from the dark limestone geodes of the pyritiferous *argillaceous schist at Bogota which attracted the particular attention of the two researchers, as demonstrated by this original specimen. Professor Fernando Etaya-Serna describes 85 new species in a monography on the ammonite fauna of that approximately 1,000 metres thick argillaceous schist, published in 1979.*

Solnhofen crab

Eryon arctiformis *(Schlotheim, 1822). Type. Upper Jurassic, Lower Tithonian, Solnhofen limestone. Solnhofen, Bavaria (Federal Republic of Germany). Length: 8 cm (see p. 2).*

This half-grown specimen is not one of the best preserved examples of this frequently illustrated species but is most important since it is the example illustrated by Schlotheim in 1822 and is to be considered by us as a type. This crab resembles living crabs but was not yet able to retract the rear part of its body under the protective shell. Related forms still exist today in deep areas of the sea.

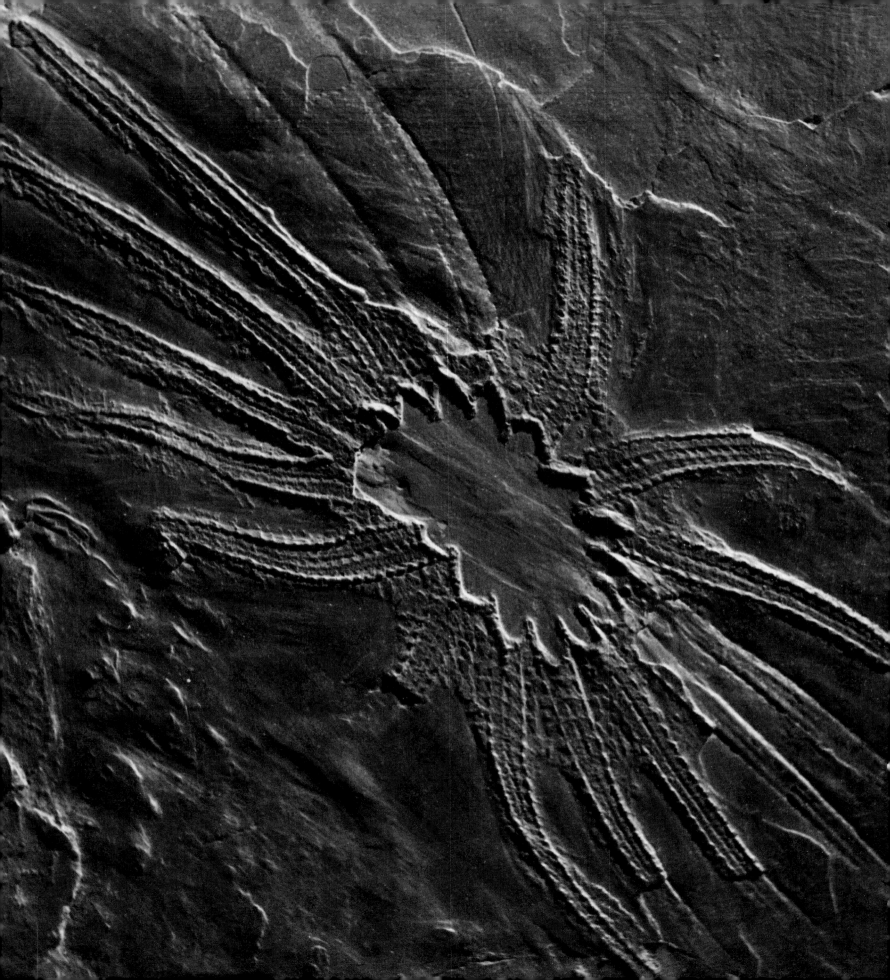

Brittle star

Heliantheraster rhenanus *Roemer. Lower Devonian, Upper Siegen, Hunsrück shale, Bundenbach, Hunsrück (Federal Republic of Germany).*
With about 50 species, the Bundenbach starfish and brittle stars largely determine our knowledge of the Palaeozoic forms of these mobile echinoderms. The old brittle stars do not always have five arms.

Trilobite

Ogmasaphus praetextus *(Törnquist). Ludibundus limestone (C2), Ordovician. Sassnitz, Rügen (German Democratic Republic). Length: 7 cm.*
In the course of their life, growing trilobites shed their exoskeleton several times and discarded the armour which had become too tight. Consequently most fossils are isolated pieces of moulted skeleton and it is only seldom that complete specimens are found as, for example, in the sugar-grain Ludibundus limestone. Our specimen clearly shows the characteristics of a trilobite. The type specimen of another species is shown on p. 60. The fossils from glacial erratics of the Central European Plain from the very start were no less interesting to emergent scientific curiosity than fossils from the bedrock. The investigation of erratic fossils has made a major contribution to the understanding of many a group of creatures but especially to that of the nautiloids and the trilobites.

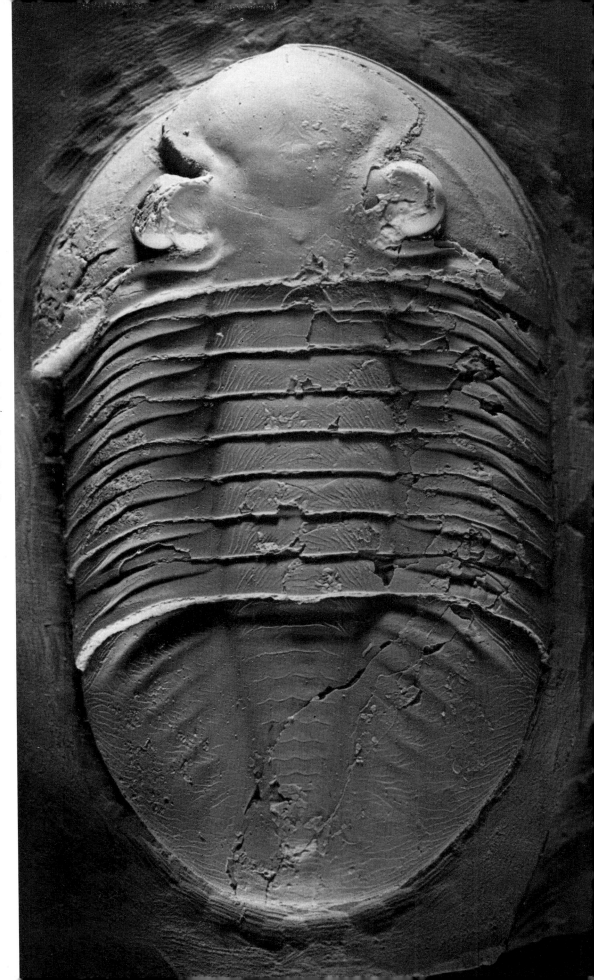

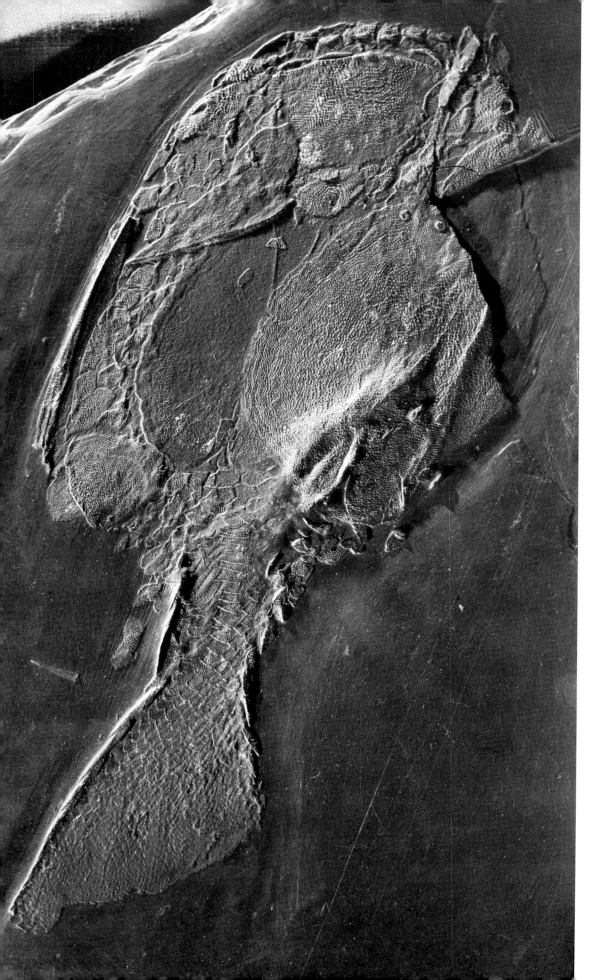

Jawless fish

Drepanaspis gemündensis *Schlüter 1887. Lower Devonian, Bundenbach (Federal Republic of Germany). Lenght: 37 cm.*

The remains of a jawless armoured fish lie before us on a slab of a Lower Devonian Hunsrück shale. This species of fish is frequently found in a completely intact state of preservation in this shale and is therefore well known. Unlike the fresh-water fish of the Old Red, this is a marine form. From the viewpoint of the evolution of the vertebrates, the Devonian is described as the Age of the Fish. The armour of our agnathan is characterized by numerous small and large plates which are covered with skin-teeth. Skin-teeth of this kind from the deep Ordovician of Spitzbergen are the oldest remains of vertebrates known. As a consequence of exfoliation, the fossil is distorted, as can be seen from its back. The larg backplate was pressed to the side already before preservation. Its curvature and the sideways deflection of the tail indicate that the body was not flat but was of an oval cross-section. In front of the rostral plate, there can be seen a long crosswise slit—lined at the front by small plates. This is the jawless mouth which is situated above this slit, as in the lampreys and hagfishes of the present day. On either side of the mouth there is a small plate with the eye aperture.

The fossils of the Bundenbach shale are pyritized. In this even the most delicate structures are often fossilized, such as trilobite legs, the cirri of crinoids or the gills of fish. This pyrite preservation of fossils enables X-ray examination of shale slabs to be carried out to confirm the existence of suspected fossils. Indeed, it is even possible to make stereo X-ray exposures of interesting objects and, if suitable exposure conditions obtain, to apparently conjure up the original three-dimensional appearance.

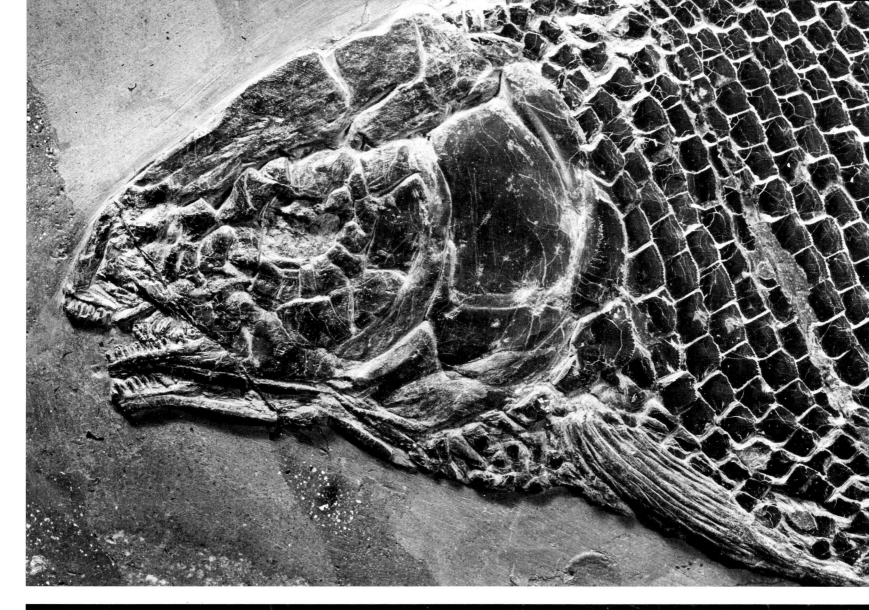

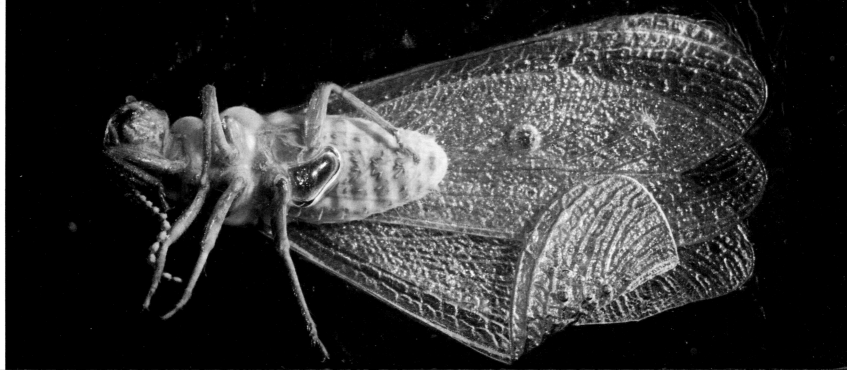

Jurassic bony fish
Lepidotes elvensis de Blainville. Jurassic, Holzmaden (Federal Republic of Germany). Length of skull: 9 cm.

The picture of this magnificent fish recalls a knight's helmet with vizor and coat of mail. It belongs to the group of Holostei which are protected by thick ganoid scales and already have a completely ossified vertebra. The eye cavity is protected by a complex ring of bone. Owing to the pressure exerted on it, the skull appears higher than it really was. The long bones of the roof of the skull have moved into the side-view and the right branch of the lower jaw has dropped.

The oil shales of the Upper Liassic of Holzmaden have supplied many fish of the most diverse species but intact finds in a good state of preservation are not common here either. A striking feature is the absence of young fish. It is mainly a question of Holostei but there are also sharks, lobe-fins, sturgeon-like fish and the first teleostei (Leptolepis).

Amber termite
Image, Eocene. Length: 1 cm.

The body of this winged termite has survived for 40 million years in the glass coffin of Baltic amber. The fantastic state of preservation in amber has permitted the precise comparison of many thousand insect and spider species of the Eocene with their relatives of the present day. This has led to the realization that the insects had already largely attained their present level of development by the time of the Early Tertiary. 70% of these were genera which still exist today. The investigation of the Lebanon amber of the Lower Cretaceous will probably provide more information about the evolution of the insects. The occurence of insects which are known today in Baltic amber enabled their ecological requirements to be transferred to the past for the reconstruction of the amber forest. It is more northerly than subtropical. Termites and oak leaves are a clear indication of a more or less Mediterranean type of climate.

Insects survive in fossil form more frequently than might be thought. They are found in the very fine grain, thin-flake deposits of the stagnant waters of lakes and lagoons—mostly as imprints. Wing-cases of beetles with the original colours have been found in the lignite of the Geisel Valley at Halle (German Democratic Republic).

Sea-lilies

Crinoids are some of the most beautiful creatures in fossilized form. Time and again in the history of the Earth, whether in the Carboniferous in the Middle West of the USA or in Moscow, in the Silurian or in the Muschelkalk, we come across these long-stemmed creatures which are echinoderms and appear in a variety of flowerlike forms. The most beautiful of them, however, are probably the pyritized forms in the Hunsrück shale of Bundenbach and in the Lias epsilon at Holzmaden (Federal Republic of Germany).

Left page:

Seirocrinus subangularis *(Miller), Jurassic, Lias epsilon, Holzmaden (Federal Republic of Germany).*
Four of the largest sea-lilies with a crown of more than a metre in diameter. The larvae of this species attached themselves to driftwood where they gradually developed into mighty specimens until they ultimately caused the wood to sink as a result of their weight. In the hostile environment of stagnant deep water, they failed to survive and became embedded. The biggest group-find, which is in the Hauff Museum at Holzmaden, shows a piece of driftwood, 13 metres long, colonized by sea-lilies, on a slab of 6 metres by 18 metres.

Right page:

Eutaxocrinus prognathus *W.E.Schmidt.*
Lower Devonian, Bundenbach (Federal Republic of Germany)
The Holzmaden lily appears to float in water but the small specimen from Bundenbach seems rather cramped. Nevertheless, it reveals the structure of a sea-lily, the tiny calyx, the dichtomized stems and the remains of the calyx veil between them.

Coral Colony
Cyathophyllum planum planum (*Ludwig, 1866*). *Devonian, Eifelian. Bensberg near Cologne (Federal Republic of Germany).*
This splendid piece of coral from the Berg country was already listed in the Quenstedt Catalogue of the Berlin University Collection of 1837.
The forms of growth of corals are largely determined by their environment. The distinguishing features of the families and genera are largely hidden from view in the interior of the calyx. Ground sections are usually the only means of obtaining additional information. However, our species displays some typical external characteristics which enable it to be used as a good index fossil of the Lower Eifelian. There is, for instance, the diameter of the calyx and its axial zone and there is the notable flatness of the colony which, in this case, is only 7 cm high and 22 cm in diameter.

Cake urchin
Clypeaster aegyptiacus. *Wright. Miocene, Gizah near Cairo (Egypt). Size: 20 cm.*
The cake urchins are the largest of the sea-urchins. The flat dome and the finely marked petals with the pores of the water-vessel system are a striking feature. This very large species from the Middle Tertiary is found at Gizah in the vicinity of the Pyramids. It must have been known to the Ancient Egyptians.

Page 72:
Snails
Undularia scalata (*Schlotheim*). *Triassic, Aphrite horizon of the Lower Muschelkalk. Rüdersdorf near Berlin.*
Slab of rare beauty with steinkerns of the species averaging 15 cm in height. Next to them there is also a specimen of Germanonautilus bidorsatus (*Schlotheim*). *The variety of forms and habitats indicates that the snails were a most successful class of the molluscs. At the present time, their range of forms is greater than ever before. This development began in the Jurassic. In the Tertiary, they account for a considerable part of fossil sea-fauna. The knowledge of recent forms played an important part in the investigation of these fossils.*

The endless stream of objects which, year in, year out, comes into the museums and their store-rooms as evidence of things past, can obviously not be displayed in the exhibitions to any real extent. Even with valuable fossils, it is only possible to select the best for the purposes of an exhibition. These are the rare specimens for which a museum is known or fossils of particular significance. These may characterize the image of an exhibition over long periods. However, exhibits are also selected to illustrate specific themes for shorter times.

Exhibition specimens of a rare and impressive quality are often of great scientific interest at the same time and must always be available for study and measurement. This is why they are sometimes missing from their place in the exhibition or are represented by a cast which can scarcely be distinguished from the original. Hardly any visitor ever wants to examine the exhibit with a magnifying glass but this is something which the researcher is obliged to.

The real treasure-chambers of palaeontology are the stored collections of the museums. Here is to be found what generations of collectors have assembled, collected, given, purchased and exchanged. It is here that the corresponding literature on the subject is kept, too. Thus the museums represent a hoard of knowledge, as it were, a mine of objects for the researcher in quest of new findings. Fossils which became the source of new knowledge, which were studied, illustrated and described, are marked as pieces of evidence.

These type and figured specimens are those fossils which have been declared the standard specimens of their species, representing as it were feedback from research to collections and enhancing their value. On the other hand, it is only when they are deposited in large, acessible collections that they are of value to science since in the final analysis they are the principal evidence for the solution of questionable interpretations and assure the priority of the first description. In the great national museums, in Prague, Paris, Vienna, Berlin, London, Stockholm or New York, for instance, there may be seen the collections of many of the classic figures of palaeontology who, in

Types Originals Sites

Et credible est per magnas illas conversiones etiam animalium species plurimum immutatas (It is also probable that, through those great transformations, the kinds of living creatures have been very greatly changed)

G.W. Leibniz 1693

the last century, described and gave their names to innumerable fossil species, names which are still in use even though later generations often disagreed with the original delimitation of the species. In the following, a review is given not only of the palaeozoic glacial erratics considered above but also of some other old examples of valuable collectors' pieces.

Schlotheim Types

The Schlotheim collection, which was acquired in 1833 on the recommendation of Goldfuss, Buch and A. von Humboldt, was once the nucleus of the palaeontological collection of Berlin University. It contains the numerous type and figured specimens of Schlotheim's studies of 1803, 1813 and 1820 to 1823. A selection of three of these types are described here.

There is first of all a specimen from the Harz Mountains which contains two species named by Schlotheim (see p. 57). These are the brachiopods *Terebratulites sarcinulatus* and *Terebratulites paradoxus*. The first case concerns two flat impressions to the left of the rock specimen. They reproduce the upper and inner side of a brachial valve and are the only evidence of Schlotheim still surviving of *T. sarcinulatus*. In 1962, Helen M. Muir-Wood selected the inner impression, which is clearly marked by radial septa, as the Lectotype of *Chonetes sarcinulatus* (Schlotheim, 1820). Whether the two impressions are the originals of Schlotheim's Plate 29 Fig. 3—shown here on page 2 (bottom left)—can no longer be stated with certainty.

The steinkern resembling a sea-gull in the upper part of the fossil slab and the corresponding impressions below it belong to a species which Schlotheim illustrated as *Terebratulites paradoxus* in 1813.

Schlotheim had a drawing made of another steinkern of this very characteristic species from the same site, however. It was only in 1971 that this original specimen was selected by Jahnke as the lectotype of the species. The species, which is now classified as belonging to the genus *Euryspirifer*, is now regarded as the index-fossil of the Upper Emsian from Morocco to the Harz Mountains.

Fossilized mussel shells with a marked arch and a shape resembling an incurved beak or prehensile toes were depicted in the 18th century in descriptions of nature as *Gryphites* (Hoppe 1745, Knorr and Walch 1768, Schröter 1775). This was not only a reference to the curved oyster shells which still bear a similar designation, the Gryphaeae, but also those brachiopods which are ususally classified under *Productus*. Thus the *Productus* bank of the Lower Permian limestone in Thuringia was regarded at that time as *Gryphites* Limestone. Schlotheim (1813, 1820) still considered the species in question in the common traditional summary manner.

The new photograph (p.58) and the old drawing in Schlotheim's contributions to the Natural History of Fossils of 1813 certainly depict the same fossil. Schlotheim named the species *Gryphites aculeatus*. *Productus horridus* Sowerby is a more recent name for the same species. *Productus aculeatus* (Schlotheim, 1813) = *Pr. horridus* Sowerby, 1823, is characterized among the Productids by a few but long spines and is also very variable. The fossiliferous rock slab, a bituminous marl slate from the upper part of the copper schist, comes from Schmerbach in the Thuringian Forest. The lace-like fossil with it, a fragmentary bryozoan colony *(Fenestella)* was still considered to be a Gorgonian fan by Schlotheim.

In addition to the Permian limestone of Thuringia, the fossils of the Thuringian muschelkalk occupy a special position in Schlotheim's work. In addition to the Carboniferous plants and the Devonian brachiopods, he also devoted himself to the Solnhofen fossils, which had already been desirable and expensive curiosities in the natural history cabinets of the 18th century, as is evident from the splendid collection of illustrations published by Knorr and Walch between 1755 and 1773. Georg Wolfgang Knorr, who began to publish the work by himself to begin with, opened the first volume with a comprehensive presentation of the Solnhofen fossils on coloured copperplates which are still a pleasure to behold. Knorr and Walch did not themselves coin any valid names or give any adequate

descriptions but later authors referred time and again to their precise illustrations. Schlotheim, who was especially interested in the Solnhofen crustaceans, did so too. The species that he described, illustrated and named in the now accepted binary form had all been depicted by Knorr on coloured copperplates in 1755.

One of Schlotheim's "Macrourites" is *Eryon arctiformis*. The original of the illustration of the species in Schlotheim's addenda on palaeontology of 1822 (p. 2, top middle) is still in existence and is shown here for the first time in a photograph (p. 63). The specimen, only half-grown and with relatively large pincers, is one of the seven examples listed by Schlotheim in 1820, p. 37, selected by him for illustration in 1822 and now regarded as the type of the species. Schlotheim writes that this was the most common of the crustaceans of Solnhofen and also "that it is so well known among fossil collectors that, in view of the illustration provided, no further description is necessary".

**Fossil Sites—
Our Sources of Knowledge**

Fossils which can be compared relatively easily with our familiar, present-day forms of life attract interest on a wide scale. This is true of land plants, vertebrates, molluscs, articulates, corals and sea-urchins, among others.

The beautiful sea-lilies, however, always irritate the unprepared museum-visitor since he assumes that they are plants. Of course, fossils which are largely complete are easier to comprehend and an incomplete skeleton on a slab is not so attractive as an intact one, even though the individual parts may be much more clearly defined and a source of information for science. This book will therefore not only show unusual details of fossils of interest in the history of science but will also turn the spotlight on unique specimens whose completeness is astonishing and whose beauty is delightful. The Archaeopteryx bird specimen in Berlin is probably the best example of these.

Impressive exhibits in palaeontological collections often come from renowned sites. With their message of life in the past, they do

not stand in isolation but are to be regarded as parts of a relationship which can be reconstructed. The remains of living creatures buried together in a single stratum can tell us something about the biological communities which once existed there or in the near vicinity. The totality of the fossils and the character of the rock of a site enable us to form a picture of the milieu which once existed there. These local results however, supplement, detail for detail, our picture of the geography of those times.

In the early Devonian, 370 to 400 million years ago, the South Pole is believed to have been in the southern half of Africa. The oceanic deposits of that time in South Africa and South America contain an unusual fossil cold-water fauna. The term employed here is the malvino-kaffrarian fauna province. Darwin was the first to come across such fossils on the Falkland Islands (= Malvinas). The Devonian fauna of the Cape was compared by the German palaeontologist F. Sandberger in 1852 with the fossils of the Rhenish Devonian while the English palaeontologist J. W. Salter found, a little later, that there was agreement with the finds of Darwin on the Falkland Islands. Extensive malvino-kaffrarian fauna were then found in Bolivia. They are also represented in Brazil and have been found, in a modified form, in New Zealand.

Our specimen (p. 155) comes from La Paz (Bolivia) from the most northerly deposits of these fossil cold-water fauna. These impressions in micaceous sandstone were originally considered to belong to *Leptocoelia flabellites*—a species from the Appalachians. Despite the close relationship, the agreement proved to be no more than superficial and so the Bolivian form was given the name *Australocoelia tourteloti* Boucot & Gill, 1956. It is evidence of the remarkable faunal provincialism in the upper Lower Devonian and indicates, on the other hand, that there was a sea-link between the Pacific and the eastern part of North America.

Numerous sites have become celebrated sources for our understanding of the history of life. Only a few unique examples will be mentioned here, together with the observation that the latest discoveries have opened up older and older worlds for us. Today, it is already possible to trace life over 3,450 million years.

Of the Pre-Cambrian rocks, special mention must be made of the cherts and silicious schists with their microflora as witnesses to this. They include those of the Pilbara Block of Northwestern Australia and the Onverwacht group in South Africa aged 3,450 million and 3,400 million years respectively, the Gunflint Iron formation at the upper lake and the Belcher group in Hudson Bay (North America), both aged 1,900 million years old and the Bitter Springs formation in Central Australia with the supposed oldest eucaryotes. The first metazoa are to be found in the 600 million years old sandstone rocks of the Ediacara Hills in South Australia in a unique diversity. The Mid-Cambrian Burgess Shale on Mount St. Stephen at Field in British Columbia gives us an insight of a special kind since the fossils in this shale are preserved in a unique manner. Jellyfish and innumerable arthropods with the most delicate structures have been preserved as a film of coal and in impressions. They show that present-day groups of invertebrates already existed in the Cambrian period, a fact proved by no other fossil evidence. Finds such as these throw a brief light on the early history of life, which is otherwise largely unknown, providing us here and there with a glimpse of the stages in development.

It is only with the Cambrian that the real preservation of animal fossils began and from this period onwards an increasing number of finds have been recorded. The more recent the sediments, the more numerous their presence among the rocks on the Earth's surface and the more familiar the fossils which they contain. Only the Triassic is an exception to this when the globe is regarded as a whole.

For a limited part of the Earth's crust, this general statement is only true if it has always been an area where sedimentation has constantly taken place. But this is scarcely the case anywhere. The Earth is pulsating, its crust is rising and falling, disintegrating into drifting plates and squeezing sedimentary strata into fold-mountains. Great areas which were once of a sedimentary nature are only accessible because they are now erosion areas—land. As a result of the varying history of such areas, there is a very great variety in the sediments from the history of the Earth between one region and another. The fossils they each contain illustrate this or that aspect of the development of life. There are thus natural limits to national research in this field and the history of life on Earth can only be written on the basis of international collaboration. For this, the great museums have the evidence—the fossils.

In many cases, it was mining interests which led to a special range of fossils being accumulated. Coal-mining has uncovered vast quantities of plant fossils which would never have been found without this economic interest in coal. The exploitation of the lignite seam, a hundred metres thick, in the Geisel Valley near Halle also revealed valuable sites of vertebrate fossils.

Since the dawn of history, slabs of natural stone have been used by Man for construction purposes. Rock slabs sometimes contain fossils of particular beauty which can be seen on the surfaces of the slabs. Would they ever have been found in such numbers if there had not been this practical interest in rocks? It is true that excavations are carried out which are concerned exclusively with the search for fossils but would there ever have been excavations on the scale of stone and slate quarries simply for the sake of knowledge? In many places mines and quarries have been worked for centuries. Thus in the course of time, as by-products, rare fossil treasures have been found in some sedimentary strata. To mention just a few, there is the Devonian roof-slate of Bundenbach in the Hunsrück, the Liassic oil-shale of Holzmaden in Württemberg, the lithographic rock of Solnhofen and the Eocene slab-limestone of Monte Bolca near Verona. There is even a classic example in ore-mining: the copper schist of the Permian at Mansfeld.

The fossils from these sites soon became famous and they quickly became associated with speculation, business and collecting. Many valuable fossils were scattered all over the world, to the delight of the museums and their visitors but to the dismay of those researchers who now have the great inconvenience of having to travel to them if they wish to study them.

The study of the Earth started in Europe and North America. It was here that the development of the productive forces had progressed to such an extent that the scientifically organized exploration of the natural resources became an economic necessity. The greatest advances were made in Great Britian. The study of the rocks there which are now included in the Palaeozoic era set a standard for other areas. Strata with certain trilobites in Wales were termed Cambrian by Adam Sedgwick in 1835—after Cambria, the Roman name for Wales. At the same time, R. J. Murchison coined the term Silurian for rocks in Central Wales. And it was in 1839 that the two geologists jointly proposed the term Devonian for the old sedimentary deposits of Devonshire. However, they were never able to agree on the dividing line between their two Cambrian and Silurian systems. It was only in 1881 that Lapworth introduced the Ordovician period as the term for the disputed strata, taking the name of the ancient British tribe of the Ordovices. System names derived from characteristic rocks (Carboniferous system and Chalk) had already come into general use in England in 1820 or thereabouts.

Following the initial classification of the early Palaeozoic in Great Britain, comparisons became possible with other deposits in Europe and America by means of their fossils. This applied in particular to the Bohemian and Balto-Scandinavian Cambro-Silurian. Gotland, Oeland, Oesel (Saaremaa) and the Estonian Glint now became famous for their extensive fossil fauna. Specimens of this fossil wealth, packed in moraines, were distributed by the inland ice of the Pleistocene over the entire lowlands of Central Europe. It was here that the fossils in glacial erratics excited the attention of collectors in the 18th century and were depicted and described by Linnaeus in various publications.

There is scarcely any major collection which does not contain specimens of mid-Cambrian trilobites from Jince and Skreyje (Czechoslovakia). The first descriptions of the species there date back to Schlotheim in 1823. The classic localities in Estonia, on Oeland and the famous Kinnekulle, a mountain in Västergötland, the sites at Beroun and Lodenice (Czechoslovakia), the Girvan district in Scotland, the banks of the River Onny and the sites at Sheinton in Shropshire or finally the celebrated "Trilobite Dingle" at Welshpool in Wales famed for the profusion of Ordovician fauna there.

Even Linnaeus gave a description of the Silurian corals of Gotland but still regarded them as formations of the Baltic Sea.

Gotland's coasts are still an Eldorado for collectors of Silurian fossils. Magnificent shell fossils from Dudley (England) were acquired by all the large collections of the 18th and 19th centuries. The *Orthoceras* fault of Lochkov near Prague was another famous locality.

Fossils from the classic Devonian of South-West England often bear the site-designation Torquay in the collections. Murchison gave the name Old Red to the reddish mainland sedimentations of the Devonian along the Welsh borders. They are particularly well-known for fossils of jawless fish. However, it was the frequency of these fossils at the northern tip of Scotland at Thurso, in Latvian and Podolic Old Red and finally in Greenland and Quebec that attracted the special interest of collectors.

The marine Devonian was soon to become most important on the Continent and then in North America, too. A distinction was drawn between the Bohemian and Rhenish forms of the Lower Devonian since they contained completely different fossils. The Eifel area, with its wealth of fossils, became the type-district for the lower Mid-Devonian. Gerolstein, with its corals, trilobites and brachiopods, has gone down in the history of palaeontology as a very great site. One could continue in this manner but for deposits of younger ages the selection of only a few major localities would become more and more difficult.

If a look is taken at the literature on palaeontology, it soon becomes evident that the names of many authors occur time and again in the naming of species. A series of great works on palaeontology published in the 19th century already contained the binary names of such a large number of fossils that these still account for a considerable number of the better known forms at the present time.

In the first half of the century, it was principally a question of private or museum collections, such as those of Brongniart, Sowerby, Sternberg, Schlotheim, Goldfuss and Münster. The range of fossils described seems to us today to be rather comprehensive. Yet even at that time special paper and monographs were published and mention may be made of those by Cuvier, Lamarck, Mantell, Salter, Martin, Phillips, M'Coy, Dalman, Wahlenberg, Buch, Beyrich. The great monographs then followed in the second half of the century such as that by Barrande on the Bohemian Silurian, Quenstedt's work on the Jurassic, Hall's book on the fossils of New York or Agassiz's work on fossil fish.

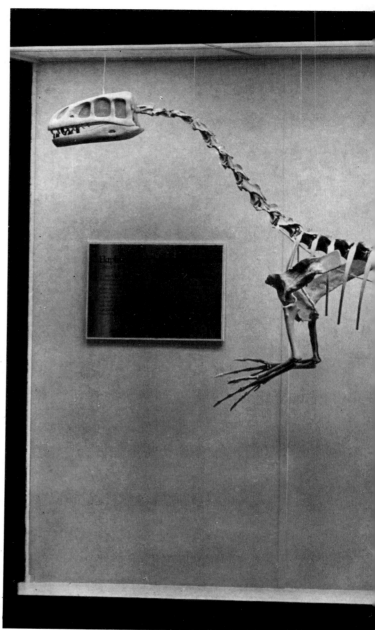

Tendaguru dinosaurs

The illustrations on the pages 77–79 show three reconstructed skeletons of various dinosaurs which were contemporaries of Brachiosaurus. *Their rather scattered bones were likewise recovered at Tendaguru from the saurian marls of the Upper Jurassic.* Kentrosaurus *(preceding page) is a relative of the North American stegosaur. Both were fat quadrupeds with a tiny head whose armoured back was lined with protruding bony plates or spines. They belong to the* group of the herbivorous bird-hipped saurians. The same also applies to Dysalotosaurus (bottom) which here, however, represents the agile, bird-footed type. The skeleton is 120 cm high. One of the predatory enemies of this species, which lived in herds, was Elaphrosaurus (top) which was also a biped, a representative of the theropods, and about 6 metres in length. The difference in the pelvis, which is here of the lizard-type, can clearly be seen.*

Flight-finger

Upper Jurassic, Lower Tithon. Eichstätt (Federal Republic of Germany). Length of skull: 6 cm.
Two groups which conquered the air emerged independently of each other from the archosaurs: first of all the flying saurians and then the birds. In the limestones of the Upper Jurassic at Solnhofen, both are represented side by side. Pterodactylus kochi Wagner (top) is a representative of the short-tailed

pterosaurs. As in the long-tailed Dorygnathus (p.19), the large skull is a striking feature here, too. The front and rear extremities are of about the same size, apart from the fourth finger which, as with all flying saurians, is very much bigger. The generic name Pterodactylus (= flight-finger) was introduced by Cuvier as early as 1809.

The skeleton of the oldest bird

Archaeopteryx lithographica H. von Meyer, centre part of the principal slab of the Berlin specimen. The skeleton was embedded in limestone ooze before it could break up. Only the shoulder girdle became detached from its position on the torso. The tail is bent at the pelvis. A characteristic feature of intact skeletons is the rearward curvature of the neck—a consequence of ligament tension.

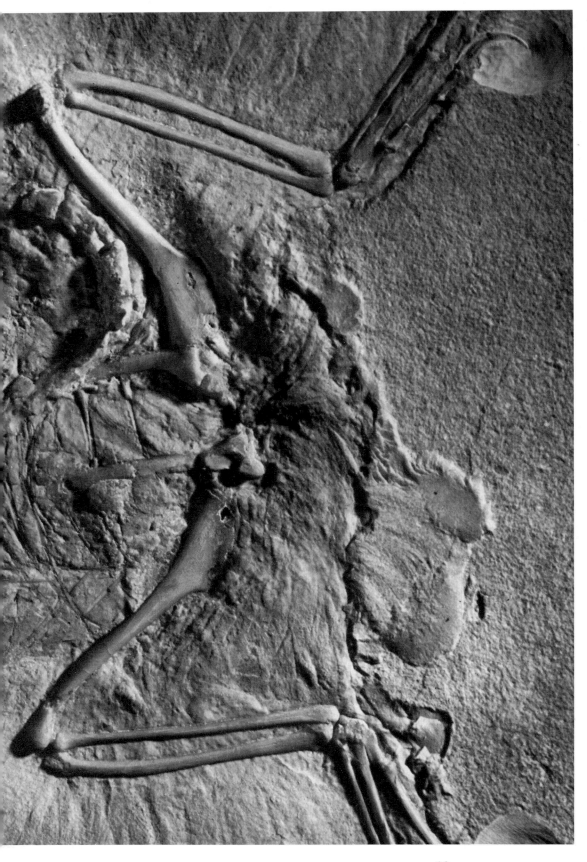

Details of the Berlin specimen of Archaeopteryx

The symmetry of the position of the front limbs excludes a position determined by chance. The V-position of the arm bones and the angular position of the hand are the consesquenses of ligament tension and indicate that the wings were originally folded. The extremely sharp claws on the toes and fingers have only recently been exposed. They can be cleary recognized here on the left hand and the left foot. More details are given on p.95.

page 84:
The feather structure of the left wing of the Berlin specimen (see pages 95 and 98).

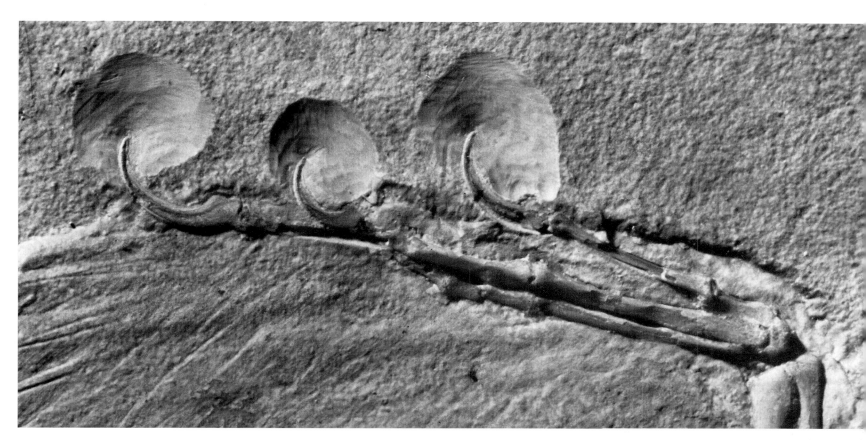

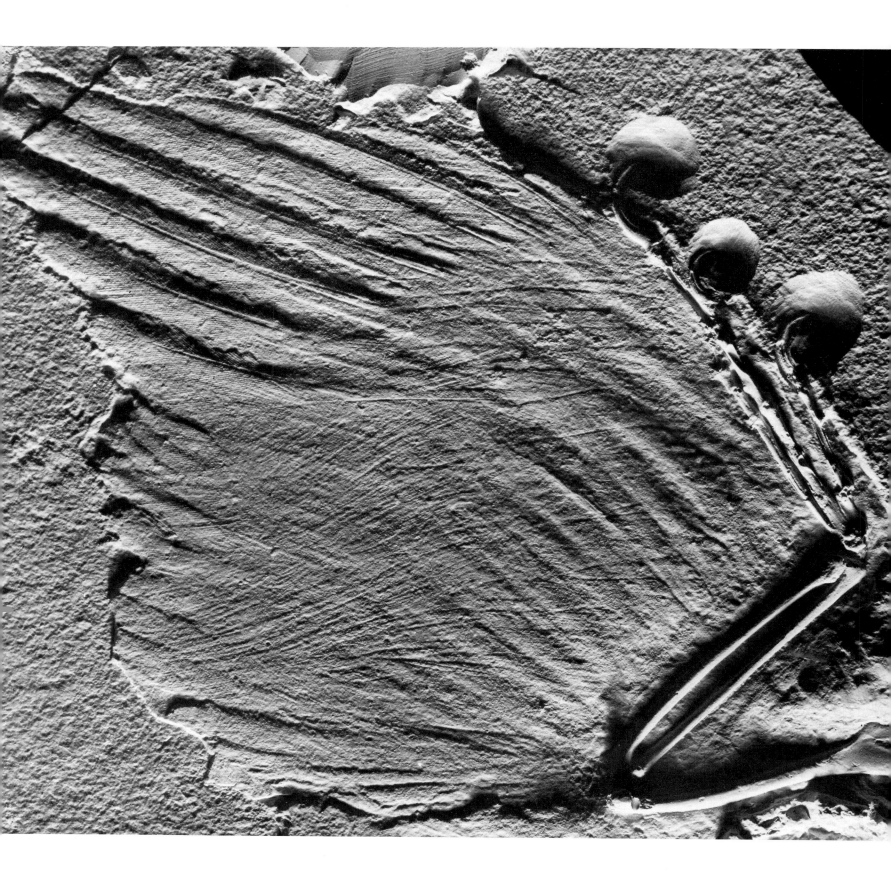

Archaeopteryx, the Oldest Known Bird

*Between **Compsognathus** and **Archaeopteryx** we are lacking only a few intermediate links. — The 'either this—or that!' is becoming more and more unsatisfactory.*

F. Engels

For more than a century, the earliest known bird *Archaeopteryx* has remained the classic example of a fossil transitional form. This is not the case with *Compsognathus*, although it had the honour of being named in the same breath with *Archaeopteryx* by Huxley, Darwin and Engels. Anyone who has recently followed the newly revived discussion of the origin and emergence of birds will scarcely be able to escape the impression, in view of the above quotation from Engels, that we are now back to square one in the hypotheses that have been advanced. After much hither and thither on the path of knowledge, the hen-sized dinosaurus *Compsognathus longipes* Wagner and the even smaller primitive bird *Archaeopteryx lithographica* von Meyer are now once again considered to be fairly close relatives. Even before the latest special study of the skeletal anatomy of *Compsognathus* (J.H.Ostrom, 1978), it seemed that the small therapod dinosaur was even a very close relative of the *Archaeopteryx* and it had been hoped that indications of the existence of feathers on *Compsognathus* could be found.

Even the first examination of the skeletons of the two species reveals such a similarity that it was not by chance that the last skeleton of *Archaeopteryx* to be discovered, the Eichstätt example, was long thought to be the remains of a *Compsognathus*. A century ago, T.H.Huxley explained the common features of the two species by their being related but the differences were subsequently given greater emphasis with the agreements being regarded as parallel and similar adaptations to the problem of walking on two feet. The scientific problem is the evaluation of the features and is thus dependent on the level of research and the theoretical position of the researcher.

Archaeopteryx and Darwinism

The note by Engels is to be attributed to the assumption by Huxley that Compsognathus also represents a form between the reptiles and the birds considering the two classes in their present systematic context. T.H.Huxley (1868) regarded Compsognathus as the representative of a systematically equal sub-order of the reptiles which was related to the dinosaurs and which he designated as Compsognatha. Shortly before E.Haeckel had similarly put the earliest birds, as a sub-class of Saururae, on a systematically equal rank with the other birds. With this, the vertebrate classes of the reptiles and birds moved closer to each other; the only question, however, was how close. Charles Darwin was more cautious in his assessment of the facts than Huxley and Engels. In the 6th edition of his *Origin of Species*, he wrote that the wide gap between reptiles and birds was filled by *Archaeopteryx* and *Compsognathus* in an unexpected manner.

The first fossil finds of both *Compsognathus* and *Archaeopteryx* were annouced by chance in 1861 at almost the same time. Both fossils come from the lithographic rock of the Upper Jurassic at Solnhofen, i.e., both species lived 145 million years ago on the southern coast of the Central European island which then constituted the northern littoral of the Mediterranean. In the 1860's, *Compsognathus* was one of the first saurian skeletons which was found in a relatively intact condition. There was consequently hardly anything available with which it could be compared. It is therefore not surprising that Huxley (1869), in the description of the skeletal remains of another small species of saurian *(Hypsilophodon foxii)* from the Wealden of the Isle of Wight (Lower Cretaceous), considered this form to be even closer to the birds. The decisive feature for Huxley was the remarkably bird-like type of the pelvis, a type which was soon recognized, with the increasing number of saurian finds, as characteristic of one of the two great groups of dinosaurs. These were called Ornithischia (bird-hipped saurians). The hypothesis put forward that *Hypsilophodon* might be an intermediate or missing link was abandoned again, this really being the result of the more extensive finds which provided more accurate information about the skeleton. In attempts to reconstruct *Hypsilophodon*, it was assumed that it had had an arboreal life-pattern and it is only very recently that studies have shown that this saurian could scarcely have lived in trees but must have been a walking animal.

The expectation of a similar natural origin of Man was inevitably associated with the emergence of the theory of evolution. In the historical context of the time, however, this was still the subject of controversy and it was here that Darwin's theory provoked heated discussion. It was in this aspect that it proved to be philosophical dynamite. As Darwinism became fashionable as "the natural history of creation", transitional forms which could be identified as such by anybody attracted great interest.

However, the identification and recognition of the development does not mean that it is already understood and seen as a process in which new contradictions appear time and again and have to be resolved. Transitional forms are the reflection of dialectics in nature. Since Engels, they show that in the examination of nature the unconditional and universal Either—Or as a method of cognition is not enough by itself but must be supplemented at the appropriate point by the dialectical aspect both this—and that for the understanding of contradictions. It may be assumed that Engels selected the example of *Archaeopteryx* on hearing the news that a second skeleton was found in 1877. The news of the find had been reported as a sensation by the newspapers of the time. There was now no longer any doubt about the former existence of creatures which combined the characteristics of reptiles and birds. The close relationship of the two classes of vertebrates which had been postulated before was now confirmed in concrete fashion for a second time.

The incompatibility of the development theory with a rigid system of classification was obvious. This was clear, at the latest, with the publication of Darwin's *The Origin of Species* (1859) with its profusion of facts. For this reason, too, the theory did not at all meet with general acceptance at first. Most biologists were still paying too much attention to first dividing up and classifying the organic world than to asking questions about general relationships and development. The Darwinists were obliged to call for, theoretically, the missing links not observed so far between the great system-units of the organic world which are now clearly separate. For their conservative opponents, however, these mixed creatures were initially inconceivable but later, follow-

ing their discovery, they were dismissed as untypical. The principal question for these scientists was which of the two possible groups were the transitional forms to be assigned to. A. Wagner, professor of palaeontology at Munich who had just described the smallest skeleton of a saurian from Solnhofen as *Compsognathus longipes*, was one of the first scientists to hear of the discovery of a feathered fossil. He recognized the problems which would result from the new fossil and, as an opponent of Darwin's theory of evolution, hastened to defame the anticipated conclusions of his adversaries since they did not fit in with his system of creation. In 1861, he wrote this about the find:

"At first sight . . . one might indeed imagine that this was an intermediate creature which was in the stage of transition from a saurian to a bird. Darwin and his followers will probably use the new find as a most welcome event for the enhancement of their reckless views on the transformations of animals."

Wagner was one of the conservative palaeontologists who regarded *Archaeopteryx* as nothing more than a feathered saurian. No time was lost either in finding an appropriate name for it: *Griphosaurus*. The concept of a feathered dinosaur was indeed seriously propounded once more in 1938 but otherwise the bird-nature of *Archaeopteryx* was widely recognized within a short time. The advocates of the bird-nature were those palaeontologists who had prepared the first detailed scientific description of the London and Berlin examples, F. R. Owen (1863) and W. Dames (1884) and then, in particular, the illustrious Darwinians Huxley and Haeckel, each of whom included *Archaeopteryx* with a very high taxonomic rank in his system of the birds.

C. Vogt represented a third group who were vigorous defenders of Darwin's theory. *Archaeopteryx* was considered to be an intermediate type which was neither reptile nor bird. In 1879, Vogt published the first details of the second skeleton of the *Archaeopteryx* before the find came to Berlin. Darwin himself expressed notable caution on the subject of this oldest known bird. In the last edition of *Origin of Species*, he remarked on *Archaeopteryx* in only two places but at that time he only knew of the

first skeleton to be found. On the one hand, as already mentioned, he noted, with a reference to Huxley, that the wide gap between birds and reptiles had been filled in an unexpected manner but, on the other, stressed that scarcely any other discovery demonstrated so strikingly how little we knew of the former inhabitants of the Earth. To understand why Darwin put such particular emphasis on the last aspect, it should not be overlooked that the discovery of a bird in the Jurassic at that time was not so surprising since it was assumed that it had been saurians resembling birds which had left the tracks in the Newark sandstones of Connecticut which had just been discovered at that time. The first skeleton of *Archaeopteryx* necessarily appeared as a solitary piece of evidence in a gigantic gap of knowledge. It was only later that those Triassic tracks of birds were attributed to bird-footed dinosaurs.

Since Darwin took *Archaeopteryx* as a demonstration of the gaps existing in the evidence of palaeontological evolution, he put it in a negative light. This resulted in a widespread prejudice towards fossils. It was asked if these remains could provide more information on the question of origins than might be deduced from the comparative anatomy and embryology of recent organisms. The problems of evolution are not, however, restricted to genealogy and many researchers interpreted Darwin's remarks as encouragement to seek the missing links and to acquire more and more concrete evidence of the actual course of the history of life.

In the meantime, an imposing amount of factual material has been accumulated and this has given rise to many hypotheses which have had to be revised, modified or abandoned time and again with every new find which is brought to light. This is how our understanding of the history of life progresses and an increasingly more profound insight obtained of evolutionary relationships. In relation to the quantity of organisms which once existed, fossils are very great rarities and are thus scientific jewels, milestones in our knowledge of the real history of life. It will be appreciated that the more unusual a fossil, the greater the burden will be which it will have to bear in the

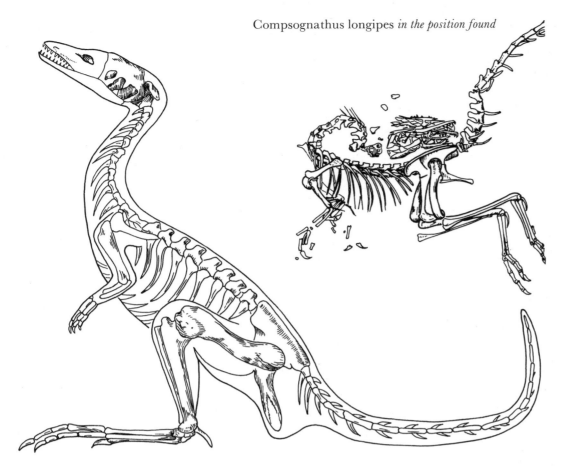

Compsognathus longipes *in the position found*

Compsognathus *reconstruction 1878 (according to Vogt)*

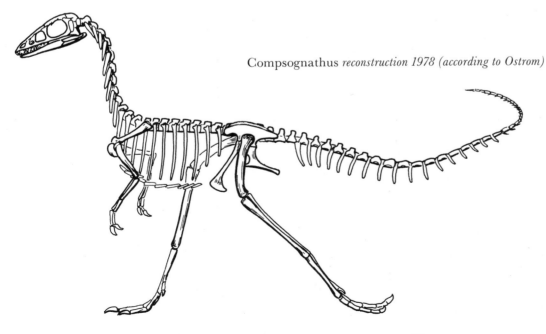

Compsognathus *reconstruction 1978 (according to Ostrom)*

sense of the hypotheses advanced. In palaeontology, there are always new surprises when something totally new is found and also when something which has been recognized as possible suddenly actually materializes but with unexpected details, forcing us to re-think our opinions and modify our hypothesis. *Archaeopteryx* from the transitional area between reptiles and birds is a good example of this. The discovery of three more skeletons in the last twenty years after eighty years had passed without a new find has once more stimulated the discussions of the problems concerning the first birds and their origin. Whether *Archaeopteryx* represents the direct line of evolution to the birds of today or whether it is a representative of a dead secondary branch is something which cannot yet be stated with any authority. However, it seems not at all impossible that *Archaeopteryx* belongs to the principal line of evolution of the birds.

In Search of Ancestors

Already at the time when the second skeleton (subsequently known as the Berlin specimen) was found the question of the ancestral group of the birds among the reptiles came to the forefront of scientific interest. It is practically equivalent to the question of the origin of *Archaeopteryx* which so far has not yet been clarified to the complete satisfaction of all. The most detailed modern investigation of this problem has been carried out by J. H. Ostrom of Peabody Museum (USA). With very great care, he studied all known skeletons of *Archaeopteryx* and, in addition, compared the individual bones with those of dinosaurs. As a result, Ostrom aquired a maximum of directly comparable data as a basis for his interpretation. In the course of his comparative studies, he discovered one of the new remains of the primitive bird while investigating the fossils of pterosaurs in the Teyler Museum at Haarlem (Netherlands). The type-example of a species of pterodactyl proved to be a specimen of *Archaeopteryx*. H. von Meyer described the supposed pterodactyl—a few years before he communicated the find of the individual feathers, the first remains of *Archaeopteryx* ever found.

Feather

1860

Solnhofen community quarry

Decscribed by H. von Meyer in 1862

*Museum of Natural History at the Humboldt
University Berlin, German Democratic Republic
Counter slab : Bavarian State Collection of Palaeontology and Historic Geology, Munich, Federal
Republic of Germany*
*Complete bird-feather which is attributed to Archae-
opteryx with relatively strong shaft. Length : 60 mm,
width : 11 mm.*
*Probably a tail-feather. Feather substance preserved
as carbonaceous film. Impression of the shaft. The
second earliest feather fossil in the history of Earth
comes from the Lower Cretaceous Amber of Lebanon.*

London Specimen

1861

*Ottmann quarry, Langenaltheimer Haardt near
Solnhofen*

*Described by F. R. Owen in 1863 and
G. R. de Beer in 1954*

*British Museum (Natural
History) London, Great Britain.*

Type-specimen of Archaeopteryx lithographica.
*Largest known specimen. Skeleton slightly decomposed;
good featherimprints; complete tail with 21 vertebrae
with conjugational feathers. Only single parts of the
abstricted skull : lower jaw with teeth, genuine
channelling of the brain cap. Joined pubis in top view;
shape of ischium, furcula and coracoid bone.*

Berlin Specimen

1877

Dörr quarry on the Blumenberg near Eichstätt

Described by C. Vogt in 1879 and W. Dames in 1894

*Museum of Natural History at the Humboldt
University Berlin, German Democratic Republic
(acquired in 1880)*

*Most impressive find. Almost complete skeleton with
imprint of the feathers (number and arrangement of
the quill feathers). Skull : shape, dentition, sclerotical
ring, elliptic nostrils.*
*Structure of extremities : bending of hands; protruding
thumbs. Pubis directed backwards (recently identified
as disturbed position) uncinate adhesion at the end.*

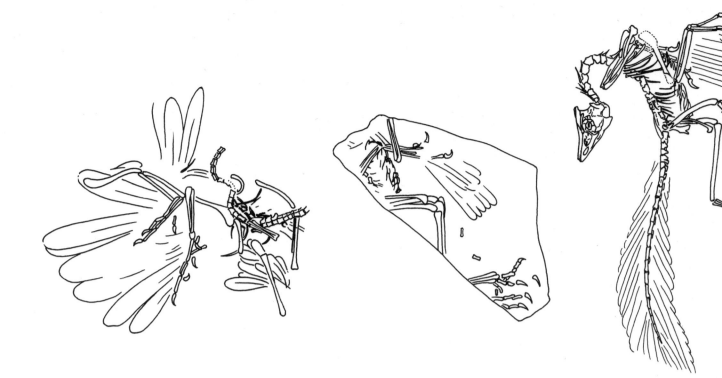

Solnhofen Specimen

1956

Opitz quarry on the Langenaltheimer Haardt near Solnhofen
Described by F. Heller in 1959

Private property. Solnhofen, Federal Republic of Germany

Almost decomposed skeleton without skull. Metatarsal grown together at the top. Metacarpal isolated. Long bones formerly hollow as filled with clear calcite.

Haarlem Specimen

1855
(Identified in 1970 as primitive bird)

Riedenburg, 40 km to the east of Eichstätt

Alt first described by H. von Meyer in 1857 as pterosaur, identified by J. H. Ostrom only in 1972 as remains of primitive bird.

Teyler Museum, Haarlem, Netherlands

Small slab showing only parts of a skeleton: the back extremities, a pubis in a steep horizontal position between the two thigh bones and isolated horny layers of claws.

Eichstätt Specimen

1951
(Identified in 1973 as primitive bird)

Frey quarry, Workerszell to the north of Eichstätt

Described by F. X. Mayr in 1973 and P. Wellnhofer in 1974

Jurassic Museum, Eichstätt, Federal Republic of Germany

Smallest specimen. Well-preserved skeleton, especially the skull: streptostyle square bone in diagonal position; one big and two small openings in the rounded triangular fenestra of the cranium in front of the eye; the outer part of the brain cap.
Pubis in steep natural position.

All six examples of the primitive bird were found within a limited area along the Altmühl river (Bavaria, Federal Republic of Germany) in the Upper Solnhofen beds of Malm Zeta 2b = lower Lower Tithonian.

In the history of discovery of the saurians, certain dinosaurs were compared with the birds, principally by virtue of their pelvic structure and their hind members. This is indicated by designations such as Ornithischia (bird-hipped saurians), Ornithopod (bird-footed saurian) or Ornithomimid (bird-imitator). For many palaeontologists, these similarities were justification enough for deriving the birds from the dinosaurs whereas other experts attributed the similarity to parallel adaptation to a two-footed gait. It is the old problem of the palaeontologist of how to assess the corresponding characteristics of species with an uncertain degree of relationship, whether they are to be considered as genetic possibilities realized in parallel in the course of the process of adaptation as the result of distant relationship or whether they are hereditary features of a direct relationship. This is what one of the early zoologists had to say about the origin of birds at a time when the dinosaurs were not yet considered in a sufficiently differentiated manner:

"We can say that *Archaeopteryx* has more similarities to reptiles than the dinosaurs have to birds and, on the basis of these observations, we can now assert with confidence that the birds must come from reptiles; that this transformation was effected through gradual changes, some of the unconnected stages of which we can demonstrate—but more than this cannot be proved with certainty. The dinosaurs may be the reptiles most similar to birds—but, as we can prove, this similarity is only based on the formation of the hind legs, which is not necessarily associated with those of the front." (C. Vogt 1878)

In his publication on the second skeleton of *Archaeopteryx*, the first description of it, Vogt 1879 overestimated the intermediate position of *Archaeopteryx* and this led him to assert that it was neither reptile nor bird but one of the characteristic intermediate types. Thus, in the argument about the systematic status of *Archaeopteryx* he merely created a new independent category.

As said already, the general view is that *Archaeopteryx* is to be seen as a primitive bird, the oldest known bird in fact. But what evolutionary information do the oldest bird fossils

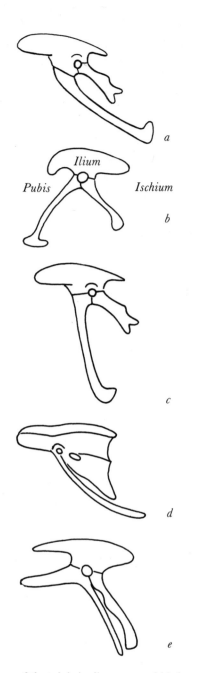

Structure of the pelvis in dinosaurs and birds

a Archaeopteryx *(Berlin specimen in position found)*
b *Theropod*
c Archaeopteryx *(reconstruction)*
d *Bird*
e *Ornithischian*

convey to us? In a monograph on the Berlin specimen, W. Dames (1884) expressed the opinion that birds and reptiles have a common ancestry. M. Fürbringer (1888), on the other hand, suspected that only birds and dinosaurs had the same ancestors which then G. Heilmann (1926) believed he had found in the Pseudosuchia of the Triassic. These thecodont saurians appeared to have a sufficiently primitive skeletal construction to be considered as the origin of all archosaurians and thus not only of the dinosaurs and birds but also of the pterosaurs and crocodiles. For half a century, the Pseudosuchian hypothesis remained unchallenged as a standard theory. Two differentiated views have since developed on the basis of this theory. One of these regards the birds as a sister-group of the Ornithischia (bird-hipped dinosaurs) while the other sees them as a sister-group of the crocodiles, whereby the common hereditary forms are believed to lie among the Thecodonts of the Triassic in either case. Without doubt, of the reptiles which still exist, the crocodiles are the closest relatives of the birds but this does not mean to say that there were no closer relatives.

In recent years, the new thesis of J. H. Ostrom has been the subject of much discussion. He does not consider birds to be directly descended from the Thecodonta but indirectly, so to speak, via the two-footed theropods which, in an evolutionary sense, are younger. These are the lizard-hipped dinosaurs with the feet of predatory animals. This bizarre set of relations includes not only the small and medium-size light-footed forms but also giant predators, such as the well-known *Tyrannosaurus rex*. With many new arguments, the new hypothesis has in fact again taken up the old assertion by Huxley that *Compsognathus* is the dinosaur with most resemblance to birds. Within the theropods, however, *Compsognathus* is only closely comparable with a few genera of the smaller forms. Ostrom lists the Upper Triassic genera *Coelophysis*, *Halticosaurus*, *Procompsognathus* and *Segisaurus* and the Upper Jurassic genera *Coelurus* and *Ornitholestes*. These forms differ from each other and from *Compsognathus* only in a few features but these features are always different. They form the outline of the group of forms to which the still unknown direct forerunners of *Archaeopteryx* belong. These were probably even closer to *Ornitholestes* with three-fingered hands than to *Compsognathus* with the specialized two-finger arrangement. Unfortunately, the delicate body-structure and the habits of the small theropods were such that they are very rarely found as fossils. The re-examination of the old finds and future fossil finds from this still inadequately known group will provide us with further information on the origin of the birds. Even now, the few fossils with their details tell us more about the real history of evolution than would ever be possible from the comparative anatomy and embryology of the forms which now exist.

A Mosaic of Different Features

From the very beginning, there was no doubt about the mixture of reptile and bird features present in *Archaeopteryx*. They are only too obvious. Even the tail by itself presents a contradictory picture. On the 22 caudal vertebrae of the tail resembling that of a lizard, there are typical bird feathers, arranged in pairs. On the London specimen, impressions of pinions are evidence that it had wings like a bird. Among the elements of the skeleton which have become detached from their original position, there is also the wishbone (furcula)—a typical bird-characteristic, even though it is present here still in an original, boomerang-like form. On none of the other skeletons has it been found in such an undamaged condition. On the left foot of the intact skeleton the big toe (hallux) is shortened and is set opposite the other toes, like the prehensile foot of a bird. Two claws were found in the area of the decomposed left hand but finger-claws are a legacy of reptiles. Toothed lower jaws were identified from the remains of the decayed skull and the brain also proved to be reptile-like; it is preserved as a natural cast. In other respects, however, and this was already the case with the London specimen, the impression obtained is that of a delicate reptile skeleton. Thus a widely varied mosaic of different features was apparent from the start.

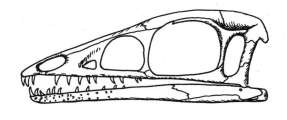
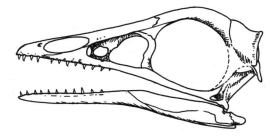

Comparison of the skull structures of Compsognathus *(above) and* Archaeopteryx

When a complete skeleton was discovered sixteen years later, it was found that the hand had three fingers which were reinforced with claws and that the head was similar to that of a bird in shape but equipped with reptile teeth. The eye was protected by bony plates in the manner of a reptile (sclerotic ring). The entire spinal column, the ribs, the presence of cervical ribs and the so-called ventral ribs (gastralia) underlined the reptilian character. The unique impression of the feather, however, revealed with total clarity that the differentiation of feathers 145 million years ago had already attained the present level of development. In fact, it is only the feathers which, as the new characteristic, are in unique contrast to the other features. If they had not been preserved as impressions, we would consequently have had no knowledge of their existence and nobody would hesitate, even today, in describing *Archaeopteryx* as a reptile or, more precisely, as a theropod. In its skeletal features, *Archaeopteryx* is further removed from the birds than from its saurian ancestors. Yet this obviously applies in a varying degree for the different characteristics and so *Archaeopteryx* has been advanced as one of the classic examples of the mosaic mode of the evolution of characteristics, as it is termed.

New Finds—New Knowledge

For eighty years, the problem of *Archaeopteryx* was discussed solely on the basis of two skeletons, those of the London and Berlin specimens. It is true that the two skeletons supplemented each other in marvellous fashion in respect of the surviving characteristics but many details were not clear enough for the possibility of incorrect interpretations to be excluded. The grandiose last word in this discussion was said by Sir Gavin de Beer with his monograph which was specifically based on the London specimen (1954). His concepts and the views of the celebrated vertebrate palaeontologist Simpson established the Pseudosuchian hypothesis as a standard theory. A further contribution to the popularization of this theory and to the dissemination of the ideas held at that time of the habits of the original birds were the coloured reconstructions of Augusta and Burian which were seen by many people.

What change in our picture of the primitive birds have been brought about by the three finds made in the last 25 years? Before coming to the answer, it must be said once more that we have learnt considerably more about the saurians too, and that we are already much more familiar with Pseudosuchia, Theropods and Ornithopods as the three possible sources of the birds.

The Solnhofen or Maxberg specimen consists of the remains of a skeleton in a fairly advanced stage of decomposition. Remains such as these are often very useful for resolving questions of detail, whether certain bones had grown together or not, for instance. In this case, the metacarpals were finally shown to be still separate whereas the metatarsals had already fused together at the top of the foot. We are confronted with the initial development of the general tarsometatarsus of birds. The humerus, filled with calcite, must have been hollow but neither on this nor on the other specimens has it proved possible to identify the pores characteristic of the pneumaticity of bird-bones.

The unfortunate limitation of the rock slab of the Haarlem or Teyler specimen allows only very little to be seen of the skeleton. A striking feature was the position of the pubis between the upper thigh-bones and this raised doubts as to whether the pubis of the Berlin specimen, which was directed towards the rear, was in the original position. On the Berlin skeleton, the connection between the pubis and the ilium had indeed been described as being without a space but the orientation of the pubis had never been questioned since, of course, it fitted in with the concept of a bird pelvis.

Individual finger-claws in a good state of preservation showed that they carried an exceptionally sharp and long horny layer. In the meantime, the entire length of the curved claws has been exposed on the Berlin specimen, too. The finger-claws must still have been capable of functioning but could hardly have been in constant use.

The Eichstätt specimen, the last to have been found, proved to be especially important for the scientific evaluation of the primitive birds. For twenty years, this *Archaeopteryx* skeleton has been mistakenly classified as *Compsognathus* in a private collection. It is the smallest example and is in an excellent state of preservation, even though, unfortunately, there is only the merest trace of an impression of feathers. The steep position of the pubis is a feature of this skeleton, too. As a result, an X-ray examination was carried out of the Maxberg specimen and this likewise revealed the same orientation to the vertebral column and also a location of the pubis and the ischium in relation to each other which differed from that known from the Berlin and Eichstätt specimens. It can now be regarded as proven that the position of the right pubis of the Berlin specimen is disturbed. At least, it can no longer be taken as evidence of the similarity of the *Archaeopteryx* pelvis to a bird pelvis or an ornithischian pelvis. The form and the joining of the pubes correspond to the conditions in the theropods but their probable orientation in the pelvis puts them between the theropods and the birds. On the other hand, the ischium of *Archaeopteryx* is of a completely independent form and with the wishbone is one of the quite specific features of the skeleton.

The Legacy of the Flesh-eating Dinosaurs

The skull of the Eichstätt specimen of *Archaeopteryx* is in an appreciably better state of preservation than that of the Berlin specimen. The old reconstruction by G. Heilmann (1926) is based on the latter. With the new find and following the investigations by P. Wellnhofer (1974), more precise information has been obtained about the position and form of individual skull-bones. He was the first to identify other elements of the skull. The skull structure very largely corresponds to that of the theropods and specifically to that of *Compsognathus*. In the form of the skull, however, in the relative size of the brain, which otherwise is of a reptilian character, in the size of the eye-cavity, in the construction of the palate and in the kinetics of the skull, there is already more of a bird-like character. Ostrom considers that the long elliptical nostrils, the triangular recess in front of the eyes with one large and two small skull-

apertures, the sloping position of the quadrate bone above the jaw-joint and finally the flat lower jaw are specific theropod characteristics. The sclerotic ring for the protection of the eye and the original type of tooth are found in various reptiles and consequently do not allow any specific conclusion to be drawn.

When we now consider the mosaic of features of the primitive bird from the five skeletons which have been found, we have to take note not only of the widespread reptilian characteristics but also, in particular, of the large number of theropod features and the varying degree of their transformation to bird characteristics. In addition to the characteristics of the skull of *Archaeopteryx* which have already been mentioned, here are some of the other theropod features of the skeleton: three-digit hand; the metacarpus construction; large, crescent-shaped carpus; narrow, parallel-sided shoulder-blade; the construction of the four-digit skeleton of the foot including the metatarsus and the raised, opposed big toe; mesotarsal joint with a rising process at the ankle-bone; orientation and hooked union of the two pubes; shape of the iliac bone; hollow structure of the vertebral column; vertebral pattern (9 cervicals, 14 dorsals, 5 sacrals and 22 caudals); obligatory two-legged posture. The number of theropod characteristics in *Archaeopteryx* speaks for itself. This was already recognized at an early date. However, since the collar bones—which are thought to have grown together to form the wish-bone—were not found in the theropods, it was assumed that the theropods had to be excluded as ancestors of birds. In the meantime, collar bones have been found in theropods and the old objection has lost its credibility. A similar argument was put forward in connection with the abscence of breast-bones in the theropod dinosaurs. It was assumed that the existence of an ossified breast-bone (sternum) found in *Archaeopteryx* was proven but the bones which were determined as sternum in the London and Berlin specimens are in too poor a state of preservation to be clearly regarded as such. In this case, the wish was surely father to the thought.

In the present state of knowledge, the theropod hypothesis of the origin of birds provides a lot of arguments. We would thus have to regard birds as the highly specialized descendants of dinosaurs, if all the arguments really would be unassailable. Tarsitano and Hecht (1980), as supporters of the Pseudosuchian hypothesis have examined the facts once again and completely questioned the theropod hypothesis.

"Fine Feathers Make Fine Birds"

The debate on the habits of the primitive birds and their forerunners is as old as the discussion on their evolutionary position. What were the preliminary stages of flight? What qualities did *Archaeopteryx* have in this respect? Our curiosity is aroused by many questions and a variety of answers is feasible. The feathers were the innovation with the most potential. Bird feathers have to perform two functions— thermal insulation and flight, when we disregard display behaviour at this point. Which of these was the primary function is still a matter of controversy. Both are conceivable and so is their dual function from the very beginning. Even the simplest feathers would have had a thermally insulating effect, thus constituting the basic condition for the development of a warm-blooded system with improved energy utilization. At the same time, even the first feathers may have improved the aerodynamic qualities of the animal body. Predatory animals, walking on two legs, may have obtained selection advantages from the two characteristics. Thus, from the very beginning, a structure could have been selected which, through constant improvements, satisfied both requirements to an ever increasing extent, flight capability and homoiothermy developing on a reciprocal basis from the early stages. Calculations have shown that the relative brain-size of *Archaeopteryx* was in the area of the lower limit for homoiothermic animals. On the other hand, by reason of the skeletal construction which it inherited, its flight capability must still have been limited.

Running or Climbing?

For the expert, a skeleton supplies a wealth of functional indices. Conclusions can be drawn as to whether certain functions were possible or impossible. The construction of the skeleton must be analyzed in a comparative manner if anything is to be learnt about the way in which *Archaeopteryx* moved. The results of such investigations have led to an increasing rejection, at the present time, of the view that the primitive birds were climbers and learnt to fly by gliding from the tress and flapping their wings. This concept was derived from the interpretation of the finger-claws as having a climbing function. The construction of the hand refutes this, however, as indicated by its angle, the ligaments firmly linking the 2nd and 3rd fingers and the feather situated on the 2nd finger. The feathers would certainly have been a hindrance to climbing and could have been damaged. Nor were the legs of *Archaeopteryx* suitable for climbing trees. Even in the forerunners, these had been developed as legs for walking and in *Archaeopteryx* were still in the stage of further specialization in this respect. The tendency to reduce the fibula and to transform the metatarsus into a unified tarsometatarsus, which was only completely achieved after *Archaeopteryx*, characterizes a selection of good walking or running characteristics but does not have any advantages for climbing.

The primitive birds and their forerunners must be conceived as creatures capable of rapid movement on two legs. They hunted small animals and had to flee from larger enemies. For this and from the very beginning, they had to use the contour feathers on the long tail as directional control feathers and the wings as stabilizers. With the increase in the wing area, flapping, gliding, and finally flight became possible. We do not know the details of this. It does not seem very likely that the primitive birds originally used their wings for swatting insects. The structure of the wing is already too close to that of present-day birds for such a function to be attributed to it. However, the flight capability of *Archaeopteryx* is scarcely to be compared with that of gamebirds although some experts now believe that their flight capability was even superior to that of fowls on account of the asymmetry of the flight feathers.

By reason of its importance in the history of development and because of the position of its discovery in the history of science, *Archaeopteryx* may be considered as the most famous fossil genus of all. As if to confirm Darwin's *Origin of Species* and only one year after the publication of this book, first a single feather and then, a year later, the first complete skeleton were found.

Without doubt, the Berlin specimen is the most impressive of the five skeletons of *Archaeopteryx*. As supplement to the London specimen in the details preserved, it dominated the concept of the primitive bird for decades. This celebrated fossil is in the Museum of Natural History of the Humboldt University, Berlin. The present book contains the first large-format pictures of details of the fossil. In the following chapter the illustrations on pages 14–17 and 81–84 are commented.

The Principal Slab

The second skeleton found (1877) remains the finest specimen discovered so far. The almost intact skeleton is depicted clearly on the rock slab, the extended wings and the feathered tail being immediately recognizable by anyone. The bird-character of the fossil is unmistakable but the characteristics of dinosaurs, its ancestors, are evident in the skeleton. The bones were fossilized by calcite mineralization but the feathers were preserved only in the form of an impression (note the impression of the legfeathers on the lower right thigh). An important new discovery is the realization that the fossil is on the underside of the rock, i.e., the skeleton is attached to the layer of limestone which once covered it up. The carcass of the bird was buried, lying on the right side of the back, in a lagoon 145 million years ago before the skeleton could disintegrate or the feathers decompose. Only the shoulder-girdle became detached from its position on the trunk. The tail is slightly bent at the pelvis, likewise the pubis. The burden of the sedimentation has tended to crush the skeleton. The head is pulled back by ligaments.

The Berlin Specimen of the Primitive Bird *Archaeopteryx*

Petrifaction is the great means of nature to keep the transitory creatures of all epochs.

G. Buffon

The Skull

Its outline with the pointed jaw looks very much like that of a bird and this also applies to the size of the cranium and eye. But the bone ring around the eye and the toothed front-jaw, as saurian characteristics, are in contrast to this. For almost a century, the skull, which is in only a moderate state of preservation, was the only basis for the reconstruction of the head of this primitive bird. The skull of the young Eichstätt specimen (1974) is in very much better condition and shows more details. Accordingly, the construction of the skull of *Archaeopteryx* has proved to be comparable with that of the theropod dinosaurs, e.g., *Compsognathus*.

The Pelvis

The arrangement of the bones in the pelvic area was, for a century, the basis of an incorrect assessment since it was considered to be the natural arrangement. Between the upper thigh-bones (femora), can be seen the right branch of the paired pubis with the symphysis extending backwards at the end. As in modern birds the pubis is parallel with the ischium. There was no reason not to consider this position as natural. The more recent finds of primitive birds have shown that the pubis orientation in the Berlin specimen must have been caused by a fracture. In its original position, the pubis of this skeleton must have been covered by the right upper thigh-bone. Ostrom's discovery has phylogenetic consequences. The right branch of the ischium lies in the shadow between the left femur and the pubis. The ilium, which runs with the sacrum on both sides and comes to a point at the rear (left, below the hip joint), can also be recognized.

Front Extremities and Shoulder Girdle

The bones of the upper arm and forearm are arranged almost symmetrically and in a V-position. The hands are both angled in the same way towards the elbow. This abduction is the basic condition for the folding of the wings. The arrangement of the limb bones in relation to each other was effected in *rigor mortis* by ligaments drying. This can also be seen in the other skeletons of the primitive bird.

The front extremity bears a good resemblance to the wing of a bird but even more so to the front limbs of certain theropods in which the same construction of the hand is found and also the same proportions of arm and hand. On the bone of the upper arm of this small two-footed dinosaur, exactly the same striking delto-pectoral crest is to be seen and this, as a muscle process, cannot be regarded with certainty as an indication of powerful wing muscles in *Archaeopteryx*. In the birds of the present time, the upper arm bone is shorter and thicker. The two narrow and parallel shoulder blades are joined to the coracoid bones. The ribs are very delicate. The much broader ribs of modern birds also have lateral processes for stiffening the thorax. On the skeleton of *Archaeopteryx*, however, another reptilian characteristic is evident: abdominal ribs, narrow slivers of bone which are to be seen lying across the ribs in the picture.

The Left Hand

In the most recent preparation work on the Berlin specimen, the claws have now been exposed, having been only partly visible hitherto. As on the other skeletons, they have proved to be sharp with a marked curvature and covered with a horny sheath. The position of the three fingers is typical. The first finger could be moved freely but the second and third fingers were permanently connected although not joined. They reinforced each other and carried the flight feathers. The crescent-shaped pisiform bone is a theropod element and constituted the joint connection between the first and second metacarpal bones.

The Right Hand

The hand, angled to the side, is embedded in the same position as the left hand. The crescent-shaped pisiform bone is less clear but another bone of the wrist can be seen between it and the radius and a further one between the third finger and the ulna. The metacarpal bones II and III are much longer than I which forms the diverging base for the two-jointed thumb (first finger). The long second finger consists of three joints and the third finger below it of probably four joints.

The function of the sharp claws is the subject of controversy. The climbing function depicted in many illustrations is extremely doubtful on account of the laterally angled hand and the feathers located on the second finger down to the last joint but one.

The Feet

It can be deduced from the comparison of the five skeletons that the foot of *Archaeopteryx* is very similar indeed to the feet of many theropods. The foot of modern birds, however, is specialized in the sense of a running-type foot to an even more marked degree. Through the fusion of the tibia and the upper tarsus in the reduction of the fibula, there resulted the lower leg-bone of birds with its supporting function. The oldest tibiotarsus of this kind is only two to three million years younger than *Archaeopteryx*.

Following the preparation work of 1978, the bones of the foot and the claws are now completely exposed and it is apparent that there is no difference from the London specimen. There are the same very curved and pointed claws.

The right foot is seen from the outside. The toes are largely superimposed so that only the third and fourth toes with their claws can be identified. The three metatarsal bones have already fused and are half-way to becoming a tarsometatarsus.

The left foot is thus seen from the inner side. In this case, too, the bones are largely superimposed but are nevertheless all clearly visible. The short first toe with its two members is situated in a very high position and faces the other three toes. The second toe (three joints) is in the topmost position, the third toe (four joints) is the longest and the fourth toe (five joints) is again somewhat shorter. *Archaeopteryx* thus has the toe-phalangeal formula (2–3–4–5). The foot of the primitive bird has been interpreted as a gripper-type foot but ist proportions make this appear doubtful.

More than 20 pairs of rudder feathers (rectrices) were located on either side of the vertebral column of the tail but only the impressions of these have survived. The remarks made concerning the flight feathers apply to these impressions, too.

The Left Wing

The photograph on p. 84 was taken in bright light falling at a low angle on the subject to show the imprinted feather-structures as clearly as possible. A deliberate optical illusion accentuates the quills. The impression is conveyed that it is the underside of the wing which is depicted here and it seems as if the pinions had been pressed into the sediment. If the picture is turned around, the space relations of the relief are reversed. The tips of the claws then appear correctly as being in hollows and not on apparent humps. When seen in this manner, the picture corresponds to the true relations of the wing imprint, the nature of which has been the subject of many contradictory opinions up till now. The feather relief on the plate opposite shows the exact imprint of the principal slab. Why the principal slab shows the relief of the underside of the wing is explained in the section "Confusion over the feathers of the primitive bird".

The existence of flight and rudder feathers on the primitive birds is obvious to anyone looking at the fossils and yet their functional value has been questioned time and again. The interpretation of their position in the history of development continues to be the subject of controversy. Whether *Archaeopteryx* used his wings may remain an open question here but it is certain that feathers, as possessed by it, became the key feature in the development of birds.

When feathers were fossilized for the first time, as far as we know at present, 145 million years ago in the lagoon of Solnhofen, the development of this special epidermal structure had already reached practically the same level which we know in the birds of today. *Archaeopteryx* already possessed pinions, rudder feathers and coverts. In respect of the evolution of feathers, the *Archaeopteryx* finds only indicate that it had already taken place to a large extent by the end of the Jurassic period. The primitive birds did not have primitive feathers, as it were. These are to be sought among the dinosaurs which were their ancestors. In their simplest forms, they certainly served as a layer providing warmth for the body. Within the scope of the history of life, the variations on this special theme may have continued until the complicated construction of modern feathers had developed and this was probably in an evolutionary line of the theropods. This provided for the possibility of new functions and especially for the development of wings. The multiple evolution of such a complicated structure is highly unlikely. This was the starting signal for the evolution of the birds which then, as we understand it, proceeded in an explosive manner. At the end of the Jurassic, there was this great chance, in the evolution of the vertebrates, to conquer the air. This opportunity was grasped and so successfully that it is hard for us today to realize that birds are the descendants of the dinosaurs.

The Berlin Bird

Of the fossils of *Archaeopteryx* the Berlin specimen, in its totality, is still the best preserved and the most beautiful of the finds, even though

Confusion over the Feathers of *Archaeopteryx*

Everybody who has a sense for bird wings will notice at the examination of the Berlin Archaeopteryx *slab that there is something wrong in the relation of the bony skeleton to the wings.*

O. Heinroth, 1923

many a detail has survived to a more complete extent in the other specimens. The principal slab of this find has been illustrated many times in manuals and textbooks. We are always hearing or reading of *Archaeopteryx* preserved as an impression but this designation is only a half-truth. It is true that only imprints of the feathers are really to be seen on the surface of the rock but the bones of *Archaeopteryx* have survived in the position in which they were originally. As is usual, they have been fossilized by calcite, i.e., the porous phosphate bone-tissue and the hollow cavities have been filled up and rendered solid by calcite mineralization.

The skeleton, which is seen diagonally from above, is compressed to a bone-thickness of only slightly more than a centimetre, but the spatial arrangement can still be identified. The bones in the rock slab have retained their natural relationship to a large extent, although they are broken in various places, the pelvis and skull having been pressed in, the left coracoid is squashed and a few fragments seem to be the remains of the wishbone. By and large, however, the bones have suffered only little damage. The bones of the extremities have even survived in their full spatial relationship. In the course of the vain search for the sternum and the wishbone, a hole has cautiously been made at the back of the limestone slab as far as the bone area.

Due to the special conditions of the sediment in which it was embedded and preserved, our specimen of *Archaeopteryx* combines in fortunate manner different states of preservation: the petrified skeleton and the imprint of the feathers. However, neither the term imprint nor the term permineralization are alone characteristic of the nature of the fossil. Of the counter part at best, it could be said that it primarily bears the character of an imprint since only imprints, with certain exceptions, of the bones are present here, too.

Astonishing Agreement

The astonishing agreement between the wings of *Archaeopteryx* and those of present-day birds have led ornithologists in particular to investigate this circumstance more closely. The discussion centred on the number and arrangement of the pinions and on the problem of the moult. The basic condition for such discussions is the correct interpretation of the fossils but in this respect there are still some strange inconsistencies. During the latest preparation work on the Berlin specimen of *Archaeopteryx*, the author therefore endeavoured to arrive at a new interpretation of the feather imprints, utilizing the latest findings on the formation of rock and fossils in the Jurassic lagoon of Solnhofen (K. W. Barthel et al.). The well-known structures were re-interpreted and the problem placed in the right perspective. For this, the ornithological arguments have had to be brought into agreement with palaeontological views on the formation of fossils.

From a Modern Viewpoint

From a modern viewpoint, the origin of the most celebrated of all fossils may be reconstructed as follows. First of all, it must be said that we do not know how the primitive bird came to be in the lagoon. Perhaps, as a poor flier, it had been driven by a storm far from land and out into the lagoon where it drowned or its dried out corpse might have been blown or washed into the lagoon. From the relative completeness of the fossil, it can be concluded that the corpse did not drift on the water for a very long time before it sank to the bottom and was embedded at an angle on its back. It is not known what caused the damage in the sternum area. The consequences of decay and the inroads of other creatures have to be considered.

The upper side of the half-spread, drooping wings was pressed into the still soft chalky ooze, on the surface of which there was a slimy layer of clay, when the bird sank to the bottom. The circumstance of the pinions being pressed into the ooze caused the feathers to be forced apart, broken and enmeshed with each other. Consequently, on the underside of the upturned wing, the shafts of the pinions were exposed. Shortly afterwards, perhaps when the next layer of chalky mud began to settle, a change took place in the position of the pinions in the left wing. They were moved outward by a few millimetres; as seen from the marks left behind by the shafts. The feathers were probably broken again by this movement.

It was in this position that the corpse was buried completely by the chalky mud. The bacterial decomposition of the corpse continued and ultimately spread to the feathers as well. There remained only the bones, the teeth and the horny sheath of the claws. While this was in progress, the chalky mud diminished in volume with the loss of water from it and became harder through the precipitation of tiny calcite crystals—a process which initially affected the corpse in particular. This diagenetic process soon spread to the bones and fossilized them. In some places of the body area, gases produced by decomposition caused buoyancy phenomena. The settling of the sediment also caused the embedded skeleton to be compacted.

The feathers around the edge of the body survived the longest, especially where they formed a single layer between the sediment below and the sediment above (flight and rudder-feathers). By the time the feathers had finally decomposed, the chalky mud was already so firm that a true imprint of the underside of the feathers, which were facing upwards, remained on the underside of the sediment above it. At the same time, the sediment directly beneath the feathers, on account of the ability of the clay mineral on the former surface of the bed of the lagoon to absorb moisture, was still much too soft for a permanent record of delicate details to be left. Only the shafts of the feathers, which were thicker than the film of clay, left lasting imprints. The continuing compaction of the sediment pressed the different imprints further and further into each other. The ultimate result of this was an embossed impression on the thin separating layer of clay which today, following the separation of the two slabs, shows the same structure on both sides as a positive and as a negative.

The essential facts of our interpretation are as follows. The imprint of the feathers is in the form of an embossed impression; the structures of the undersides of the wings and the tail provide the details. This is believed to be due to the properties of the clay partings. Primary and secondary imprints of feather-shafts (double impressions) indicate that the counter part was the original lower slab. The principal slab is the upper slab.

Heinroth's Experiment

The old and new arguments about the character of the wing impressions will now be described in somewhat more detail. As already stated, an astonishing number of inconsistencies has been associated with the interpretation. The basic and at the same time the most careful examination of the feather impressions was carried out by Oskar Heinroth, the Berlin ornithologist and founder of the Berlin Aquarium. He wrote the following lines in 1923:

"Anyone with a feeling for bird-wings will notice, on examining the slab of the Berlin *Archaeopteryx* that there is something wrong about the relationship of the skeleton to the wings. But what? We see the body of *Archaeopteryx*, i.e., the bones, from above, i.e., from the back, but what about the wing-feathers? Unless we have got completely the wrong idea, what we have before us is the underside of the wing. The somewhat confused coverts, which certainly look like the coverts of the under-wing, support this view, and the fact that the inner webs of the pinions are mostly lying over the outer feathers, reinforces us in our opinion. On examining them very closely, we find a lengthwise barrel on various feather shafts, i.e., the impression of a furrow, and on all the birds living at the present time this is only on the underside of the feathers. On the counter part, which exists only in fragments, the barrels of the pinion-feathers are smooth, thus it is to be assumed that we are concerned here with the top-side of the wing but the conditions here are not so clear as on the main slab. It is not at all easy to orientate oneself in this confused picture: body and wing-bones from above, wing-feathers from below.

"To clarify the situation still further, we embedded jay and partridge wings in semi-solid plaster and then poured liquid plaster over them; we allowed the whole to solidify, peeled the wings out of it again and examined the casts, or rather the imprints of the upper and lower sides. It could be seen by this, too, that *Archaeopteryx* slab shows the wings from underneath. Furthermore, it was noted that breakages easily occur at the inner webs and specifically those of the primary feathers, protruding downwards from the surface of the wing, and that these often make the feathers appear narrower than they are in fact and we find the same thing in *Archaeopteryx*". (O. Heinroth, 1923)

The original plaster slab of Heinroth's experiment is still to be found at the Berlin Museum of Natural History. It shows in two imprints the underside of a partridge wing in moult and the top-side of a jay wing. The experiment and Heinroth's observations created the basis for the interpretation of the feather-impressions of the Berlin specimen. The quill-furrows and the overlap arrangement of the feathers are clear evidence of this, as confidently recognized by Heinroth. Later critics were not so precise in their examination of the overlap arrangement in particular but regarded the clearly free and uncovered position of the feather-shafts as a counter-argument since with a half-spread bird wing the feather-shafts on the underside are covered by the inner feathers. Heinroth had no reason to see a counter-argument in the exposed position of the feather-shafts. He made an empirical investigation of the behaviour of bird wings when embedded but the critics have not paid due attention to his remark on the separation of the webs of the primary feathers (last sentence of above quotation).

An important observation regarding the character of the wing-impressions was made by R. Rau (1969). He had noted, contrary to Heinroth's opinion, that it was not the top-side of the wing which was imprinted on the counter part. What was on the counter part was the exact negative of the principal slab, both slabs consequently displaying the same structures.

Above or Below?

The knowledge of which side of the wing is imprinted on the principal slab of the Berlin specimen of *Archaeopteryx* and what is above and

what is below on the skeleton does not, as such, say anything about the original position of the slab in the rock formation. One cannot simply look at detached slabs from the Solnhofen strata and say which was once their top-side or underside. As with many old collectors' items from the lithographic limestone area, no note was made of where the Berlin bird was found. In these cases, the difficulty has always been solved by referring, in a neutral manner, to the principal slab and the counter part. Many authors have consciously or subconsciously assumed that the principal slab with the principal part of the fossil was synonymous with the lower slab and this also applied to Heinroth who regarded it as the lower slab and the other as the top slab. It is only fairly recently that palaeontologists, in the systematic examination of the circumstances of finds, have realized that the principal slabs of Solnhofen fossils are usually the upper slabs. We can show, for the first time, that this is also true of the principal slab of the Berlin *Archaeopteryx*, as suspected by several authors in recent years. It must therefore not be regarded, as was the case until now, as the lower slab. The famous fossil must have originally been discovered by quarrymen on the underside of a slab when they were raising it.

The Fossil Site

For a better understanding of the fossil, the special features of the sediment and its fossils will now be examined in a little more detail. The Solnhofen strata at the Old Mill are deposits of a large lagoon of the Jurassic period which was situated between coral reefs in the South and the coast in the North. Even such apparently different terminology as platey limestone and lithographic limestone for the same rock are a reflection of the diversity of its appearance.

The rock, usually of a pale yellow colour, comprises dense, pure limestones with intermediate layers of chalky clay. The deposition of a limestone layer took place relatively quickly but that of a clay layer was a very slow process. The thicker beds usually show very delicate partings which enable them to be

split into thinner slabs. Every parting is evidence of an interruption in limestone sedimentation, in the course of which a clay-like film was formed. Recent investigations suggest that algae may have played a part in the formation of some of these partings. The fossils are found, pressed flat, exclusively on the surfaces of the partings and not inside the slabs. This means that organic remains accumulated on the floor of the lagoon where the clay surface isolated them from the underlying chalky ooze in a more or less effective manner. It was only when the next layer of sediment was deposited that the corpses were buried in chalky ooze. As a result, the fossils are now largely found adhering to the undersides of the slabs above the partings. This is also the case with our *Archaeopteryx* skeleton; it is on the underside of the principal slab.

The Strange Impression of the Left Wing

If we now examine the impression of the left wing in detail, we will find all those structures together whose evaluation led to the interpretation of the feather impressions described above. To begin with, we, like Heinroth, are confused by what we see. We automatically assume that what we see is the top-side of a fossilized wing since we are looking at the upper side of the skeleton. The curvature of the primaries, the exposed view of their shafts and outer barbs and the apparent overlap-arrangement of the feathers lead us to see the object as such. But our attention is caught by the impressions of the feather-shafts which Heinroth too had recognized as belonging to the underside. What appears to be the top-side of a wing is really something else and we have to look consciously at the relief as an impression, as a negative of the underside of the wing. To imagine this negative as the underside of the wing is unnecessary since we only have to look at the counter part on the lower slab. Here we have an actual picture of the underside of the wing before us. The overlap condition, with the "inner barbs on top", the decisive feature of the underside observed by Heinroth, immediately catches our attention. All that disturbs us are the exposed shafts and outer barbs of the primaries and we see the shafts of the secondary quills covered by the inner barbs, as we would expect.

The sharply outlined positives of the secondary shafts are slim and clearly raised on the underlying slab. Towards the base, they then increase in width just as rapidly and have collapsed on either side of a central seam above the marrow which had once been there. Such a picture can be the underside of a squashed shaft, even when the profile and the proportions of the feather shafts of *Archaeopteryx* do not quite correspond to the present-day standards.

On the principal slab, the imprints of the wings give the impression that they are supported by pedestals. As long as the slab was regarded as the ground slab, an explanation was needed for this, such as that vague supposition, for instance, that the wings had protected the sediment for a while from decomposition or being washed away. On the real underlying slab, however, on that piece of the floor of the one time lagoon, the wing imprints are recessed in the shape of a tub which can be explained by the sinking in of the relatively rigid wings supported on the soft ground by their tips. It will also be noted that the curvature of the pinion feather imprints appears fairly natural but it must be remembered that in the compaction of the sediment a reduction in height to about one-tenth took place, i.e., the differences in height were considerably greater when the bird was embedded. The primary quills, dragging their barbs, were pressed, relatively hard, into the mud of the floor of the lagoon which was still soft enough. In the course of this, the barbs came into conflict with each other, broke off or were pushed out at an angle. As a result of this, the broad barbs on the inside no longer covered the following feathers. The shafts of the primaries and the barb areas around them were now directly covered by sediment as the preliminary condition for the survival of their sharply drawn underside imprints.

If an attempt is made to determine the number of primary quills by counting the shaft-imprints, difficulties are encountered because blurred imprints occur between the sharp imprints. Sometimes these have also been included in the count or it has been assumed that these are a second row of pinion feathers. The ornithologist Heinroth considered these to be moulted and newly growing feathers but de Beer, the former director of the British Museum of Natural History, London, recognized these structures in his monograph on *Archaeopteryx* as double shaft-imprints made before the final embedding. It can be seen at the primaries that a sharp and a faint impression run together at the tips of the feathers. When the two imprints are compared, it will be noticed that there is a clear distinction between the first and the final imprint of a feather shaft. The two have an opposing relief. The first imprints thus appear raised on the principal slab. But all the other imprints are also raised which have to be associated with the shafts of the secondary quills. How can this be explained? R. Rau (1969) interpreted the raised "double imprints" as contact marks. In our opinion, if this were the case, they would be much more even and, on the other hand, they would have been obliterated again by the barbs, bearing in mind the assumed consistency of the sediment. In contrast to Rau, we have turned our attention to the genuine lower slab.

The positive and negative reproduction of the same structures in the imprints on the two slabs can now no longer be regarded as the one-way transfer of the relief on the principal slab to the underlying slab. It is rather the case that this is a two-way impression of the imprints, an embossed image, which we see. This, however, has its special features. It is clear that to begin with it was only relatively coarse structures such as the shafts which could be imprinted in the underlying slab. In our view, it was a slimy film of clay which was responsible for this. It completely covered the chalky ooze of the bed of the lagoon even before the body of *Archaeopteryx* sank to the bottom and after the rock had become hard formed the dividing surface between the underlying slab and the top slab, the basic condition for the discovery of the fossil and also for the isolation of the two-way reliefs from each other.

The upper surfaces of the feather-shafts always left the same imprints on the bed of the lagoon, whether they were in the first position or in the second and final position. In the first position, the shafts left imprints which we can regard neither as a sign of life nor as the fossil itself but only as the result of passive movements by dead objects. These brush marks made by the feather-shafts were produced as the consequence of a sharp movement by the wing in the time between the settling of the corpse and its becoming embedded. In contrast, we must regard the shaft imprints of the second position as genuine fossils. It was in this position that the remainder of the organism was finally embedded and survived, even though it was only as an imprint.

Each feather-shaft made only one imprint when it came into direct contact with the sediment. In the case of the primary quills, this applies to the top surfaces and the undersides. With the disappearance of the horny substance, the shafts, which had become squashed in the meantime, were changed into hollow shapes, the top surfaces and undersides of which were then pressed into each other under the weight of the sediment.

This is how the strangely flat embossed relief of the shaft-imprints came about on which the more marked relief of the underside predominates. As can be recognized from the impressed barb-structure, the brush marks of the primary shafts were covered, flattened and in some places even obliterated by the inner barbs when the feathers were shifted. With the secondary quills, it is not possible to distinguish between the short brush marks and the shaft-imprints, which causes a problem in the counting of the feathers. On the underside of the wing, turned upwards, inner barbs and wing coverts naturally cover the pinion shafts so that no imprints of their characteristic undersides could be left behind in the chalk ooze covering the creature.

It will be noticed that the four longest primaries display clear double imprints of the shafts but not the primary quills in front. There is probably a connection here with another phenomenon which likewise divides the two groups of feathers. The curvature of the shafts of the large wing feathers at the front is normal but that of the long flight feathers is in opposition to this. It is clear that the long shafts were in a forcibly extended position, which could be indicated by the accumulation of sediment pointing backwards at the tips of the feathers. The same can be seen less clearly at the secondary quills but nothing like it at the leading flight feathers of the primaries. When the body of the bird settled on the bed of the lagoon, the hanging left wing was obviously pressed backwards at the tips of the feathers into the ooze, the leading primaries not yet leaving an imprint perhaps. The still rigid wing, together with the flight feathers, was subjected to elastic tension which gradually ceased with the progress of decay. The position of preservation of the flight feathers was apparently caused when the hand became detached. The quills were drawn forward and the shafts, which had already become softer, were bent even more.

Attention has repeatedly been drawn to the fact that the imprint of the feathers on the underlying slab is sharper than that on the principal slab. However, this only appears to be so partly because of the structure of the feathers and perhaps also as a consequence of earlier cast-making techniques. Even if both slabs display the same details of the feathers, a flat relief with sharp ridges is depicted more sharply in light striking it at a low angle than its counterpart with narrow furrows. Narrow furrows have been impressed by the barbs in the top layer but their imprint in the underlying layer caused narrow ridges as the natural duplicate of the barbs and thus the apparently sharper relief of the underlying slab.

It is quite evident that the embedding of the Berlin bird took place under particularly favourable conditions since none of the other fossils of *Archaeopteryx* displays the phenomena discussed to anything like the same clear degree. The feather imprints on the base slab of the London bird are very ill-defined.

It is only at various few places on the right wing that occasional tiny pieces of sediment show the sharp relief. The pieces of sediment are presumably what is left of a layer of chalk which flaked off when the find was made and on which there was an impression of the delicate structure. Of critical importance for the good preservation of a fossil are rapid entombment, the structure of the sediment, the thickness of the clay isolating layer and the interaction of the bacterial decomposition of the corpse and the settling and compaction of the sediment.

The strange imprint shown by the left wing of the Berlin bird with its apparently contradictory structures can only be logically understood in the aspect presented here as a two-way embossed impression. Since brush marks as concave shapes can not characterize underlying slabs, they prove that which we postulated at the beginning as being usual for fossils from Solnhofen, i.e., that the principal slab of the Berlin specimen of *Archaeopteryx* is the original top slab.

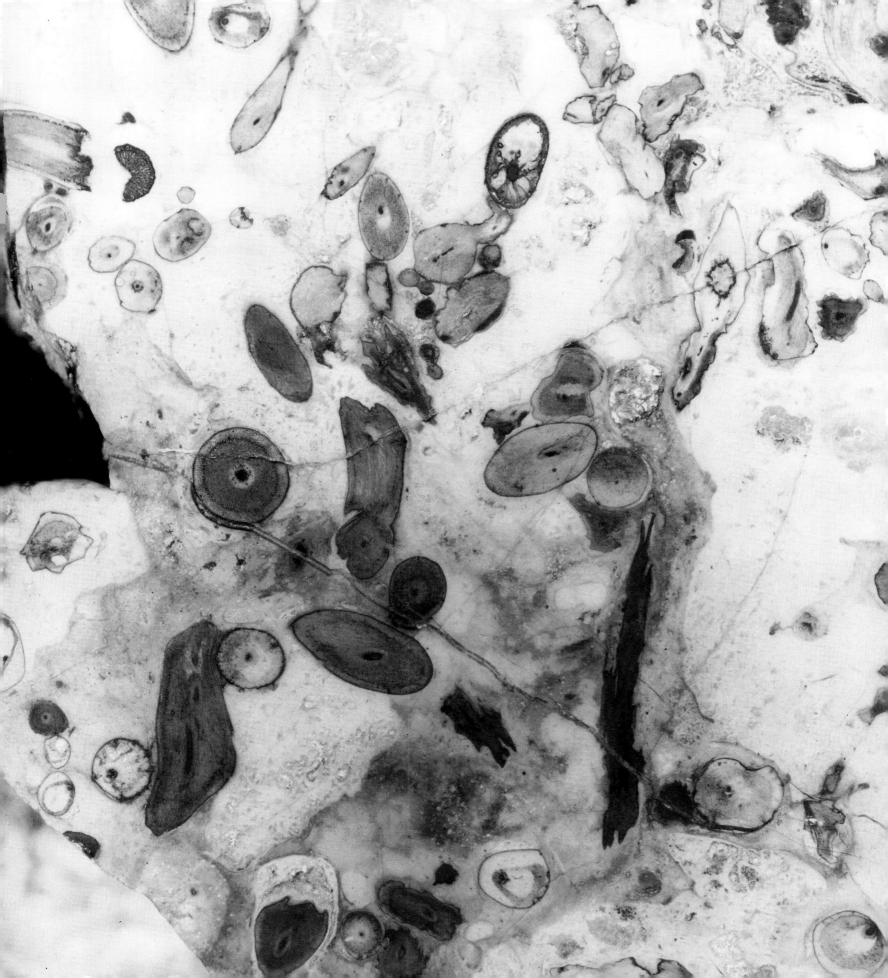

Preceding page:
Rhynie chert
In 1916, William Mackie drew the attention of palaeontologists to the Middle Devonian chert at Rhynie, 30 miles to the west of Aberdeen in Scotland. The polishing of this blueish-grey rock, which looks somewhat like Wedgwood ware, reveals numerous cross-sections and longitudinal sections of land plants (Psilophytes) of about 370 million years of age.

Rhynia cross-section
The real excellence of the preservation produced by silification processes at Rhynie 370 million years ago often only becomes apparent when the material is ground, when one can look into the cellular tissue of round axes: in the centre there is a black strand of the water-conducting cells (xylem), surrounded by cells with exceptionally delicate walls which probably conducted the sap, and then the inner and outer cortex. The outermost cell-layer is formed by the epidermis in which stomata (not shown here) are incorporated. Magnification: 36×

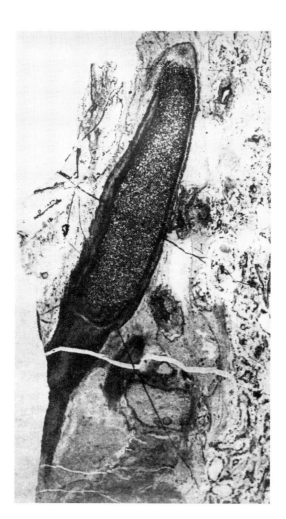

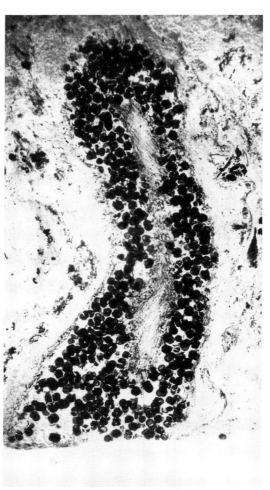

Rhynia gwynne-vaughani
Original illustration of a Rhynia *sporangium (Rhynia gwynne-vaughani) from the treatise by R. Kidston and W.H. Lang, 1917. Some of the round-stem shoots in the Rhynie chert in longitudinal section show a thickened end part which is filled on the inside by tissue which changes to spore tetrads. Magnification: 5×*

Horneophyton lignieri
Thin section produced by W. Hemingway, Derby (England).
A so far unsolved problem is posed by the sterile tissue in the interior of the spore tetrad mass of the sporangium of Horneophyton lignieri. *This fossil plant was described by R. Kidston and W.H. Lang in 1920. A sterile tissue of this kind in the interior of the sporangium is known from recent mosses. Are the mosses descended perhaps from these land plants of the Scottish Devonian? Magnification: 55×*

Horneophyton
Thin section produced by W. Hemingway, Derby (England).
It seems incredible to a botanist but even the delicate root hairs (rhizoids) of the Horneophyton *rhizome have survived. Magnification: 20×*

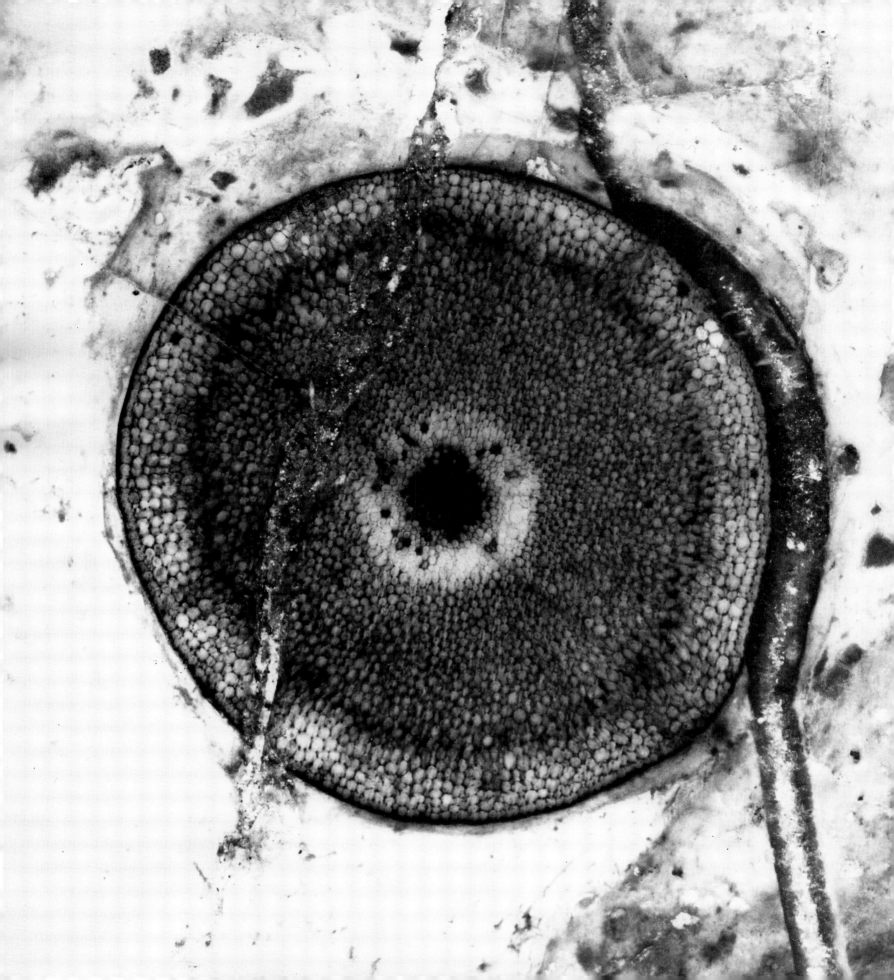

Asteroxylon mackiei

Thin section produced by W.Hemingway, Derby (England).

It is apparent that 370 million years ago land plants of a more complicated construction with star-shaped wood-bodies existed side-by-side with land plants of a very simple shape and internal construction. The thin section shown contains five such cross-sections of Asteroxylon mackiei. R.Kidston and W.H.Lang named this species in honour of William Mackie in their treatise of 1920. Magnification: 4×

Asteroxylon mackiei

Thin section produced by W.Hemingway, Derby (England).

A longitudinal thin section shows that Asteroxylon was a plant with primitive leaves. There is no strand leading outwards from the xylem (black) to these assimilation organs. Magnification: 5×

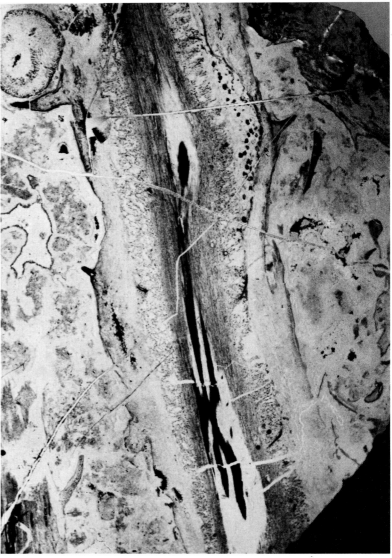

Asteroxylon mackiei

Thin section produced by W. Hemingway, Derby (England).

Magnification of the xylem allows the annular thickening of the water-conducting cells (tracheids) in Asteroxylon *to be seen. Magnification: 120×*

Asteroxylon

This illustration from the treatise by R. Kidston and W. H. Lang of 1920 is one of the classic documents of palaeobotany. In the centre, there can be seen the xylem as a black star-shaped form (Asteroxylon = star wood); the very pale thin-walled tissue is sap-conducting tissue (which had not yet developed as phloem). The inner cortex appears in the thin section as fine points and in the longitudinal section as long cells. The middle cortex, however, appears as an air-chamber system. There then follows a thick outer cortex and the bases of the leaves. From the star-shaped stele of the centre xylem strands lead outwards into the outer cortical layer where they end before reaching the leaves.

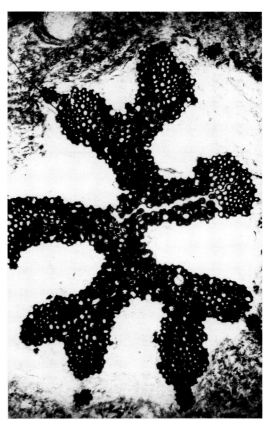

Asteroxylon

Thin section produced by W. Hemingway, Derby (England).

A fairly high magnification of the star-shaped stele of Asteroxylon *shows that it is a question of thick-walled water-conducting wood cells. Are the xylem patches located outside and now becoming separated really leaf conducting strands or simply xylem transformations in the cortex where initial xylem had already been? The point in the upper centre does indeed show protoxylem on the inside which has been joined concentrically by metaxylem on the outside. Magnification: 50×*

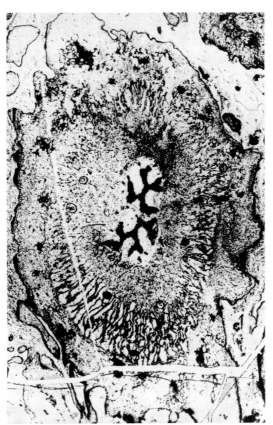

Medullopitys sclerotica

A piece of gymnosperm wood, 280 million years old, from Namibia. An original specimen from the collection of R. Kräusel (1928). Permian Karro strata, in Namibia contain tree-trunks and wood which have been transformed into calcite and whose wood structure under the usual transmitted-light microscope can only be seen as a vague longitudinal structure (left; magnification: 60×). In polarized light, however, the wood structure (260 million years old) appears as a clear picture which can be measured in every detail. The water-conducting cells of the wood (tracheids) can be recognized as longitudinally oriented structures with closely packed dots (bottom left; magnification: 225×). In the crosswise direction, medullary rays dominate the picture (right; magnification: 150×). Depending on how the stage is turned, different parts of the picture appear in light colouration.

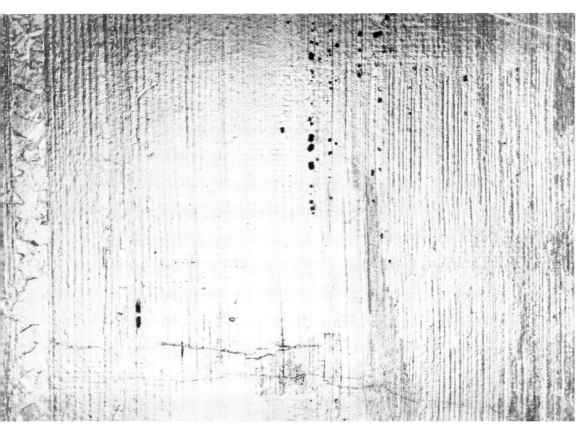

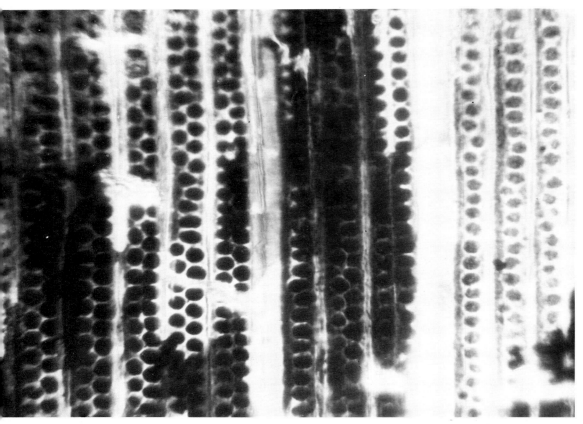

Conifer wood

Woods transformed into marcasite are sawn with the rock-saw and ground. The polished surface, gleaming like metal, allows every detail of the wood structure to be seen, even when examined under the microscope. Unfortunately, the surface shine clouds over within a few hours and the precious finds disintegrate within days or weeks. The finds shown here are from a clay pit of the Tertiary period (Miocene) in Lusatia (German Democratic Republic).

Cupressinoxylon *spec.*

Cross-section of conifer root wood. The cell cavities are filled with clearly regulated marcasite crystals. Magnification: 250×

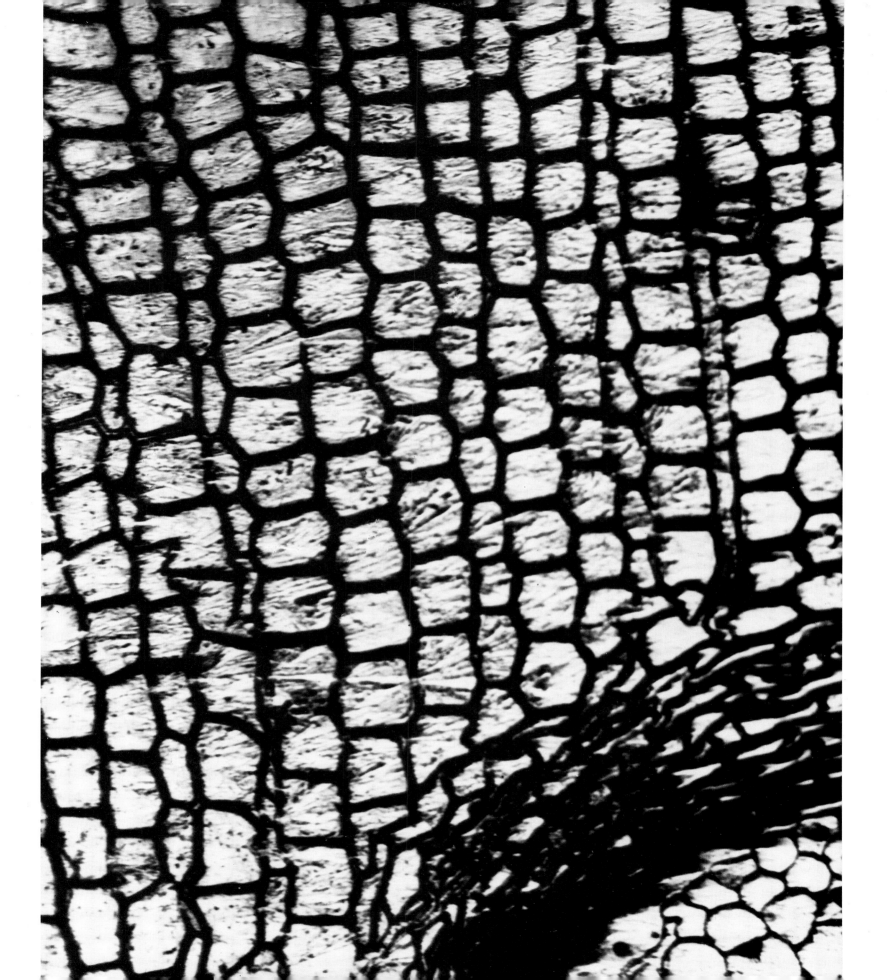

Cupressinoxylon *sp*.

Radial long section of the root wood. The water-conducting elements (tracheids) are cut up longitudinally; on the bottom of the picture the pits in the tracheid walls are to be seen, medullary rays cross the picture. Magnification: 120×

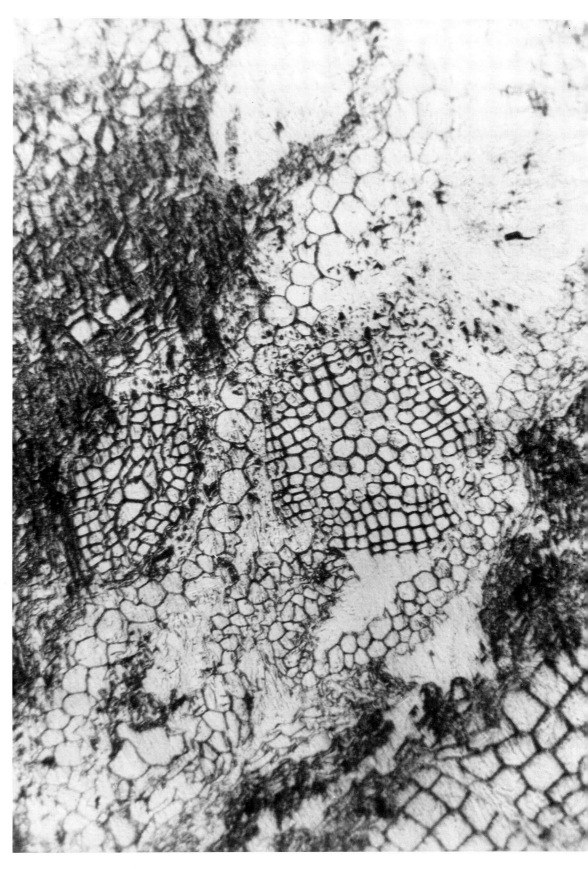

Cross-section of small roots which sank in decomposing wood 20 million years ago and were also marcasilized. Magnification: 150×

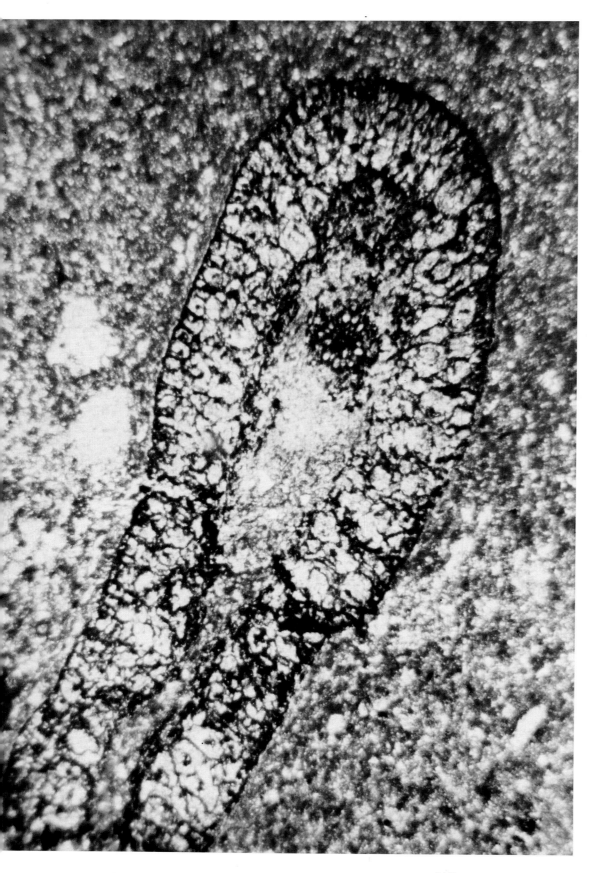

Psilophyton dawsoni

Canada, Gaspé peninsula, Atlantic coast of the Province of Quebec, upper Lower Devonian.

To counteract the disintegration of material or to obtain whole series of specimens for examination under the microscope, cellulose-acetate peels are prepared from the ground surfaces. In this manner, long-lasting sections can be produced from very rare finds. The originals shown in the illustration belong to the Palaeobotany Collection of Cornell University, Ithaca, N.Y. and are the subject of a paper published by H.P.Banks, S.Leclercq and F.M.Hueber in Palaeontographica Americana VIII, 48 1975. For the first time, these pictures showed the anatomical structures of the Psilophyton plant, dating back 370 million years. This is one of the oldest land plants on Earth.

The pictures show an initially small (left; magnification: 160×) but subsequently larger wood body (right; magnification: 200×) enclosed by a large-celled cortex, which is lined on the inside by perishable, delicately walled cortical tissue. Its initial cells (protoxylem) are in the centre with large-celled water-conducting tissue (metaxylem) enclosing the thin initial strand. This is a particularly ancient wood body, a protostele, which was common 370 to 400 million years ago in the very first land plants.

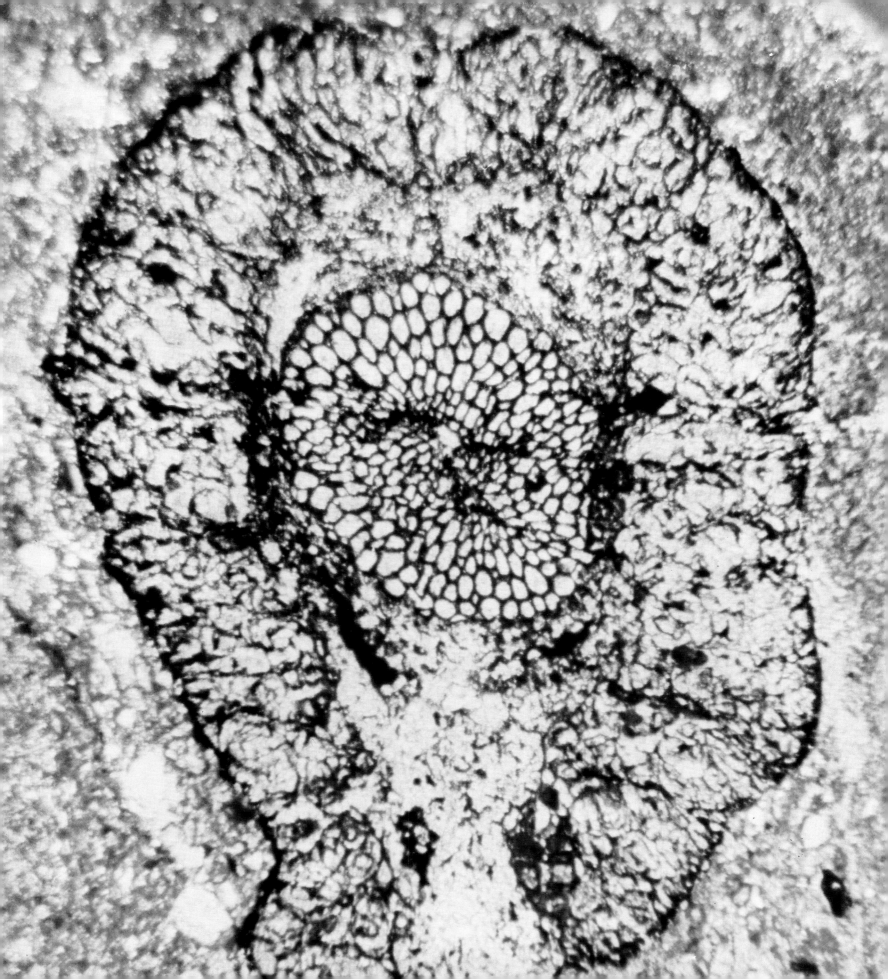

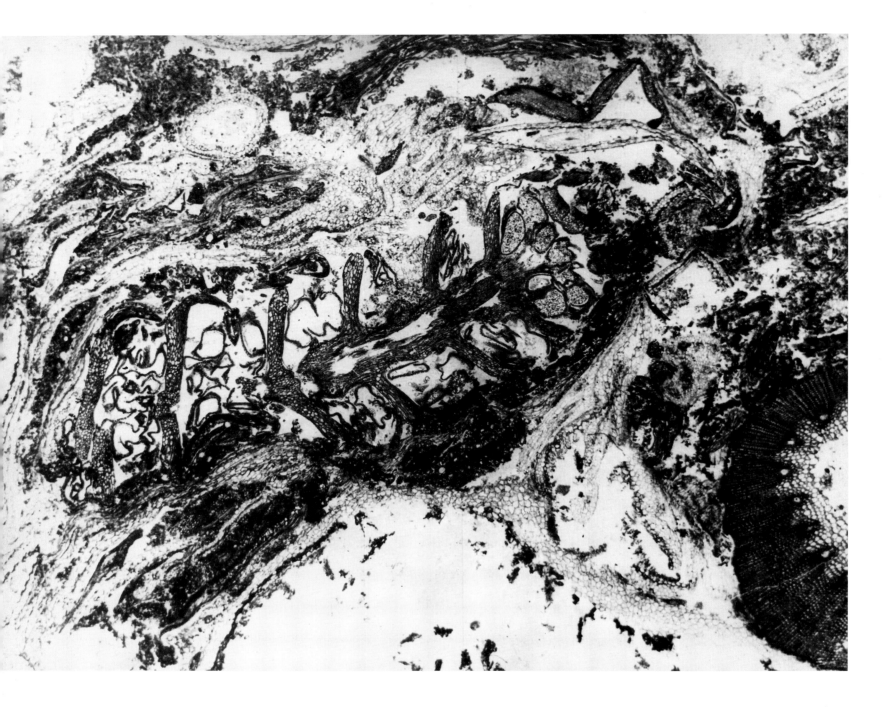

Calamostachys binneyana

Thin section produced by James Lomax from a chalk-dolomite body of the Hard Bed horizon at Halifax. Magnification: 25×.

Calamite cones are not uncommon in coal-balls but a longitudinal section through such an axis with whorls of sterile leaves between the whorls of sporangia on their own stems (sporangiophores) is rare.

In the upper part of the cone shown, the sporangia are cut. The picture also shows a calamite cross-section with the remains of pith cells and secondary wood but without the cortex which has not survived. Magnification: 25×

Sphenophyllum

Cross-section of a Sphenophyllum *axis with cortex. There is a zone of narrow thin-walled cells between the wooden body and cortex which realized the growth in thickness of the axis. Magnification: 60× Older* Sphenophyllum *axes display a round cross-section of the entire wood. The inner cortical layers (periderm) also show the close-packed arrangement of the cells subsequently formed. Specimens prepared by American scientists—D.A.Eggert and D.D.Gaunt, Chicago and Iowa (USA), 1973—also show the cambium and phloem material directly following the xylem and in 1972 C.W.Good and T.H.Taylor, Illinois University, Chicago (USA), finally succeeded in revealing the tetrahedral apical cell of* Sphenophyllum *in a thin section.*

Page 116:

Calamites *and* Sphenophyllum

This thin section comes from a coal-ball from the Katharina seam, which forms the division between the Westphalian A and B levels in the Upper Carboniferous of Westphalia, of the former Karl mine at Essen (Federal Republic of Germany).

Thin sections of Upper Carboniferous coal-balls reveal a confusing picture of the cross-sections and longitudinal sections of axes, roots and leaves of a tropical vegetation *which existed long before the saurians, birds and mammals. Particularly valuable finds have been made in England and Westphalia. The calamite stems usually reached a diameter of 5 to 10 cm; in the present case, the fossil axes are 3 mm in diameter and come from a very young plant. A large hollow space will be noticed in the centre resulting from the disruption of the delicately walled pith tissue in the course of the growth of the axis. Delicate pith tissue has survived at the outer edge of this hollow pith area. The numer-* *ous conducting bundles began their growth outwards with small initial tracheids (protoxylem) which, in the process of the extensive growth of the axis, soon disrupted so that another set of hollow spaces (more than 25 here), the carinal canals, resulted. Metaxylem formed around the protoxylem with secondary wood appearing on the outside (centrifugal). Cortical layers have not survived in the case of this thin-section picture.*

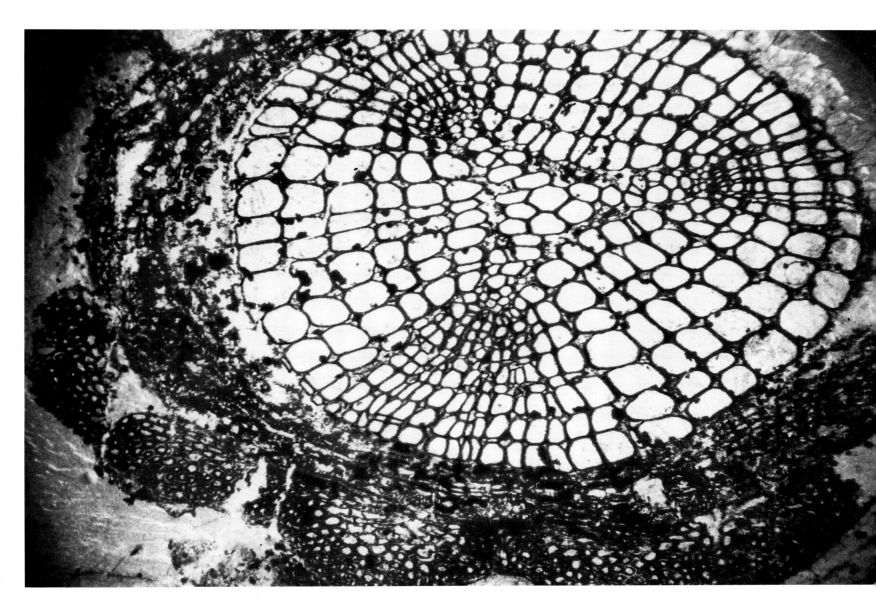

Natural science has been on a war footing with miracles for time immemorial. Modern encyclopaedias are very reserved and clearly disapprove of the use of this term in connection with science since only that is considered to be true which can be comprehended as true in the sense of logical thought and by the senses. Despite this, the vague term of the natural miracle is to be found in many contexts.

In comparison with what was known in the past and with common-sense which knows that everything is transitory and that history, especially natural history, is not necessarily omnipresent, the following seven states of preservation are very close to seven miracles.

1. Transformation to stone (petrifaction).
2. Mineral substances infiltrate plant cells and enclose them.
3. Plant substance becomes coal to varying extents.
4. Preservation in transparent resin (amber).
5. Imprints are only left behind in some sediments.
6. Preservation of long-lasting parts of plants in coal and fluviatile sediments.
7. Modelling of highly perishable parts of plants by parts of other organisms resistant enough to survive.

It is only in the course of the last 200 years that science has turned its attention to the surviving remnants of organisms from the geological past and it has often been difficult for it to accept the hundreds of millions of years of the history of the Earth. Even the great thinkers of evolutionary research were very reserved with their optimism and expressed doubts. Charles Darwin (1859) spoke of the gaps in geological documents and of the inadequacy of our palaeontological collections. This scepticism has continued down to the present time and hindes theoretical thinking.

Transformation to Stone

Miracle No. 1, the genuine petrifications, must have come as a shock to those who first saw them and this still the effect today.

The Miracle of the Seven States of Preservation of Fossil Plant Remains

*Astonishment,
today as in the past,
stimulates man
to philosophize.*

Aristotle

The finds of early land plants in the greyish blue Devonian chert at Rhynie in Scotland between 1916 and 1921 were not the first silicified plant remains but they are the most astonishing of silicified plants. The longitudinal and transverse sections of plant tissue can scarcely be matched in beauty by those of modern plants. To obtain a view of the inner structure of a plant stem, a living plant is sliced with a sharp razor or a microtome. In the case of soft and easily damaged tissue, it is first embedded in a suitable substance, by saturating the delicate tissue with it, and allowing the whole to solidify before cutting thin slices.

When special geological circumstances happen to coincide, nature's method of producing genuine petrifactions is not very different.

In many cases, free silicic acid was available, especially when streams and small areas of water were enriched with it by volcanic activity and the intrusion of deep-seated rock and mineral veins. This silicic acid solution with the consistency of gel probably penetrated the hollow spaces of the plant. It is scarcely likely that this took place while the plant was still living when the protein material with its semi-permeable membranes in the living cells would still have prevented this to a large extent but it must have taken place soon after the plant had died when, after the dissolving of the protein material, vacant cellular chambers became available for the flocculation and precipitation of silica gel. The resulting siliceous rocks can conveniently be examined when peel-sections or polished sections are made from them.

The transverse and longitudinal sections of the axes of previously unknown plants in the Rhynie chert revealed the spongey aerial tissue of swamp plants and even enabled pictures of apical growing point to be obtained. They prove the existence of root hairs, delicate hairs able to suck up moisture from the ground, at the rhizomes which cannot yet be described as roots since this step in development with its anatomical consequences was still to come. The sections also demonstrate the existence of a little column of sterile tissue in the centre of a type of sporangium which is full of unripe spores: *Horneophyton*. A state of preservation so rich in information was and is incredible and science had to accept that such an inconceivable possibility nevertheless did exist.

It is known that entire tree-trunks, layers of leaf remnants, of fungoid hyphae growing in them and unopened blossoms of Cretaceous bennettites have been preserved in this manner and are awaiting scientific examination.

Details of many of the ages of the Earth have been preserved in this way. The petrifactions were not always so favourable for scientific study as in the case of the chert from Rhynie in Aberdeenshire. Nevertheless, the trunks from Karl-Marx-Stadt (formerly Chemnitz) have provided materials for generations of researchers and the stem of a Bennettite with recessed and unopened flowers found two centuries ago in the vicinity of Wieliczka (Poland) was once used by G. R. Wieland (1934) as a foundation and link in his comprehensive chain of evidence on the history of development of the Bennettitales in the Jurassic and Cretaceous periods. The trunk already mentioned on page 33 as a 4300-years old finding is also such a petrifaction. It is always quartz which we see as the end-product of the siliceous process. Opal is unknown as an end-product of petrifaction. Many investigators thought that the fine crystalline form of many woods, from the Miocene of Hungary, for instance, resembled opal but mineralogical examination has not confirmed this.

Another genuine petrifaction which alternates with, and is obviously very close to, silicification is preservation in fluorite. A series of siliceous woods from Karl-Marx-Stadt display parts which are encrusted and impregnated with fluorite and all the details of the anatomy of the wood have survived here, too. It is possible that in the initial stage silica gel was replaced by fluorite mineralization without the wood, consisting of innumerable empty cells (tracheids), being destroyed. Unlike the Rhynie chert, it appears that nothing survives any longer of the original substance of the wood in such a petrifaction in quartz and fluorite and that the very last organic giant molecules have been replaced by mineral substance. Fortunately, colouring through iron and manganese mineralization in the cell-walls of the plant indicates their position without the original substance having to be preserved for this. Investigations with electron microscopes of fossil siliceous woods prove that in favourable circumstances even the delicate fibrillary structure of the walls is mineralized and preserved. This gives rise to the hope that perhaps one day the structure of the protein material or even of the chromosomes may be found to have survived in the form of silicic substance. So far, however, such finds have not been made.

Calcified pieces of gymnosperm wood are known from the Permian Karroo strata in Namibia, in South-West Africa. In natural light they appear translucent but in polarized light calcite crystals appear either dark or light, according to their position in the rock. If such a microsection is viewed through a petrological microscope which can be changed over from normal light to polarized light, the miracle becomes reality: where there was hardly anything to be seen before, there now appears the magic picture of the structure of the wood that had once existed. The varying position of the calcite crystals is the sole reason for this wonderful state of preservation. We owe the originals of our illustrations to an investigation by W. Gothan, made known in 1908 at a monthly meeting of the German Geological Society at Berlin. His published communication contains a sketch of it. Later, in 1928, R. Kräusel and P. Range published a detailed treatise on it. An illustration by Kräusel was published in a German textbook but the illustrations in the present book now make this known to the general public.

It might be thought now that rock sections exhaust all the possibilities but this is far from being the case. Even completely opaque rocks can be made to reveal plant structures when their surfaces are polished. In argillaceous rocks, remnants of wood became concretion centres for iron sulphide millions of years ago with the result that marcasite was deposited there. Such a piece of marcasite, whose appearance is still recognizable as that of wood displays, when cut and polished, a surface with a metallic shine and the delicate outline of the original wood structure. The photographs do indeed show the cross-sections of delicate roots or anatomical details of wood. Hard grades of photographic paper show the marcasite crystals in the cells of the wood, the wall-structures which are obviously of a very delicate crystalline nature and stand out as dark areas from the general metallic shine. Unfortunately, marcasite remnants of this kind disintegrate to a large extent in the course of time. Fifty years ago investigations of such marcasite and calcite fossils were made much easier by the development of the peel technique. Not long ago, the author of this book was sent a valuable work on the anatomy of *Psilophyton dawsoni* from the Lower Devonian of Quebec (Canada) whose author H. P. Banks, President of the International Organization of Palaeobotany at the time, enclosed one of his peels.

The value of such a scientific publication is increased many times over, of course, when the original peel is available. This method allows the making of many original sections from rare and perishable pieces of evidence.

Mineral Substances Infiltrate Plant Cells and Enclose Them

We shall continue the series of our examples with tropical peat, 300 million years old, from the Carboniferous swamp forests. To be sure, logical doubt is justified here, too, since a tropical climate and the formation of peat are not really compatible, at least not today. In the system of the numerous named and unnamed seams of coal where mining is or was carried out, there are also a few in which round nodules of calcium and magnesium carbonate, black on the outside, are to be found. Above these seams an horizon with sea fossils is regularly to be found so that it may readily be surmised that the still young coal seam had been affected by infiltration from the sea. This supply of calcium and magnesium carbonates have led to the concretions mentioned above. The area in which they are found extends from Rhine-Westphalia to Holland, Belgium, France and England. These coal balls are also known from North America and the Donetz Basin. Their value is revealed by cutting and polishing or by making peel sections. In an almost uncrushed condition, plant parts are embedded in the carbonate matrix which can be dissolved away by acid. This is preservation, therefore, in a completely intact state, even though its substance has been somewhat transformed by carbonization. Essentially the vacant cell chambers have been filled out and fossilized by mineral substance.

The fact that the mineral substance can be easily dissolved led John Walton to develop the peel technique for these coal balls which had previously been sectioned by cutting, grinding and polishing. The smooth cut face of a coal ball is etched in dilute hydrochloric acid. As the matrix dissolves away plant material is exposed on the surface. The etched face is carefully washed and left to dry and then a thin layer of cellulose acetate is poured on. When this is dry it can be peeled off as a thin section of the plants in the coal ball. Walton demonstrated his technique on the occasion of an international congress at Cambridge (England) in 1931. One of his gelatine peels, more than 30 cm in size, can be seen at the public exhibition in the Hunterian Museum of Glasgow (Scotland). Nowadays the technique is slightly modified: the etched face is flooded with acetone and a piece of cellulose acetate sheet carefully laid down.

Plant Substance Becomes Coal

Miracle Number Three, carbonized preservation enclosed by sediment, has been rendered visible by a chemical method of investigation known as maceration. The fact that plant substance is present in coal in widely varying forms of preservation has been revealed by polished surfaces and thin sections and these methods of using the microscope for the study of fossil plant structures are remarkably old. Even Hooke's *Micrographica*, published in London in 1665, contained a direct light illustration of fossil wood. However, it was only in 1830, in England, that the method was developed of processing rocks and therefore fossil plant remains as well as polished thin-sections. In 1831, Witham of Lartington published the first thin-sections of fossil woods.

It was only later that this technique was also applied to coal.

The preparation of thin-sections of coal is still customary today but the first really admirable pictures of the coloured constituent parts of coal were obtained by E.C.Jeffrey of the Botanical Institute of Harvard University, Cambridge, Mass., USA. He was able to produce exceptionally thin microtome sections of coal. For this, he developed a complicated method of softening the coal in question before it was cut with the microtome. He placed cannel coal, for example, which is rich in spores, for a week or longer in 70% alcohol heated to 60 to 70°C and saturated with sodium hydroxide (NaOH) or potash (potassium carbonate K_2CO_3). The hydroxide or potash solution was then removed in another alcohol bath which was followed by a two- to three-week treatment with concentrated hydrofluoric acid (HF). Other coals were treated with aqua regia or other acid mixtures. After these acids had been washed out, the piece of coal was embedded in a flexible substance and sectioned. These sections were again dehydrated in high-percentage alcohol or chloroform and decolorized in benzene or xylene. The section was embedded in canada balsam, a transparent resin widely used for permanent preparations of this kind. Jeffrey produced true works of art in the scientific and technical sense between 1910 and 1914 and gave some of his collections of sections to famous museums. Thin sections of such excellence have never again been produced.

Shown here is a section of Zwickau coal prepared by Jeffrey in which particularly fine small pores and large megaspores (yellow), constitutent parts of wood and bark substance (ochre) and fossil charcoal (black) can be identified. The plant substances, which contain suberin, are changed so little by the process of carbonization that they still appear yellow after 300 million years. The other plant parts, largely consisting of wood and bark tissue, are homogenized in ochre tones but in some cases also still display the crushed cellular structures. Only charcoal is black in appearance and the extent to which the cellular structure is crushed depends on the degree of carbonization.

Coal, 300 million years old, can therefore still reveal its onetime hues although it is only in thin sections that the black pieces of coal actually show its colours. Coals with a high degree of carbonization (fat coal, lean coal, anthracite) no longer provide such coloured pictures since all the plant substance is now subject to the enrichment process of compounds rich in carbon. The black colour increases until the graphite stage is reached.

The black carbonized substance of fossil plants known as compressions is a thin film of coal. Such plants yield much more useful information to the palaeobotanist than coal itself. Each leaf of a plant is covered by a thin skin of cuticle which supplies a true copy of the outer layer (epidermis) of both upper and lower sides of the leaf. Of course, it was not long before science succeeded in treating compression fossils with certain chemical substances and in decolourizing the dark remnants of plants with acids (HNO_3) or oxidizing solutions (H_2O_2).

The method of investigation most widely employed for the maceration of plant remnants is that developed by the Berlin botanist F.Schulze in 1855. The Schulze mixture consists of nitric acid (HNO_3) varying in concentration from weak to concentrated to which a few crystals of potassium chlorate ($KClO_3$) are added. With this solution, it is not only possible to break up modern wood into its cells by the dissolving of the pectine lamellae but also to decolourize carbonized leaf remnants until a brown colour remains. After the acid has been carefully washed out in water, the piece of decolourized fossil leaf is placed in dilute caustic solution (e.g., NH_4OH), thus dissolving all the dark, carbonized substance. A.Schenk, in the 1860's, was probably the first palaeobotanist to employ this method of maceration.

Other chemical dissolving operations can be carried out before the maceration process. The piece of rock can be disaggregated by H_2O_2 or hydrochloric acid (HCl); or when silica has to be dissolved, hydrofluoric acid. After the acids have been washed out, an entire collection of tiny plant remnants is then obtained which can be studied further by maceration. The illustration on p.194 shows a

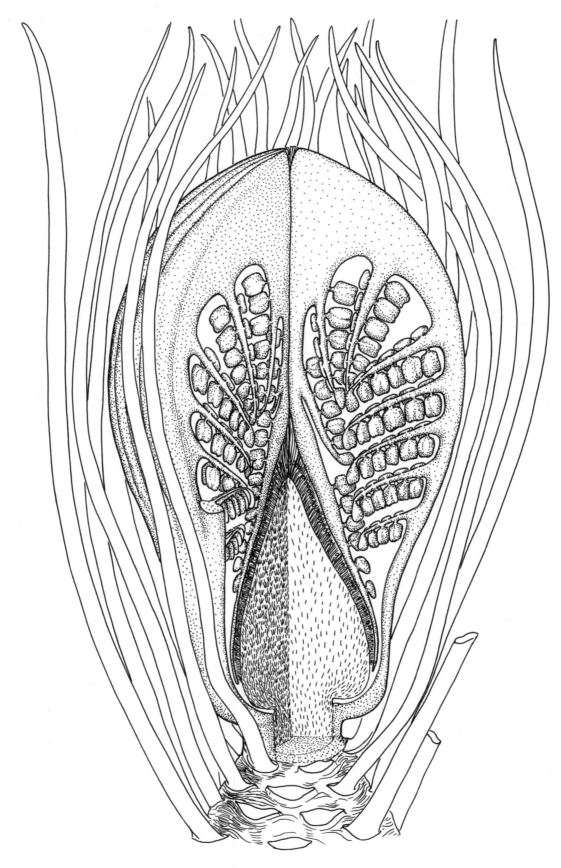

Cretaceous bennettitalean flowers of the genus Cycadeoidea *have survived as closed buds in fossil form.
This view, reconstructed from grinding-finish illustrations, shows curved stamens and a many-seeded fruit-
cone. (reconstruction according to G.R.Wieland
1906, T.Delevoryas 1968, W.L.Crepet 1974)*

Diagrammatic reconstruction of the Ptilophyllum-
leaved Williamsonia *sewardi plant, assembled from
many partial finds by B.Sahni 1932. A life-sized
model based on this drawing now graces the foyer of
the Birbal-Sahni Institute for Palaeobotany in Lucknow (India).*

piece of rock drill core from a geological bore-
hole and its separate constituent parts under
water in a porcelain dish.

Frequently with conifer needles or pinnate
cycads and bennettites, a tiny piece of coherent cuticle is obtained which formed the
cuticular outer covering of the needle or leaf.
The two sides of the cuticle of the leaf are
separated with thin needles and mounted on a
slide in such a manner that the upper side of
the leaf (on the right in the picture) and the
lower side (here with numerous stomatal
openings in a longitudinal strip) can be studied
together. The piece of leaf is remarkably well
preserved for a bennettite leaf from the Lower
Cretaceous period (Wealden).

The illustration on p.194 shows another
bennettite cuticle preparation from the Wealden in which the stomatal openings are
arranged in lines meeting diagonally at the
edge. Greater microscopic magnification
reveals the complicated structure of the
stomata, the characteristic wavy cell-walls
and a lenticular spot of light on every cell.
This is a species of the genus *Ptilophyllum* which
covered wide areas in the Jurassic and Cretaceous periods and of which a reconstruction
has been prepared by Indian palaeobotanists.
Air-exchange apertures arranged in strict
lines are also revealed by a section of the interior of the leaf which, in the following
photographs, shows us remnants of the long
prismatic cells of the mesophyll which contained the assimilating chlorophyll grains.

Providing that the degree of carbonization
was not too high, it is possible to make preparations of this kind from all the ages of the
Earth. In this way, plants have been studied
from the beginnings of land plant development
in the Lower Devonian, from the Carboniferous Period, from the Mesozoic and from the
Tertiary. It is as if plants, in an apparently
unchanged state and enclosed on all sides
were only waiting to be removed and to appear
under the microscope as if they were still living. The space of time between the present
and the past seems to melt away even if, in
most cases, there is only the thin layer of cuticle covering the once living leaf like a thin film.
Our understanding has found a way of making the past come alive again. News has re-

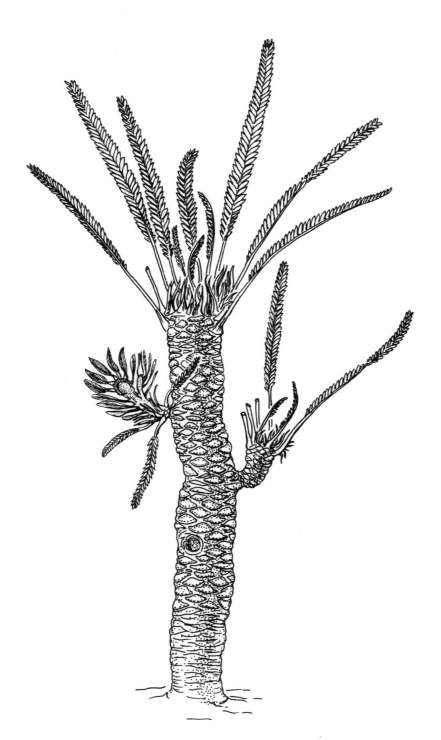

cently been published of the structures of the interiors of cells, including cell nuclei and chromosomes, from the North American Carboniferous period (Pennsylvania). S. D. Brack-Hanes (1978) is of the opinion that the humic acids in the original coal swamp area might have killed off and fixed such protein structures. Microspores of a *Lepidodendron* cone are shown, including prothallial cells and also chromosomes, l to 2 μm in length.

Preservation in Transparent Resin

Now that it is understood, it is no longer a miracle although it should be our miracle of Nature Number Four. Even the natural philosophers of Greece mentioned fossil resin and it was also noted by the authors of the 16th century; mention has already been made of the reference to amber in the book by Encelius, 1551. C. A. Gerhard, in his Outline of the Mineral System for Lectures, Berlin 1786, wrote: "In many pieces of amber one finds wood, leaves, moss, drops of water and air-inclusions . . . From all these circumstances, compared with the constituent parts of amber, it is clearly evident that amber is a vegetable resin, originating from great resin forests and their destruction and passing into the Earth. . .". Incidentally, Gerhard expressed his astonishment that so many strange insects (in amber) had come to Prussia. He was certainly right in this.

The amber to which Gerhard referred comes from the Eocene of an area now covered by the Finnish and Swedish parts of the Baltic. It has been found at sites along the entire Polish Baltic coast but also at Eberswalde near Berlin, in the Ukraine (USSR) and even on the Kola peninsula (USSR). It has been mined for centuries on the Samlan peninsula (formerly East Prussia, now part of the USSR) where it is found in deposits of the Oligocene "Blue Earth" there.

This Baltic amber is famous for its inclusions. There are vast numbers of small insect inclusions but many plant inclusions are also found such as remnants of the branches of Cupressaceae, parts of mistle and oak leaves and even remnants of a small palm branch.

Although rare, they include parts of flowers of special interest. A cinnamon blossom is known to have been found and there is the largest flower discovered so far in amber, *Stuartia kovalewski*, a Theaceae flower of almost 3 cm in size, whose petals and stamens are magnificently preserved. Capsule fruits of the genus *Stuartia* are known from the Rhenish lignite area and from the Lower Pliocene of Frankfort-on-Main (Federal Republic of Germany). This flower exemplifies how much can be learnt from the objects preserved in amber resin.

However, only the outer appearance of insect and flower remains are shown. The objects are hollow on the inside. In the case of insects, the highly resistant chitin shell can be released from the amber. Chitin has proved to be very durable in coal, too, and can be removed by maceration or can easily be shown up on polished surfaces in reflected light. This also applies to sclerotia, the hard permanent spores of fungi. In amber, however, the remnants of other particularly delicate plants such as mosses have been preserved. In this case, it has not yet proved possible to obtain any detailed structures by separation from the amber. It is only the outer appearance which has survived, the substance itself having obviously fallen victim to oxidation processes.

The value of preservation by amber not only lies in the individual object but also in the great quantity of objects in a uniformly good state of preservation from a cohesive area of former biotopes of the Swedish and Finnish parts of the Baltic.

This Baltic amber clearly supplies the most comprehensive view of the world of small fauna of a wooden area of geological prehistory. In a review published in 1969, W. Hennig wrote that about 1,000 amber species of the order of dipterous insects alone have been described whereas in the present dipterous fauna of Central Europe about 6,000 species are considered to exist. This supports observations indicating that in the Baltic Eocene amber area there must have been regions with widely varying conditions of life, that a part of the amber area must have been mountainous and crossed by numerous, rapidly flowing streams. This conclusion is founded on the

large proportion (73 of a total of 152 species) of caddis flies found in Baltic amber, the modern larvae of which live in the fast-moving waters of springs, streams and rivers.

Amber has been found at other sites of different geological ages and accordingly containing remnants of other flora and fauna. Even though the general public knows very much less about these other sites, it can safely be forecast that these other occurrences will supply knowledge of great importance about the natural history and phylogeny of many a group of insects or plants. Hennig in 1969 listed eight important amber sites in all the Northern continents of the Cretaceous and Tertiary periods: Lebanon (Lower Cretaceous), Canada (Upper Cretaceous), Alaska (Upper Cretaceous), Baltic (Eocene), Sicily (Tertiary), Haiti (Tertiary), Mexico (Tertiary) and Burma (Tertiary). Mrs. Langenheim, in her work between 1967 and 1969, concerned herself in particular with American fossil resin sites. She has supplied us with the results of modern methods of investigations on the origin of the resin. In the past, it was assumed that only species of pines provided the resin. In Baltic amber, there are indeed definite remnants of pine but also of branches of Cupressaceae; apart from the fact that bark-beetles found in Baltic amber live in cypress trees. Mrs. Langenheim studied these questions by comparing the wavelengths of the infrared spectra of fossil resin samples and found that a whole series of sources of resin were probable. Her list of more than 50 fossil resin sites names the following genera or families which furnish resin:

North-East Angola (age: Pleistocene to recent) Leguminosae (Copaifera)
Israel (age: Pleistocene) Anacardiaceae (Pistacia)
Victoria/Australia (age: Pliocene) Araucariaceae (Agathis)
Para/Brazil (age: Miocene) Leguminosae (Hymenaea)
Central Sumatra (age: Miocene) Dipterocarpaceae
Haiti/Dominican Republic (age: Oligocene) Taxodiaceae
California/USA (age: Eocene) Pinaceae

Baltic amber (age: Eocene) Pinaceae (Pinus)
London clay/England (age: Palaeocene)
Burseraceae
Alaska (age: Upper Cretaceous) Taxo-
diaceae
Kreischerville, N.Y./USA (age: Upper
Cretaceous) Taxodiaceae, Pinaceae
Maryland/USA (age: Lower Cretaceous,
Alb) Araucariaceae, Taxodiaceae,
Cupressaceae, Pinaceae.

The oldest resin-supplying trees may have been cordaites and a few seed-ferns (Pterido-sperms) in the Upper Carboniferous. Regular resin glands are known since the Triassic in *Araucarioxylon arizonicum*. Up to the Tertiary, resin-supplying trees were to be found only among the conifers. In the Upper Cretaceous, they were probably joined by liquidamber as the first resin-supplying dicotyledenous plant.

The Miracle of Nature Number Four thus turns out to be a special botanical case in which many details, such as the cell mecha-nisms secreting the resin, are still awaiting scientific clarification. Long before the science of mineralogy thought of using canada balsam for embedding its sections, nature was already using this method.

Imprints of Plant Remains Left behind in Sediments

Various types of impressions occur in rocks of certain types. Sometimes preservation must have been on the slightly moist surface of a type of sediment which was then covered by a slightly different sediment. The banks of flat areas of water were probably especially suitable for this. When the two different types of sedi-ment subsequently split at the line where they join, surfaces supply an accurate negative of the impression on the lower surface and the corresponding positive on the overlying surface. Many museums possess upper infill slabs of the spoor animal *Chirotherium* (*Ticino-suchus ferox* B. Krebs) and visitors who give their attention to such matters ask in surprise how it is possible for the footprints to have been preserved.

In the lower New Red Sandstone (Permian)

period, wave patterns, animal spoors, four-sided rock salt crystals, raindrop imprints and the impressions of brances of conifers (Wal-chia) can be found on the surface of many a stratum. The tracks of insects, resembling dotted scratches and the undulating lines of the feeding marks left by molluscs can also be identified. In these traces and impressions, no organic substance has survived but never-theless a picture of a moment of time from 270 million years ago has been preserved.

It happens far more frequently, however, that the characteristic outer surface of a *Sigil-laria* or *Lepidodendron* is imprinted in fine clay. The finder will see the uninteresting and smooth inner surface, which as rock easily splits away, of the outer bark which has be-come a layer of carbon several millimetres thick. It is only when the actual plant sub-stance is freed from the surrounding mate-rial—pit-coal splinters easily and can be re-moved without difficulty with the aid of wooden spill—that the marvellously preserved sculpture comes to light as an imprint in the clay. Its value is now evident and the removal of material from the other direction—the taking away of the clay to obtain the positive of the pit-coal bark surface—is no longer possible. When *Lepidodendron* and *Sigillaria* finds are found only as imprints of the outer surface and not with actual carbonized material this is not such a disadvantage. W.G. Chaloner and M.E. Collinson of London published the re-sults of their investigations of such imprints in 1975. They took casts from the clay negative imprints with all their details and then ex-amined them under the microscope and also with the scanning electron microscope. Aston-nishingly enough, it proved possible with this technique to investigate the cell surface net-work of the epidermis including the stomatal openings.

The centimetre-large leaf cushions of the stem surface with the various scars can be identified without the aid of magnification. The illustration shows a drill-core with the impression of a *Lepidodendron aculeatum* stem. The rhombic outlines of the leaf-cushions bear the actual leaf scar, the area with a length-wise division above this with a pit where the ligule was situated and the two lower areas of

the thicker part of the leaf showing their pa-richnos scars (collapsed aerenchyma). Such an impression does not provide as much infor-mation as the cuticle of the actual plant but is very useful.

It is often the case that plants in sandstone are preserved only as moulds. Quite frequent-ly the hard and durable cones of conifers were buried in such strata and when these sand-stones were subsequently permeated by circu-lating water the organic substance totally disappeared leaving a hollow space in the now hardened quartzite. To obtain a replica of the cone casting compound is poured into the hol-low space and an accurate cast obtained. Such hollow external moulds of pine cones are occa-sionally found in sandstones of the Tertiary period.

Many plants of earlier times were charac-terized by internal cavities. The Carboni-ferous *Calamites* and *Archaeocalamites (= Astero-calamites)* and the stems of *Equisetites* frequently found in red marl have large pith cavities along their length (see p. 116). It is not really known how fine sediment penetrated these cavities (clay, volcanic ash) but a great num-ber of infillings of *Calamites*, known as pith-casts, decorate the collections of museums. These cylindrical infillings of the central cav-ity, which show lengthwise stripes represent-ing primary wood, are really steinkerns or internal moulds rather than casts.

Trunks, thick and thin petioles and even leaves with their veins and, in the case of ferns, with their sporangium clusters may be preserved as mere imprints in sandstones. Thus there are innumerable holes in the Low-er Cretaceous sandstone of Quedlinburg (German Democratic Republic). Some layers of this perforated sandstone have been shown to be former root-soils. Other rows of holes are so regular that the rock can be struck with the hammer along them. It then splits exposing fern fronds of the genus *Weichselia* up to a metre long. The thick stems of the fronds form an empty hole in the rock but the innumerable little leaves only a thin slit. Such a state of preservation is not ideal for scientific purposes but it has enabled particularly large remnants of leaves and fronds to survive and has thus made an important contribution to our scientific understanding of the living world of the past.

An aspect of brief duration is more likely to be preserved in sandstone than in clay which is subsequently compacted. The Upper Cretaceous sandstones of Quedlinburg-Altenburg contain the furled leaves of *Credneria triacumitata*, certainly originating from the autumn fall of the leaves in dry weather conditions. Only the external mould of plant remains survives in travertine, too. Where springs, laden with calcium hydroxide, emerge at the dividing line between clayey red sandstone strata and overlying muschelkalk, tiny chalk crystals are precipitated in the water as it becomes warmer and enclose the leaves, cones, branches, mosses, algae (characeae) and bones lying in the water. The travertines of Weimar-Ehringsdorf (German Democratic Republic) are known as an example of such a site and have supplied many leaf and early human remains. Only bones and pieces of carbonized wood survive in their original physical form, all other remains consist only of the hollow moulds and the imprints.

Preservation in Coal and Fluviatile Sediments

A first sight, our sixth example does not seem so miraculous but in the case of natural history covering millions of years one does not think of such a possibility: there are also hard parts in plants which can survive for millions of years. The hard shells of walnuts and palm-seeds are evidence of this. In actual fact, large quantities of Tertiary seeds and fruit remains are found in lignite seams and fairly often as well in the sandy, clayey strata accompanying them. They range from the tiny pips of the wild vine (*Vitis teutonica* and *Tetrastigma chandleri*) to subtropical dogwood plants (Cornaceae such as *Mastixia*, *Ganitrocera*, *Tectocarya*) and palm seeds.

In the course of the last fifty years, notable advances have been made in the systematic study of these seeds from the lignite period. What was considered to be firm knowledge on the basis of the leaf finds now has to be re-examined from the aspect of the associated

seed finds. Many characteristic seeds have puzzled researchers and have led to long drawn out comparisons. In 1957, F. Kirchheimer published his book of 700 pages on fossil seed studies. D. Mai, in 1976, informed palaeontologists about 28 kinds of fruit and seeds from the Middle Eocene period of the Geisel valley.

Seed finds date back to much earlier times of the Earth's history but their classification always presents problems which is why science contented itself with giving seed finds names which merely expressed their characteristics: *Cylocarpus* (the round seed), *Trigonocarpus* (the three-edged seed). Seed finds date back to the Lower Carboniferous period. In Great Britain, over the last 20 years, important microscopic studies have been made of such petrified seed finds from the Lower Carboniferous period. At the International Botanical Congress of 1964 in Edinburgh, A. G. Long reported on his seed finds, resembling angiosperm ovaries in the upper Lower Carboniferous of Scotland and in 1972 J. M. Pettitt and W. S. Lacey published their work on Lower Carboniferous seeds from North Wales. These individual seeds, preserved in a compressed form, were subjected to a maceration process and displayed all their anatomical details under the microscope. No seed plants are known before the Lower Carboniferous.

Cones are also of great durability. What is true of pine cones today was also true of conifer cones in the past. Pine and *Sequoia* cones are found in lignite strata. In older strata, cones have been found from conifers which are still something of a mystery. When the fruit and seed scales are freed from the substance surrounding them, it is possible to clarify their systematic position and then to classify them with the Taxodiaceae or Araucariaceae or to identify them as representatives of unknown genera and families. The oldest conifer cones are found in some places in the Stephanian stage of the Upper Carboniferous and also in the Lower Triassic.

R. Florin, after much painstaking work, propounded a theory of the origin of the conifers in these old finds. His thorough investigations between 1942 and 1944 showed convincingly that the seed and fruit scales of pre-

sent-day conifers probably come from reduced short shoots in the cone.

Pieces of wood can also be so tough that they survive the march of time. Pieces of Miocene to Oligocene wood in moist soft lignites (50–65% water content) can still be cut with a razor blade or with a microtome. It is not difficult to see from the size of the cross-section of the water-conducting cells whether it is coniferous or decidous wood. The barks of many trees, while they were still growing, contained latex channels. The latex in them hardened to fossil rubber. The miners of the Middle Eocene Geisel Valley lignite at Halle/ Merseburg (German Democratic Republic) were familiar with these fossil barks, which looked like pieces of fur, and called them monkey hairs. When such fossil rubber is ignited, it leaves behind the unmistakable smell of old, burning rubber. The wood structure of these fossil rubber-bearing trunks is similar to that of the present-day *Couma* genus of Tropical America.

The dormant spores of the fungi (sclerotica) and all plant pollen and spores have proved to be exceptionally long-lasting. In polished sections of coal, the dormant spores of fungi have always attracted attention by virtue of their great reflectivity. As reflective round bodies, almost white in colour, they lie between the other plant constituents of coal. With but little variation in form, they have not yet yielded any further information despite systematic studies. It is quite a different matter with the innumerable spores and pollen which have produced a great deal of palaeontological information. Their protective outer layer of sporopollenin like the cuticles mentioned in the third paragraph on maceration, remains relatively unchanged and it is consequently possible to free them from the clayey rock. They are cleaned by weak maceration and separated from the rock by sieving and centrifuging. Under a light-optical microscope and recently under the scanning electron microscope, these spores and pollen show countless important features which permit systematic descriptions and classification into certain fossil plant genera and families. In many cases, far more species of spores and pollen are known than the corresponding leaf, wood and seed re-

Lepidophloios harcourti

Thin section produced by James Lomax, Bolton (England). Site: Hough Hill Colliery, Stalybridge near Manchester.

The branches of Carboniferous clubmoss trees, about 1 m in thickness, show a surprisingly small xylem strand, surrounded by a thick cortex. James Lomax held a noteworthy lecture at the Geological Society of Manchester on 13 June 1899 entitled "Recent Investigations on Plants of the Coal Measures" mentioning that he had produced several hundred thin sections. A large number of his thin sections and of the coal-balls which he investigated now form part of the collections of the British Museum of Natural History, London. Many other museums and collections have also acquired precious examples of thin sections from the James Lomax collection.

In the thin section illustrated, the water-conducting cells (tracheids) appear as a round strand 2 cm in diameter, filled with pith tissue. This tubular column of water-conducting cells (siphonostele) was enclosed by delicately walled tissue (cambium, phloem, inner cortex) which has not survived in the present case. On the outside, there is a strong outer cortex with leaf-bases which appear to be large in this specimen.
Magnification: 12×

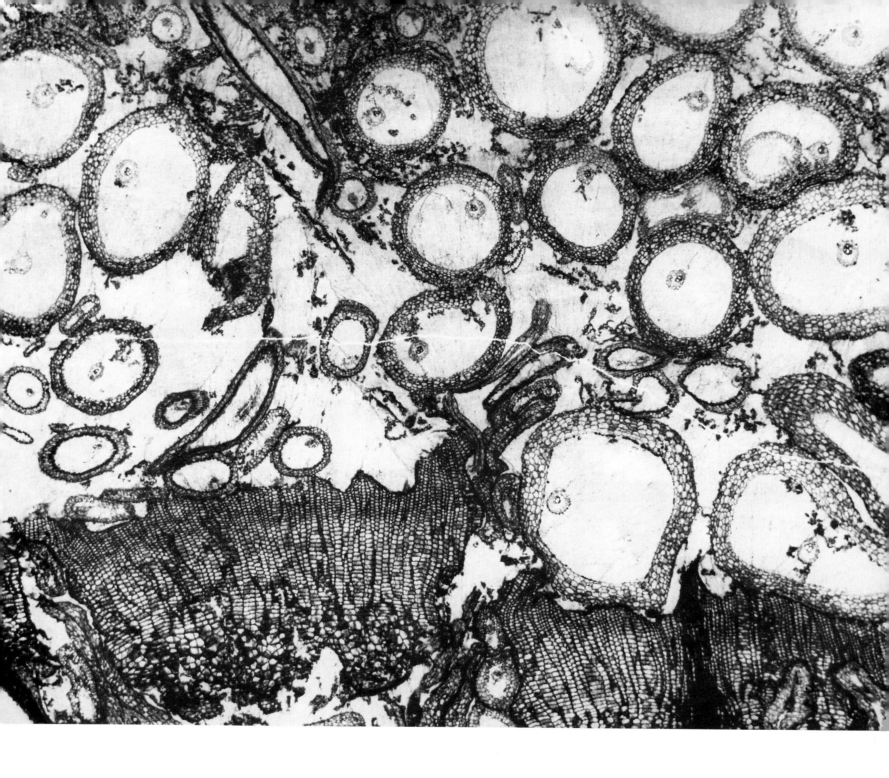

Stigmaria-roots

This thin section comes from a coal-ball from the Katharina seam of the former Karl mine at Essen (Federal Republic of Germany).

It shows the rootlets, only a few millimetres in thickness, of a Lepidodendron *tree. In the centre, the small, water-conducting xylem strand is attached to a mostly very thin ribbon of cells. These rootlets extend in every direction through the peat substrate which certainly had a low oxygen content at that time. They were attached to the large rooting organs of* Lepidodendron, Sigillaria *and* Bothrodendron *trees which are known as* Stigmaria. *Magnification: 25×*

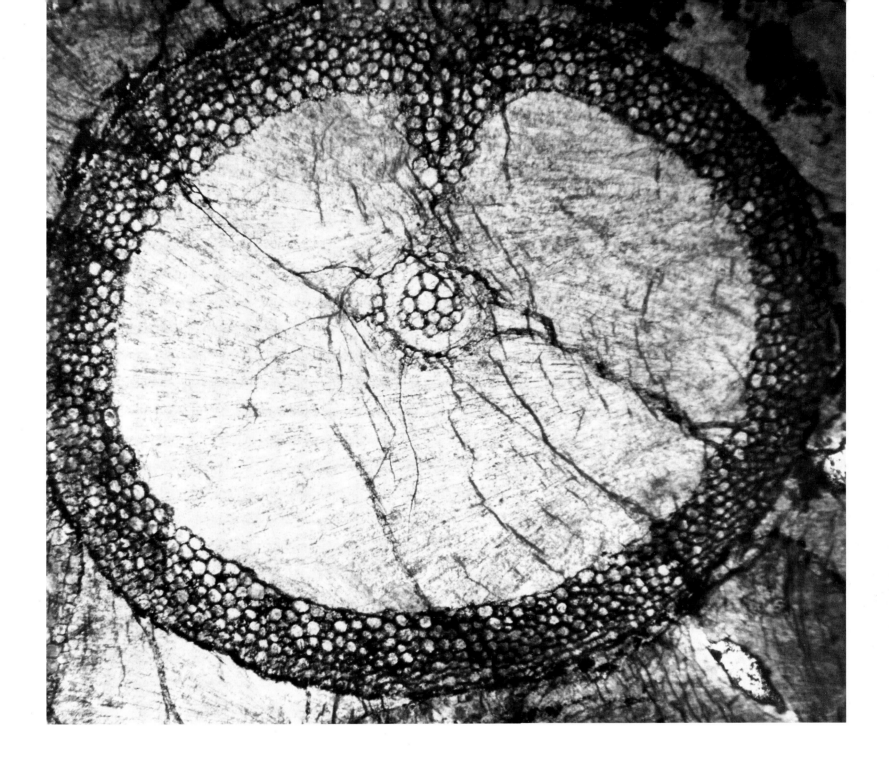

Stigmaria

A view of the inner structure of a stigmarian rootlet (cross-section). The central xylem strand is attached to a thin ribbon of parenchyma cells. Delicate aerial tissue, which has not survived, or a totally empty chamber enclose this centre of water-conducting cells (tracheids). This unusally well-preserved appendix was found at Oldham, England.
Magnification: 70×

Lepidodendron aculeatum

Lepidodendron trees of the Carboniferous period had an outer surface covered with characteristic diamond-shaped cushions each of which bore a narrow leaf. These cushions remained after the leaves had fallen off. The scaly bark of a Lepidodendron acu-leatum *shown here was found in a geological bore-hole far from the classic Coal Measures of central Europe, on the Baltic island of Hiddensee, near the island of Rügen (German Democratic Republic). Magnifcation: 3×*

Lepidodendron

Site: Dulesgate, near Manchester (England). The Lepidodendron *leaves situated on the scaly bark are occasionally found in coal-balls. When pre-served in this manner, it is apparent that they were not flat leaves but succulent and fleshy ones. In the case of the genus* Lepidophloios, *the lower half of the rhombic base of the leaf was tapered or folded in-wards. This thin-section probably belongs to the genus* Lepidophloios, *too, since the leaf cross-sections are closely packed. Magnification: 8×*

Lepidophloios laricinus

Goethe, the great German writer, also possessed a large collection of minerals and fossils which is still to be found in its original location, in the attic of his garden-house in Weimar (German Democratic Repu-blic). Goethe was given a fragment of Lepidophloios laricinus *from the coalmine at Radnitz by his friend Kaspar von Sternberg of Bohemia. Sternberg first published the name as* Lepidofloyos *in 1825 and, in actual fact, his spelling has priority but the customary spelling of* Lepidophloios *is too well established to be changed.*

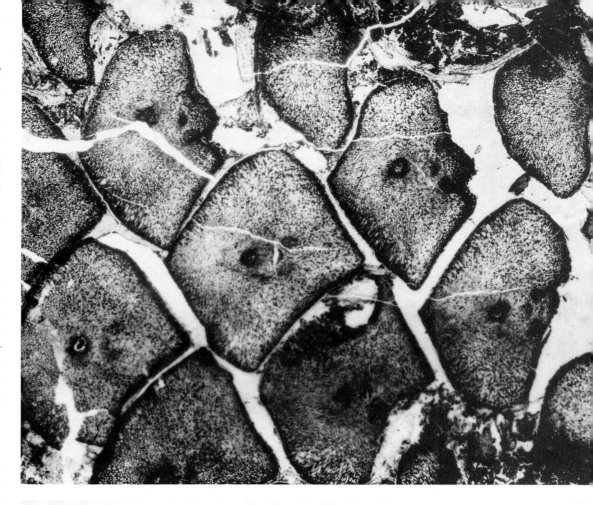

Carboniferous forest floor in Glasgow

There are remains of fossil forests from the Carboniferous period in the most diverse areas of Europe and North America but especially in those areas where the exploitation of the Coal Measures led to the growth of industry. Various bases of Lepidodendron and Sigillaria trees are to be found in museums but in Glasgow stands a small part of a Caboniferous forest floor. The picture shows the tree-trunk bases with their outstretched stigmarian roots. The city of Glasgow can be justly proud of this unique fossil grove which is now covered by a glass building in Victoria Park. No other city in Great Britain—or anywhere else for that matter—has such a Carboniferous forest floor. Glasgow is situated on the western edge of the great Central Scottish coal basin, the Clyde Basin. A total of 11 tree-bases were exposed here in 1887.

Right: A trunk base from the Fossil Grove with extensive, dichotomously bifurcated Stigmaria.

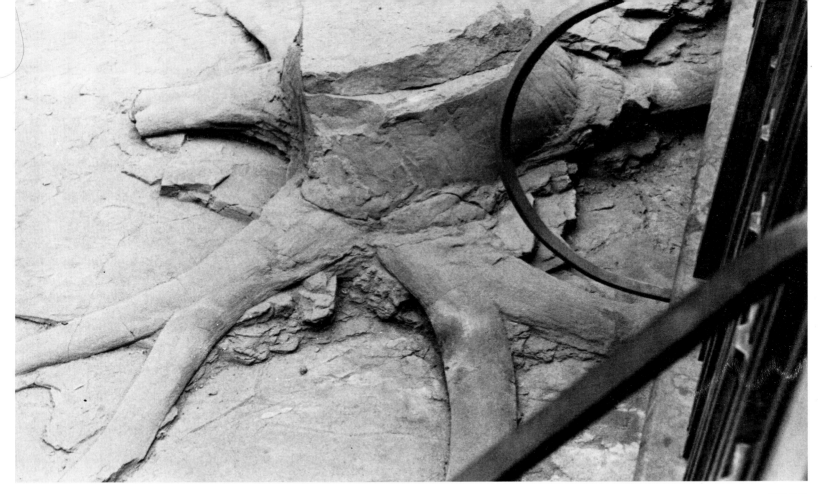

Main shaft of Snowdon Mine (Great Britain)

For centuries, the shafts of coal-mines have been producing not only coal but also a great deal of information about conditions underground, uncovering fossil plants, coal-balls and animal remains. England and Scotland are countries with a very long history of coal-mining. In recent years, many of the old classic coalfields have been exhausted but completely new districts are beginning to be exploited. The Kent coalfield to the south of the Thames in South-East England is one of these new areas.

Drill-core from a depth of more than a thousand metres

The stratum surface shows several species of fossil plants (Annularia sphenophylloides, Alethopteris subdavreuxi). Did they grow together at a single spot or were they only embedded together? This is an Upper Carboniferous (Westphalian D) horizon in the Zwickau coalfield (German Democratic Republic).

Drilling-rig in Zwickau coalfield (German Democratic Republic)

Drill-cores in core-crates

Geological drillings explore areas where no mining has prevoiusly been carried out. They bring up drill-cores of up to a thousand metres in length from a depth of many hundreds of metres, providing information about the nature of the coal seams and the accompanying rocks.

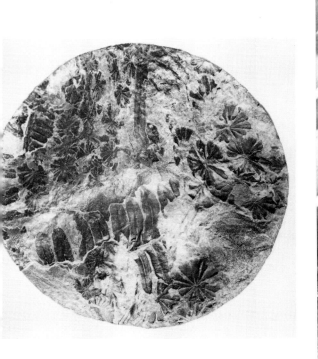

Palaeobotanists at work in a Miocene clay exposure

Almost like panning for gold!
Seeds and cones of plants are to be found in the accompanying strata of lignite seams, in the sands and clays. The precious plant fossils can be obtained by washing and screening. London clay, which is about 50 million years old, is famous for its pyritized fossils, seeds of the Nipa palm and sharks' teeth.

Pteridophyte structure: Pietzschia

Only a small axial fragment—a part of the trunk—a thin branch? A piece only a few centimetres in diameter and about 360 million years old, it was found by a schoolboy in 1924 in the oldest Upper Devonian strata (Manticoceras level) of the Wildenfels hills on the edge of the Erzgebirge (Ore Mountains) (German Democratic Republic). At that time, the evolution of the land plants was still in the early stages. They had only been in existence for 40 to 50 million years! Gothan described this plant fragment on account of the fine preservation of its inner structure which so surprised him that he presented his cross-section in his treatise (1927) as a completely new and previously unknown pteridophyte structure. In 1968, S. Leclercq of Liége (Belgium) and K. M. Lele of Lucknow (India) referred to this find once more and compared it with the inner structure of the Middle Devonian Pseudosporochnus nodosus axes investigated by them.

Our cross-section of 2.5 cm shows more than 30 radiating cell groups which served for the conduction of
water (xylems). Between them, there are wedges of
sclerenchyma. Numerous individual water-conducting
strands have been formed on the inside, in the large area
of pith tissue.
Right: enlarged detail

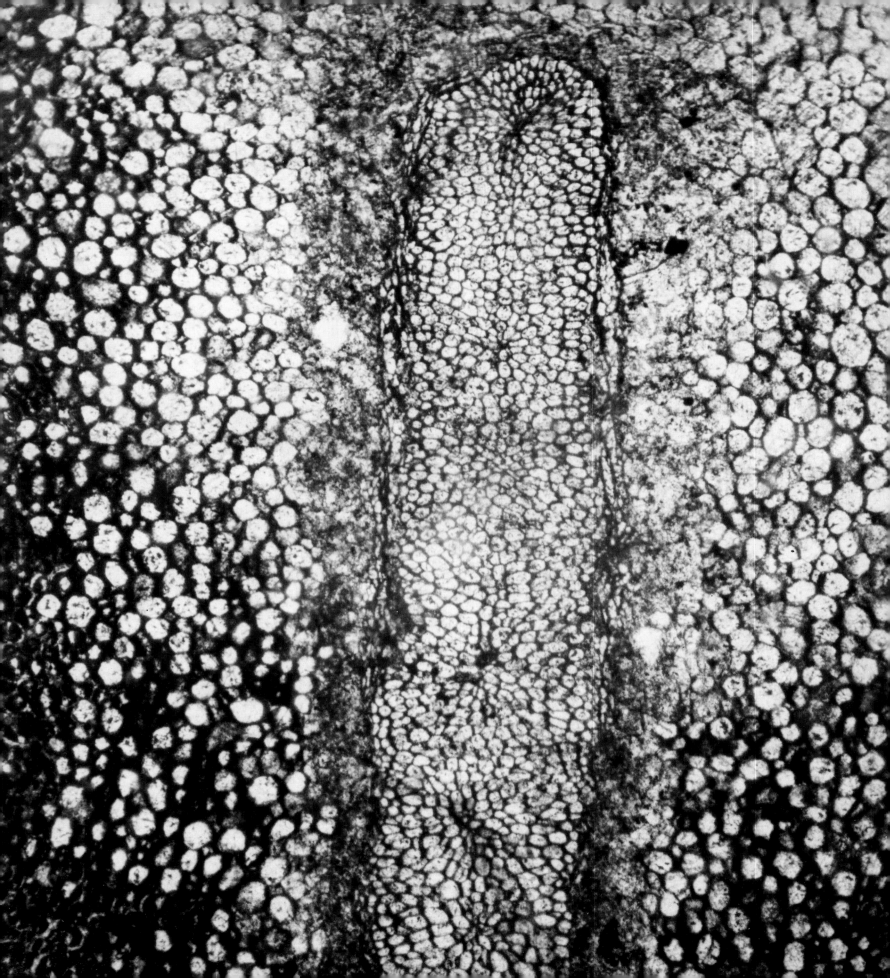

Pietzschia schülleri *Gothan*

The fairly powerful magnification of these xylem plates reveals centres containing small water-conducting cells (protoxylem) in their core; at least six such initial centres, arranged like a string of pearls, can be identified. The individual strands (bottom left) also have a protoxylem. The longitudinal section (top right) shows that in both the tissues mentioned (xylem and sclerenchyma) it is a question of tissue from extended cells.

At that time, there was obviously still no secondary growth in thickness in land plants. There was a multiplication of the water-conducting strands (individual xylems) as here in the centre. Areas between these individual strands were transformed into such tissues (metaxylem) and on the outside these radiating organs emerged for the conduction of water. Hard fibre-tissue was formed between them. The path of development towards wood constantly growing outwards was still a long one. It is evident that the outward growth here has been completed and perhaps the entire growth of the axes upwards took place more with the still undifferentiated tissue located in the centre.

Pietzschia schülleri *is the complicated preliminary stage of all subsequent trees.*

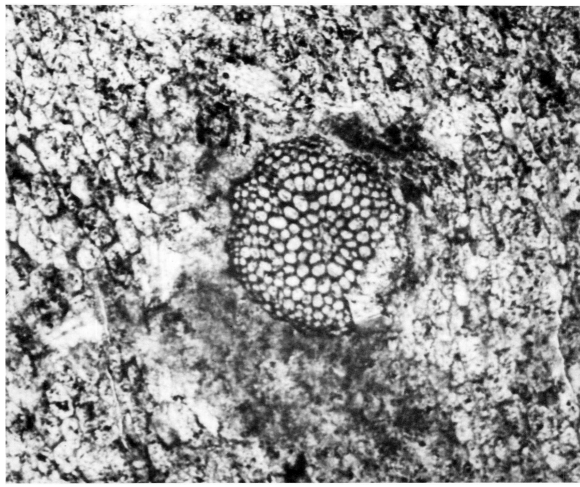

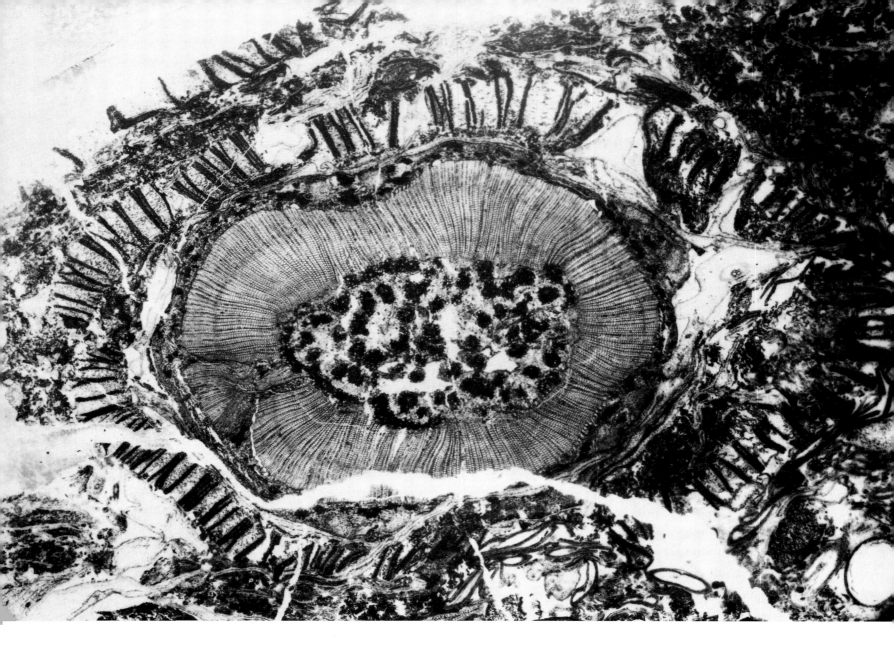

Lyginopteris oldhamium

Site: Dulesgate near Manchester (Great Britain).
Thin section produced by James Lomax.

For a characteristic geological period—the beginning
in the topmost layer of the Lower Carboniferous
(Visean) of Europe and North America and ending
in the middle part of the Upper Carboniferous
(Westphalian B)—there exists a stem-structure which
is regarded as typical for the group of seed-ferns (Pte-
ridospermae) existing at that time. On the outside in
the cortical layer, we can see anatomizing, radial
bands of fibres in cross-section: It was just such fibres
that we saw directly next to the water-conducting radii
(xylem) in Pietzschia, which is about 40 million years
older. They are now arranged separately in the cortical
layer and a longitudinal section (bottom) shows how
these cell-groups have developed further into a network
structure strengthening the cortex. The wood, located
further in displays the growth of secondary wood
outwards so that a coherent body of wood is present
although annual rings are still lacking. The beginning
of the growth of this wood (protoxylem) was on the
inside in the stem and some secondary wood—but not
much—was also separated towards the inside. A large
area in the centre of the stem is occupied by the pith in
which there are numerous nests of dark-coloured cells.
When a branch separates from this stem, an entire
segment of the woody member becomes detached (see left
of picture), loses its secondary wood and moves as a
characteristic, divided W-structure into the bifurcated
frond.

The stem-structures which preceded the present-day
forms were thus of a complicated character and it
would scarcely be possible to gain an idea from the
present ones of the earlier forms if they had not been
found in the fossil state.

Page 140:
Lyginopteris oldhamium

Coal-ball thin section with two Lyginopteris stems
from the Katharina seam of Langendreer near Bochum
(Federal Republic of Germany). Magnification: 6.5×

mains. The study of the pollen and spores of all geological periods, from the Devonian to the Post-Ice Age forests, has opened up a new era of knowledge for biostratigraphy, plant geography and phylogeny.

A few years ago, the American palaeobotanists R. W. Baxter and G. A. Leisman (1967) succeeded in finding in Upper Carboniferous calamite spores the watchspring-like elaters which are so familiar from present-day horsetail spores; and G. W. Rothwell (1972) obtained a picture, resembling a pollen tube, of an Upper Carboniferous seed-fern pollen grain. Attention was first drawn to rare genera of the Tertiary by pollen finds (*Rhoiptelea*, *Reevesia*, Bombacaceae, Sapotaceae, Buxaceae, Araliaceae, Araceae, Ilex) and it was only through the demonstration of ephedroid pollen that the wide dissemination of *Ephedra* plants in the period of the development of the steppes was recognized as probable. And it is hoped that the question of when the first angiosperms appeared in the upper Lower Cretaceous period or even earlier will one day be clarified by pollen finds. It is known that the norma pollen was widely disseminated in Europe during the Upper Cretaceous period but the extinct plant which produced this type of pollen remains unknown. All that is known is that the norma pollen plant must have played an important part in the Upper Cretaceous period. So far, nobody yet knows whether it was a tree whose leaves have remained undiscovered or a herb or a perishable shrub.

It was only in the processing of pollen that delicate traces of algae were found to be exceptionally durable although it had seemed certain that nothing of them could survive. When maceration of the appropriate weak degree was carried out, planktonic fresh-water algae with floating outgrowths or even flagella were found. It is clear that many albumin compounds were more resistant in earlier times than had previously been surmised. Planktonic organisms of this kind, which have even survived regional heat build-up resulting from the deep geological location of the rock or from volcanic intrusions, have been discovered in very old strata. These planktonic organisms are thus in many cases the only durable remnants of organisms which have

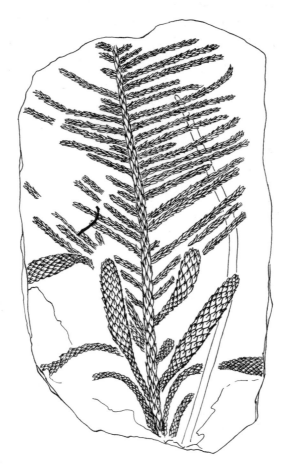

Female (vertically upright) and male (hanging) cones—really cones which are made up of small cones—on the needle-covered branch of Walchia piniformis.
Site: Lodève (France)

survived the passage of time and provide information about the events of the Silurian, Ordovician or Cambrian periods, i.e., of the time 400 to 600 million years ago. The scientific miracle is therefore not that it is known that hard parts of plants also exist but that there is a great deal more of plant substance, including the most delicate substance, still in existence than could ever have been imagined only a few decades ago. Probably, yet unknown, more enduring transformations of otherwise transitory organic substances play a role, perhaps silicified protein.

The Moulding of Perishable Substance by the Immuration of Sessile Animals

It was in the mid-1950's that E. Voigt drew attention to this hitherto overlooked possibility of bringing to light the highly perishable life of past ages. Many palaeontologists had come to accept only too readily that fossil communities would only survive in an incomplete form since the highly perishable organisms would be lacking. Voigt now had the idea of studying the underside of sessile animals such as oysters, bryozoa and larger foraminifera. Since every sessile animal clings tightly to its base, an impression is taken of the relief of the substrate in all its details. However, a basic condition is that the objects sought have themselves settled on a perishable substrate so that the underside of the immurating creature can be studied and has not grown too firmly on to the base. O.S.Vialov (Lvov, USSR) in a study of 1961 used the terms "biomuration" and "immuration" for this, biomuration being applied to the case where the organism is still alive when immured.

So far, most of the examples have come from the Maastricht tufa chalk in Belgium. Examples are also known, however, from the writing chalk deposits of Rügen which make it possible for the frequently discussed problem of the depth of the water at the time and in the area of the formation of chalk sediments to be studied from a new angle.

In addition to many perishable animal remains of sponges and hydrozoa, the soft parts of bryozoa have also survived—moulded by biomuration. The immured plant remains are of special interest here since it is often the case that round holes are the only sign of the enclosure of stalks and stems.

Of the higher plants, the structure of the epidermis and the course of the veins in the leaves have been recorded on the underside of bryozoa. Of course, the reproduction of the epidermis is not such that would allow systematic determinations to be carried out but nevertheless the difference in comparison with algae is clearly evident. Sessile foraminifers also mould the pattern of the epidermis of higher plants.

Through preservation in this manner, it was possible to demonstrate sea-grass in the Belgian Upper Cretaceous (Maastrichtian). It is difficult to identify algae which can be given a botanical classification since these usually leave only a smooth surface.

In the 1950's, silicified aquatic plant remnants in a surprisingly good state of preservation (belonging to the Potamogetonaceae family: *Thalassocharis bosqueti* Debey ex Miquel) were found in the Upper Maastrichtian of Kunrade/Holland (E. Voigt and W. Domke, 1955). The leaves, stems and roots were preserved by incrustation in all the anatomical details—corresponding to our first state of preservation. The finds are found embedded with molluscs, brachiopods and numerous bryozoa. Growths of bryozoa are often found on the roots. All the physically preserved remains are silicified or transformed into a rock resembling flint.

Coal-like remains are also found in certain locations. Accordingly, it must have been a question of the interplay of various preservation conditions in this case and immuration may have played a part in this, even if this cannot be determined with any certainty. The subsequent preservation under hydrogen sulphide conditions and in the presence of free silica may well have completed the preservation begun by biomuration. Perhaps this is

The cone of the Permian conifers did not consist of scales but of an assemblage of small shoots of limited growth carrying a forked pinna, sterile bract and an ovule (shown by dots): fertile shoot of Walchia piniformis, *reconstructed after the preparation and maceration of large cones (see Fig. on p. 141) by R. Florin 1938.*

the explanation for the preservation of a little silicified palm trunk as a flint boulder which was found on the island of Rügen.

Seen in this manner, all the seven examples contain unexpected possibilities for an understanding of natural history. What was thought to have been lost for ever has been preserved under sometimes rare and sometimes not so rare geological and mineralogical conditions. Many of these possibilities of preservation were unexpected for science and, for many educated people with a solid fund of knowledge, astonishing, wonderful and perhaps even a shock.

We have learned to see the history of the development of plants and animals as being less straightforward in its course than might be assumed from the simplified presentations of relationship models. The importance of transitional species in the history of development (Darwin once called them "missing links") has increased.

Finds of such clarity have made the history of nature more meaningful in the conclusions which can be drawn. Some periods of the Earth's history have proved to be formative times for a great part of the plant tax of later times and thus of the present, too. At the Carboniferous period the equator crossed Middle Europe and the winds raining themselves out over the variscic mountains caused a unique tropical laboratory in Europe and North America. The miracles of knowledge which are discovered time and again have brought about an upsurge in activity in the study of natural history.

The limits between what is probably possible and that which is improbable have moved, at times, into areas which hitherto seemed improbable. This is the achievement of human experience and the scientific comprehension of complicated relationships; of the coincidence of factors able to influence each other in a favourable manner. Complex possibilities have thus emerged at times and this applies then to what was hitherto improbable. Some years ago, in the coal of the Geisel Valley at Halle/Merseburg, green leaves were found. And indeed, in certain coals (dysodiles), sufficient fossil chlorophyll can be demonstrated by the usual chemical techniques to justify the use of the term chlorophyll coal, as was actually proposed a few years ago. In the same coals of the Geisel Valley, fossilized red corpuscles from a lizard of the Eocene period and polygonal frog-skin epithelial cells with one cell nucleus each were demonstrated! Such results are matched time and again in other and older strata. In 1977, a publication by the University of Columbus (Ohio, USA) reported on the preservation in limestone of cytoplasm in gametophyte cells of an Upper Carboniferous fern species: T.N.Taylor and M.A.Millay believe that in their maceration preparations they can identify the granular structure of cytoplasm and concentric bodies. In another communication of 1977, G.W. Rothwell describes a pteridosperm seed ovule which was fossilized at the fertilization stage. The ground section shows a noncellular substance which was released by the micropyle

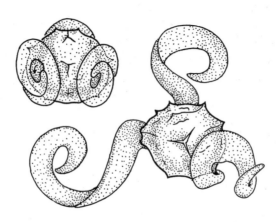

Not only modern horsetail spores possess the strange hygroscopic bands of an outermost spore-wall layer: such elaters are also described by R.W.Baxter and G.A.Leisman in connection with calamite spores of the Upper Carboniferous

of the ovule (pollination drops) which had taken up several grains of pollen.

Such interpretations cannot be regarded as self-evident. The marvel of such rare and highly developed possibilities of preservation are the driving force of knowledge. The mere taking stock takes no account of that which follows, the pleasure of re-experiencing perception. Perhaps, everybody will know one day, from the days of childhood onward, that the way of the world is a much more complex matter, that even in Space it is not the elements which float alone and emit light but also fragments of complicated compounds, a fact demonstrated by radioastronomy in the last decade and totally unsuspected hitherto. In the future, too, the discovery of new perceptions—complex possibilities—will be a source of pleasure and astonishment.

Saurians

Faded lettering on the dignified sandstone facade of an almost century-old building promise us news of Nature. In the interior there indeed ready to receive us are the dinosaurs. We abruptly step from the vestibule of the building into a lofty hall, flooded with daylight. Astonishment, curiosity and perhaps also a slight shudder are what we feel when we see this herd of skeletons of animals which in their lifetime never saw a human being and there is undoubtedly a breath of times long past hanging over them. Our imagination soon comes to our aid and we recall the pictures created by others of that departed world with saurians of flesh and blood.

In the middle of the scene, there stands the lofty form of *Brachiosaurus*, its massive body supported on four pillar-like legs and with its head slightly inclined as if to greet us. To the right and left, the scene is lined by two gigantic and more compact skeletons with long tails. The one on the right, only medium-sized, is *Dicraeosaurus* and he has had to be satisfied with a relatively short neck, quite in contrast to his opposite number on the left. This, the longest of all saurians, appears to be the black sheep of the herd since a black skeleton distinguishes him from his loam-coloured brothers. *Dipolodocus* is the name given to this sombre fellow. Unfortunately, he was unable to appear on parade in person—he resides at the Carnegie Museum in Pittsburgh—but they have sent a plaster representative in his place.

In the shadow of the giant dinosaurs, at the back of the hall, there are smaller saurians to be seen, including an agile predatory dinosaur which ran on two legs. These are imprisoned in glass cabinets to protect them from children's curiosity.

The excavated remains of dinosaurs have always excited the imagination of mankind since the time of the first discoveries. Whenever interest in these strange giants from prehistory declined, it was never long before new discoveries or theories hit the headlines again. Natural science at one time banished the giants of our world of legends but then provided a new stimulus for our powers of imagination when giant creatures were proved to have existed in earlier times. Curiously enough, it is not only the special characteristics of the dinosaurs which engage our attention but, in particular, also their end. Why did they become extinct? New answers have repeatedly been given to this question but so far none of the possibilities considered has been able to provide a satisfactory solution for this complex problem. We will return to this subject again later on.

In recent years, the door to another set of problems has been forced open. Greater attention is beginning to be paid from the biological standpoint to the profound differentiation in the skeletons of the saurians. Some experts consider that the dinosaurs possessed a higher physiological level than that which is known from present-day reptiles. The new hypothesis that the dinosaurs were warm-blooded creatures has stimulated scientific discussion on the subject to a quite incredible extent. The indicators have got to be studied once again, on the basis of the available facts. These are solely the fossilized bones which have often been recovered with great effort, freed from the surrounding material and classified in collections. An aspect of considerable importance here is the exact documentation of the circumstances in which they were found as a possible indication of the way of life of the departed. In many cases, fossil spoors are all that remains of saurians. The scientific interpretation of spoors has shown us that large herbivorous sauropods lived in herds and that the adult animals kept the young ones on the inside of the herd. This will remind everybody of the behaviour of modern mammals.

It was only recently, in the North-West of the USA, that the first saurian nest was found, containing 15 young hadrosaurs. Clutches of eggs from dinosaurs were already known from the Gobi Desert, of course. The fact that the babies only 60 cm in length and 20 cm in height, from the Rocky Mountains had already used their teeth indicates that they had already ventured out from the nest in search of food. It is only exceptional conditions which lead to fossilization. In many cases, it was events of a catastrophic nature which led to the bodies of dead saurians being buried or their bones becoming saturated. Of great interest is the discovery of a new mass-grave of dinosaurs at Salt Lake City. In a giant quarry there, a great pile of *Allosaurus* bones was brought to light but not a single intact skeleton. The find is believed to comprise about 10,000 bones from some 70 individual creatures.

The find at Bernissart was famous over a century ago. Miners in a Belgian coal mine, working at a depth of 320 metres, were confronted with loamy rock containing strange "tree-trunks" in 1878. Experts were quick to appreciate the significance of the find. The miners had found a unique dinosaur graveyard after passing beyond a fault from the coal-bearing strata and into deposits from the early Cretaceous period. The work of excavation lasted for over three years and ultimately 31 skeletons were recovered. An entire herd of saurians had met their death at this spot 125 million years ago. Strangely enough, only adult animals were found. Some of the skeletons were reconstructed in lifelike positions and set up as a group in the Royal Museum of Natural History at Brussels, others were exhibited at the place where they were found. Since that time, *Iguanodon* has become one of the best known of saurians. It was fifty years before this event that the first traces of this dinosaur had been found in England—a few teeth which were initially classified as rhinoceros teeth until it was realized that they resembled giant forms of the teeth of the American *Iguana*. They were thus described as *Iguanodon* meaning iguana tooth. Soon after this, skeletal remains were discovered to which the generic name was now applied. *Iguanodon* was a herbivore which walked on two feet, could reach a height of five metres when upright and weighed between four and five tons.

A number of plaster casts were taken of the best preserved skeleton in the Brussels museum and now the visitors to the natural history museum in Vienna and the Senckenberg Museum in Frankfort-on-Main can all marvel at the Belgian *Iguanodon* with its mighty three-toed hind feet and its strange thumbs which have turned into powerful spikes.

The best known sites for saurians are usually in the dry regions of the Earth where vegetation and soil formations have scarcely been able to cover the fossil-bearing rock strata. These areas undoubtedly still contain many

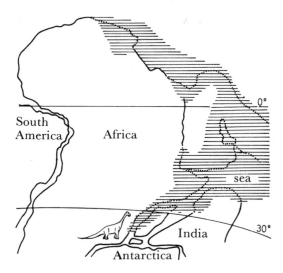

At the end of the Jurassic period, delta deposits of a river system buried the remains of saurians in the East African Gulf.

fossils but their remoteness, the increasing complexity of the equipment needed and political developments have increasingly raised the cost of excavating expeditions. However, it is not only the large-scale excavations which help to complete our knowledge of life in prehistoric times; in many cases, it was individual finds or even single bones which revolutionized our concepts and led us to take a new look at old evidence. The rapid advances made in the field of vertebrate animal palaeontology in particular has now made it necessary for a review to be made after only twenty years in many areas, a new examination of the evidence on which previous and now outdated studies were based.

Seen in this, one cannot help but realize the importance of the great museums of natural history where the unavoidable dust of decades in their storerooms is ever more frequently being disturbed in the quest for indications overlooked in the past. This was how comparative studies of material in the collections of many museums made a significant contribution, for example, to the evidence supporting the revolutionary concept of the warm-blood nature of dinosaurs.

Natural history museums have a double function. On the one hand, they serve the interests of popular education with their selected exhibits while on the other they are the central establishments of the systematic storage and examination of the scientific material of natural history. A report by American palaeontologists states that in the USA alone there are 25 museums with more than 10,000 catalogued fossil bones from vertebrate animals. Many of these museums have collections of reconstructed skeletons in their exhibitions but not only of saurians. In some cases, it is the remarkable mammals of the Tertiary which predominate. Cities with famous natural history museums include New York, Washington, Chicago, Berkeley, New Haven, Pittsburgh and Denver.

Two of the most illustrious collections of fossil vertebrates on the European continent are in the German Democratic Republic. A great deal of skeletal material from fossilized vertebrates has been recovered in the last 50 years from the old Tertiary lignite of the Geisel valley and now determines the profile of the Geisel Valley Museum of Martin Luther University, Halle, with about 80,000 to 100,000 remains of large vertebrates including more than 100 crocodiles, over 200 lizards, about 300 turtles and 160 frogs. The very valuable mammal material includes primitive horses, lophiodons and lemurs. But even greater than the international reputation of the Geisel Valley Museum is that of the Saurian Collection of the Berlin Natural Science Museum. Without doubt, the Berlin saurian exhibition is one of the attractions of international tourism. It includes not only the largest of all the dinosaurs but also the biggest collection of East African saurians from the Late Jurassic period and is thus a unique counterpart to the great collections in the USA of North American saurians of the same age. There is a surprisingly great similarity between the saurians of Tanzania on the one hand and those of Wyoming, Utah and Colorado on the other.

What had been the connection ·between these two sites? The answer was a long time coming and it was only the continental drift theory which solved the riddle. In its modern form, it postulates the development of the Earth's crust from great drifting land masses. From this aspect, there is now no difficulty in conceiving of an area of land corresponding to the present-day Africa-America in that far-distant epoch. It was only at the beginning of the Cretaceous Period 120 million years ago that the South Atlantic began to open up and was comparable with the modern Red Sea between the African and the Arab land mass. The Atlantic is still moving apart in the middle where there is a healing basalt scar and its bed is becoming wider by two centimetres every year. Consequently in the shape of the bed of the Atlantic, we possess an impressive instrument with which to measure the inconceivable period of time which has passed since the idyll of the dinosaurs.

It has also been proved that the saurian fauna of Tanzania existed in Southern Argentina. Even millions of years later, scarcely changed descendants of these creatures were still living on the territory of the modern Niger in the Southern Sahara. From the iguanodonts of Bernissart and the frequent trackways, it is evident that the great dinosaurs also populated the European islands of the early Cretaceous period. At Osnabrück, for instance, the spoors of various kinds of dinosaurs were found on steep sandstone strata.

Complete skeletons of saurians are a rarity; finds usually being incomplete and species very often described solely on the basis of a few skeletal elements. The simultaneous exhibition of the skeletons of five different species of dinosaurs from a single fossil fauna is thus worthy of special attention. This is why, as an example of the many famous collections which exist, the saurian collection of the Museum for Natural Science of the Humboldt University, Berlin, is described below. This exhibition features the skeletons of five saurians from Tendaguru in the southern coastal area of Tanzania.

A Life for the Saurians

Tendaguru, a hill of no particular importance in the south of Tanzania, kept its ancient secret until the beginning of this century. It was by chance that a mining engineer came across it when he noticed great bones protruding from the naked rock in the bush during the dry season. The graves of prehistoric giants

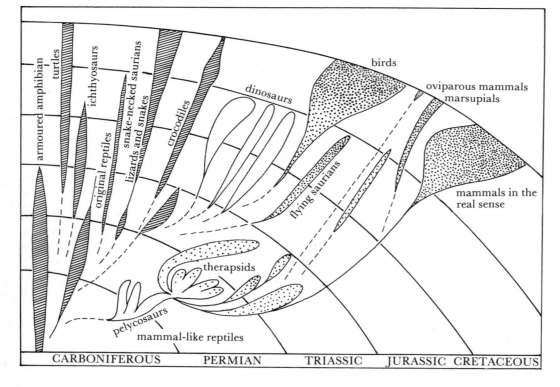

Genealogy of the saurians. The warmblooded groups are shown by interrupted lines. The dotted lines indicate an increase in warmblooded features. The classification of the dinosaurs is left open since differing views are held at the present time in respect of their metabolic level.

had been discovered quite by accident. Just as the rulers of Ancient Egypt had built pyramids as their tombs, nature had done the same here for the kings of the reptiles. 145 million years ago, a great river had buried the saurians in its delta. Movements of the Earth's crust had subsequently lifted up the compacted sediments and weathering had then moulded the shape of the burial mound.

On hearing the news of the mighty bones, Professor D. Fraas, although gravely ill, travelled to the spot in 1907 and brought the first evidence back to Stuttgart. As a result, an expedition was sent from Berlin to excavate in the then German colony. It proved to be one of the most successful in the history of palaeontology (1909–1912). The expedition was led by W. Janensch with E. Hennig as his capable assistant.

Fragmented and even brittle petrified bones, very often buried deep in marl strata, were freed from the material enclosing them by nimble black hands and prepared for transportation. 225 tons of this scientific raw material had to be carried between 20 and 60 km to the coast. Digs were only excavated during the dry periods and while the excavation area grew larger and larger as new sites were discovered the scientists and restorers in the Museum at Berlin had already commenced the gargantuan task of processing the stone avalanche of Tendaguru.

On his return home, W. Janensch was appointed professor. The task awaiting him at the Museum became his life's work: the scientific examination of the bone material recovered and the reconstruction of the skeletons. A vast quantity of bones had to be completely freed from the rock adhering to them and restored or replicas made. It was an enormous scientific project. But it was not long before the push forward to new knowledge, to the reconstruction of skeletons as a highly effective demonstration of nature for the purposes of popular science, met with serious setbacks. Hostilities caused the work to be interrupted and post-war difficulties reduced the budget. And the great skeletons had scarcely seen placed in position when they had to be taken away to a place of safety to protect them from the bombing of the Second World War.

The continuity of the Berlin saurian programme was largely the merit of Professor Janensch. He was fortunate enough not only to be entrusted with a great task but also to retain his intellectual energy to an advanced age. He made good use of both these blessings and, with perseverance and modesty, devoted five decades to the completion of the great work. Professor Janensch (1878–1969) was tireless in gathering together again the threads of saurian research in Berlin which had almost been destroyed by the Second World War. Two generations of restoration experts working under his direction did a splendid job. Although only small in numbers, their skill and his scientific work created a monumental memorial which has become the symbol of the Berlin Museum of Natural History and will be associated with it for ever—the saurians in the glass courtyard of the museum. Of equal interest for scientists and the general public, the saurian skeletons in characteristic postures have now been viewed with awe by millions of visitors and studied by innumerable scientists from all over the world. However, it is not only dinosaurs from Tendaguru which are to be found in the Berlin Museum. Under the direction of Professor Janensch, a *Plateosaurus* skeleton was also set up in the museum—a result of the excavations in the Keuper of Halberstadt during the 1920's—together with an impressive cotylosaur and various saurian skulls from South Africa, acquired during collecting expeditions led by him and others (1929, 1932, 1937).

The Saurians of Tendaguru

The material recovered in the excavations of Tendaguru does not consist solely of the five skeletons on show in the Berlin Collection. In actual fact, the results of the excavations were very much more comprehensive than might appear to visitors to the exhibition. The storerooms contain incomplete skeletal material of other specimens of the species on show and also form other saurians. In all, the excavations of Tendaguru revealed evidence of fifteen different species of dinosaurs, even though the details of this evidence vary greatly in extent.

Numerous isolated bones of flying reptiles were also discovered.

Between the marl strata in which the bones were located at Tendaguru, banks of rocks were found containing sea-shells. Most numerous here were the Trigoniae with their sculpted shells. It was only the occurrence of marine deposits containing index fossils associated with the estuarine strata at the saurian sites that has made possible the biostratigraphical classification of the saurians. The fossils we now possess are known to be Upper Jurassic in age.

To return to the dinosaurs, a few words should initially be said on systematics. The popular term dinosaur is not used by the systematists since it covers two independent lines of descent within the archosaurians, these being the saurischians and the ornithischians which vary greatly in the construction of the pelvis. As reflected in the technical designations, the pelves of the former resemble that of the lizard while those of the latter are similar to bird pelves. The principal lines developed among the saurischians—the quadruped and very weighty sauropods, which were vegetarians, and the two-footed theropods like their ancestors, were adapted to a predatory way of life. There was a similar differentiation in two- and four-footed forms in the case of the vegetarian ornithischians. The two-footed ornithopods were paralleled here by three different groups of quadrupeds, the spiny stegosaurs, the armoured ankylosaurs and the horned ceratopsids.

How were these groups of dinosaurs represented in the material excavated at Tendaguru? The most striking remains are those of colossal sauropods of which there are five species. Two complete skeletons were reconstructed and put on display: *Brachiosaurus brancai* and *Dicraeosaurus hansemanni*. Together with a third sauropod skeleton, they dominate the saurian exhibition of the Berlin Museum with their great size. The third, however, the *Diplodocus* skeleton, is not an original but a plaster cast of an American relation of the Tendaguru sauropods. The theropods are probably represented by eight species. Their skeletal parts are so incomplete in some cases that the number of represented species is not absolutely certain. The type skeleton of a species has been reconstructed and put on exhibition: *Elaphrosaurus bambergi*.

The two ornithischian species identified at Tendaguru were found in massed accumulations of bones. Consequently, the assembly of one skeleton of each was not a problem. These herbivores obviously lived in herds and, when catastrophes occurred, were killed in large numbers. This applies especially to the ornithopod *Dysalotosaurus lettow-vorbecki* but is also true of the stegosaur *Kentrosaurus aethiopicus*.

The Biggest of all the Saurians

A live weight of no less than 80 to 100 tons is attributed to the animal whose skeleton of 12 metres in height and 23 metres in lenght towers over the other dinosaurs in the Berlin Museum of Natural History—*Brachiosaurus brancai*. A few isolated bones from the limbs and ribs of other specimens of this same species indicate that it had by no means reached the maximum size of this species. It is reported from the USA that the remains of a *Brachiosaurus* have now been discovered which must have been 30 metres long. It is assumed that the dimensions of the upper thigh bone convey an idea of the weight of the animal. Up to now, the skeleton of this giant from Tendaguru is the largest intact skeleton of a land vertebrate to have been put on show. This saurian is unique not only in its dimensions but also in its appearance which is quite different to that of the other sauropods. Not only has it been possible to take a cast of the brain case but the arrangement of the semicircular canals of the inner ear are also known.

The particularly striking feature of *Brachiosaurus* is its towering, giraffe-like form. If it is compared with other sauropods such as the *Diplodocus* or *Dicraeosaurus* of the exhibition, it will be noticed that the front legs of *Brachiosaurus* are much longer than is usually the case. In general, the front legs of sauropods are much shorter than the hind legs—a legacy of their biped ancestors. The opposite is true with *Brachiosaurus brancai*, hence its name: *Brachiosaurus*, arm-lizard. As a consequence of the considerable height at the shoulder (5 metres),

the line of the back declines towards the rear. The tail is relatively short but the long neck rises up to a dizzy height. Its colossal vertebrae are extended. Finally, the head of this massive creature was incredibly small in comparison with the size of its body and followed practically the same line as the neck. The brain weighed 200 g at the most. This represents a ratio of about 1:400,000 in comparison with the weight of the body.

A skull located at a height of 12 metres is not easy to study. For this reason, the skeleton on show has a replica skull of plaster but visitors can study a real *Brachiosaurus* skull face to face. A glass cabinet at the foot of the saurian contains the extremely precious skull of another animal. Seen at close sight, its dimensions are formidable after all since it is no less than 70 cm long. Massive jaws catch our attention. They give the skull a wide-jawed look but the rest of the skull, in contrast, looks lightly built.

The bones of the skull curve up gracefully over the brain case and frame the large apertures for the nose and eyes. A central ridge of bone curves up to a strangely high extent. This marks the enlarged nose area. The nostrils, set far back and raised upwards obviously enabled the creature to breathe while reposing in the water since the skull, with its disproportionately heavy snout, hung at an angle in the water when in the resting position. The position of the snout, slanted diagonally downwards, must have played a specific role in the animal's feeding habits. This head posture has also been chosen for the reconstruction of the skeleton with the raised neck. It was found to be the normal position of the *Brachiosaurus* skull, following the examination of all the other skulls found. The entire face is sharply angled downwards, against the axis of the cranium. With one of the skulls, it proved possible to remove the natural stone filling of the labyrinth and thus, for the first time, to establish its form in the sauropods. However, it is the horizontal position of the lateral semicircular canal of the equilibrium organ, which characterizes the normal position of the skull.

The powerful teeth of *Brachiosaurus* are impressive, even though their arrangement has been deformed somewhat by the weight of the rock. The finger-sized teeth are closely packed

in the jaws which also still contain spare teeth like a magazine. When the strong teeth were compared, it was found that they displayed a varying degree of wear at the sharp cutting edges and must therefore be considered to vary in age. The way in which, in all likelihood, the teeth were quite frequently replaced is not comparable with the conditions in recent reptiles.

What did this giant saurian eat? From his examination of the teeth, Professor Janensch was of the opinion that the teeth were not suitable for cutting delicate plants and that *Brachiosaurus*, unlike *Diplodocus*, did not live on aquatic plants but was certainly capable of biting the great cones, rich in food value, of cycadaean trees. This certainly fits in with the giraffe-like form of the brachiosaurians but is scarcely compatible with their weight. They probably stayed on dry land at times but the moving of this great weight must have called for a vast amount of energy.

It is certain that water supported much of the weight of the sauropods so that they could swim and move with alacrity. But what is the explanation for the divergent form of the brachiosaurians? Many illustrations show them standing up to their necks in deep water and grazing off the bottom. But did the buoyancy of the water permit this? The constant alternation of pressure on the head and neck between grazing and breathing appears problematical. *Brachiosaurus* would not have felt really comfortable either on dry land or in deep water but, by reason of its exceptional height at the shoulder and its long neck, it was probably able to reach food in swamps and areas of water which was beyond the reach of other sauropods. Such a gigantic creature as the brachiosaur must have spent most of its time in feeding.

The prevalent concept today, in a very general sense, is that the sauropods inhabited mainland waters and their banks and lived on aquatic plants. Spoors have been found consisting solely of the slots of the front feet. From this the conclusion has been drawn that the sauropods were characterized by a floating mode of locomotion in which they repeatedly pushed themselves along by their front feet on the bottom. Similar behaviour is known

Preceding page:

Copper fish

Platysomus gibbosus *(Blainville). Permian, copper shale. Mansfeld (German Democratic Republic). Length: 18 cm.*

Copper has been mined in the Mansfeld field since the Middle Ages. Since that time, people have known about the plants and fish in the copper shale. Even Leibniz, the founder of the Berlin Academy of Sciences, had a correct understanding of the Mansfeld fossils. Much rarer than Palaeoniscus *or the copper herring is the genus* Platysomus. *Both are members of the ganoids (Chondrostei) which predominated at that time and are now represented only by the sturgeons and* Polypterus.

Fish

Ophiopsis attenuata *Wagner. Upper Jurassic, Solnhofen limestone. Eichstätt, Bavaria (Federal Republic of Germany). A thick-scaled holostean with forked ray-fins. Length: 14 cm.*

Priscara pealei *Cope. Tertiary, Eocene. Green River, South-West Wyoming. Freshwater teleostean. Length: 13 cm.*

Lates gracilis *Agassiz. Tertiary, Eocene. Monte Bolca near Verona (Italy). Length: 20 cm.*

Naseus nuchalis *Agassiz. Tertiary, Eocene. Monte Bolca. Length: 20 cm.*

Since the Carboniferous, the great majority of all fish have ray-type fins. To begin with, they were characterized by rhombic ganoid scales (Chondrostei and Holostei). With the Jurassic there appeared, and from the Upper Cretaceous there predominated, forms with thin, bony cycloid scales and with an inner skeleton which was now entirely ossified. These Teleostei with more than 20,000 species at the present time are a hundred times more numerous than all the other groups of fish put together.

Although fish are the most frequently found intact vertebrates and, at some sites, provide a profound insight into the variety of the past, relatively few species are known as compared with the present day. The fish shown represent four of the most important sites: the copper shale of Mansfeld (German Democratic Republic), the limestone of Solnhofen (Federal Republic of Germany), the oil shale of Green River (USA) and the limestone of Monte Bolca (Italy).

Ammonites
Peltoceras annularis *(Reineck). Monstrous.*
View of the normal and of the pathologic side.
Middle Jurassic, Callovian. Turnau, Upper Franconia.
Dia.: 4 cm.

Right:
Quenstedtoceras marie *(Orbigny). Juvenile macro-*
conch. Middle Jurassic, Callovian. Łukow (Poland).
Dia.: 3.1 cm.
Whether shells or steinkerns, ammonites have always
attracted exceptional interest. They delight both the
collector and the researcher with their simple beauty
and the variety of their forms, especially when the
iridescence of the mother-of-pearl shell has been pre-
served (right). They are very frequent in many marine
strata and from the Jurassic onwards they are the
index-fossils par excellence. Since they were charac-
terized by a rapid rate of evolution, they are valuable
objects for studying evolution since in addition, in their
spiral shells, they preserve the development of the indi-
vidual creature down to the larva stage, enabling
conclusions about their phylogeny to be drawn from
their ontogeny. Pathological conditions can also be ob-
served, as on the gold snail shown at left whose shell-
forming programme was once unilaterally disturbed.

Index-fossils

Fossils of certain animal and plant species which existed for only a relatively short time but were common and widely distributed serve as index-fossils for the stratigraphic comparison of layer geological systems. They are the chronological markers of the history of the Earth. The ammonites and trilobites achieved classic importance in this connection. There are also other groups, examples of which are shown on these pages.

Spirifers

Brachyspirifer carinatus *(Schnur, 1853).*
Lower Devonian, Lower Emsian. Coblenz (Federal Republic of Germany).
The spirifers are considered to be an important group of index-fossils among the brachiopods. They are usually found as imprints and steinkerns in the sandy Rhenish facies. The species illustrated was selected as the type of the Brachyspirifer *genus, Wedekind, 1926.*

Beyrichiae

Nodibeyrichia tuberculata, Hemsiella *cf.* maccoyiana*; next to it stem-members of* Entrochus asteriscus. *Beyrichian limestone boulder, Upper Silurian. Niederfinow, north of Berlin (German Democratic Republic). Length: 4.5 cm.*
Typical Beyrichian limestone with an accumulation of the large, eponymous ostracods which represent numerous index-species in the Silurian. 150 years ago, the age of this type of rock was still spoken of as transitional (see pp. 40).

Hallstatt mollusc

Monotis salinaria *(Schlotheim, 1820)*.
Alpine Upper Triassic, Nor, Hallstatt limestone.
Sommeraukogel, Upper Austria.
Height: 16 cm.
This easily identified mollusc species has proved valuable as an index-fossil. Like our specimen, the type of the species comes from Hallstatt limestone of which there are several classic sites. The wealth of fossils existing there was known at an early date since the rock was used for lining purposes in the salt mines of the Salzkammergut.

Southern brachiopod

Australocoelia tourteloti *Boucot & Gill, 1956.*
Lower Devonian, Lower Emsian. La Paz (Bolivia).
Index-fossil of the Lower Emsian for the coldwater fauna of the Southern Hemisphere of that time. These brachiopod imprints were once determined as belonging to Leptocoelia flabellites—*a species from the Appalachians.*

Page 156:

Coral-like mollusc

Hippurites heritschi *Kühn. From the type-locality Hippurite Riff Kalchberg at St. Barthelemä, Styria (Austria). Gosau chalk, Upper Campanian.*
Dia.: 6 cm.
Cross-section of a mollusc from the unusual group of the Rudistae. The right valve of this extinct creature, stuck in the sediment, grew like a rugose coral while the left valve, as a flat lid with long lock-teeth, closed the calyx. In the warm, shallow waters of the Cretaceous seas, they stood shoulder-to-shoulder in some places. The hippurites could grow up to a metre in length.
The sectional view shows the thick walls with two pillars projecting into the sediment-filled interior. The same pillars can be seen also on the shell of the larvae which colonized the abandoned shell. The two-coloured sediment in the old and the young shells tells about two steps of filling the calyxes. A short time after the young hippurite colonization the roof was destroyed. Sinking down the shell was filled with a grey-green marl.

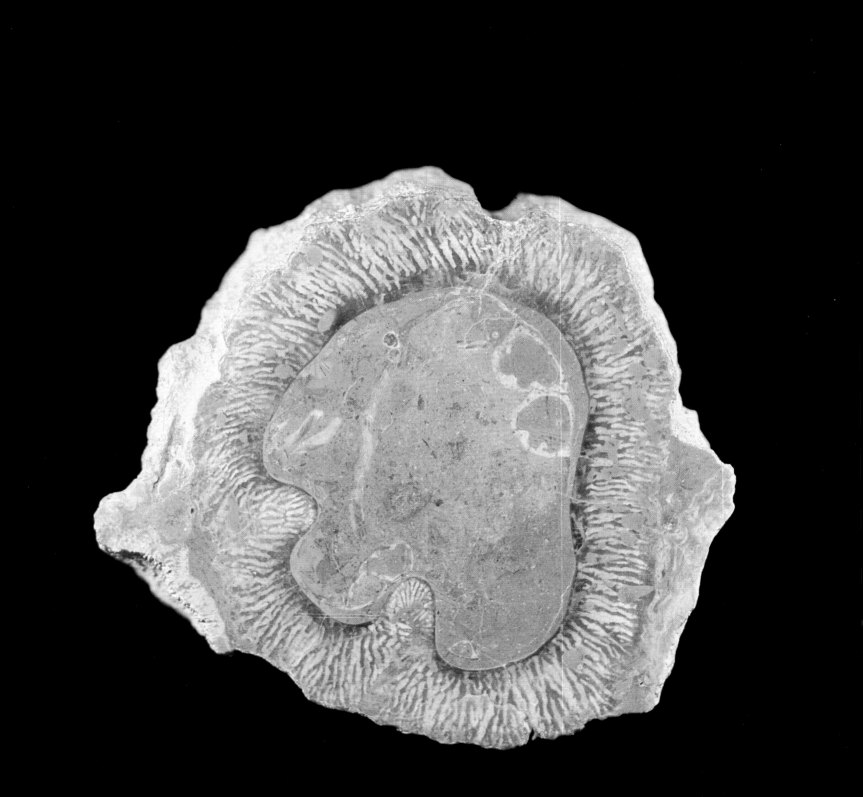

today from the hippopotamuses which, after some ten million years, have obviously resettled a part of that habitat occupied by the sauropods for a hundred million years.

It is considered that the special modifications of the sauropod skeleton conclusively indicate that the sauropods lived in the water. The large vertebrae were not at all so heavy as they might appear. The vertebrae of the back were hollow and those of the neck were of a particularly bizarre construction since their lateral hollows may have provided space for 'air bags'. The neck of the creature could well have floated on the water. This would certainly have been an ideal resting position for this colossal creature. On the other hand, the solid vertebrae of the tail would have made this long member tail-heavy, allowing it to sink to the bottom like an anchor. Finally, the heavy bones of the extremities would have given it stability in the water, acting in the same way as the lead boots of divers.

Dicraeosaurus

Single bones of brachiosaurs had already been described in the USA before their discovery in Africa. However, what was completely new at the time of the excavations of Tendaguru were the practically complete skeletons of a form of sauropod of only medium size whose neck and chest vertebrae were characterized by spiny appendages which were long and divided. This was why Professor Janensch chose the generic designation *Dicraeosaurus*. The skeletal material recovered consisted of the remains of two different species. Three skeletons of *Dicraeosaurus hansemanni* were found. The most complete of these was subsequently supplemented and put on show. This sounds perfectly straightforward but this too represents an enormous amount of scientific work and great skill in the work of restoration and reconstruction. The replica of the skull is based on individual bones which were found. The remains of a second species of *Dicraeosaurus* have been placed in the storeroom where they are available for scientific studies.

For a sauropod, *Dicraeosaurus* has a relatively short neck and, in comparison with *Brachiosaurus*, the skull is also much more compact and even somewhat smaller. It bears a greater resemblance to that of *Diplodocus*. As in the latter, the snout is long and rather like a beak. The protruding peg-like teeth are arranged like a palisade in the jaws. Professor Janensch, who was responsible for the reconstruction, considered that this arrangement of the teeth would be appropriate for catching small fish in shallow water and thought it unlikely that the creature would have lived on plants. The nostrils situated high above the eyes are clear evidence that it lived in water.

The Cousin from America

The cast of the skeleton of the North American *Diplodocus* presented by Andrew Carnegie is a splendid counterpart to the East African saurians. Furthermore, the cast of the skeleton has become a kind of international parameter for the saurian collections of several great museums since this cast is not unique. Tourists will find this gift by Carnegie in the British Museum in London, in the Palaeontological Museum in Moscow and in the Natural History Museums of Vienna and Paris. In London, the representative of Diplodorus carnegii stands alone in the entrance hall while in Moscow it is flanked by a mighty Tarbosaurus from the Gobi Desert, a close relative of the fearful *Tyrannosaurus*, in the midst of numerous Permian saurians from the Northern Dvina. All the *Diplodocus* replicas were produced in black to reproduce the original bones from Wyoming which contained asphalt. The porous saurian bones, buried deep in sediment millions of years ago, acted as traps for mineral oil. They absorbed the oil, which subsequently turned into asphalt, like a sponge.

The genus *Diplodocus* is one of the best-known sauropods. It is documented by several complete skeletons from North America. One of the original skeletons has been brought to Europe and set up in a quite unconventional manner in the Senckenberg Museum at Frankfort-on-Main. The type skeleton of the *Diplodocus longus* species is on show in the U.S. National Museum in Washington. A skeleton of the same species is also to be found in the Denver Natural Science Museum where it forms part of a dinosaur group with *Stegosaurus* and *Anatosaurus*.

The unprejudiced visitor who studies the skeletons of the giant dinosaurs will be impressed by the colossal bones of these creatures. He will be interested in the question of whether the bones are genuine, how old they are and where they come from. But scarcely anybody doubts their correct arrangement. Yet it is precisely this which is the real problem in the reconstruction of skeletons and, in the final analysis, of the real-life pictures which we produce of prehistoric animals. Nobody has ever seen live saurians and even comparisons with modern reptiles can only be made to a limited extent. The palaeontologist specializing in vertebrates must not only be a good anatomist but, in particular, also needs imagination.

When visitors to the Berlin Natural History Museum inspect the parade of the sauropods, they are taken aback not only by the black bones of *Diplodocus* but also by its posture. The front legs of *Diplodocus* are held differently to those of its African cousins. The reconstructions of these skeletons reflect a scientific controversy which has been going on for decades.

The original question was whether the sauropods walked around with legs apart like lizards or upright and with their legs under their body like mammals. For anatomical and static reasons, it was shown that they could not have had a crocodile-like posture. But while some considered that they walked fully upright others were not totally convinced of this and took the view that the front legs were maintained in a more bandy stance, as demonstrated in the reconstruction of the Tendaguru sauropods and in contrast to *Diplodocus*. The view now prevailing is that the sauropods had vertical pillar-like legs, resembling the gigantic limbs of elephants but carrying many times their weight. This theory is supported by the huge weights which have been calculated for the sauropods and also by their gait which is evident from the many spoors found. In the bed of the Paluxy River at Glen Rose (Texas), a particularly long spoor of an apatosaur was discovered. Its tracks were followed by a two-footed predatory saurian. The sandstone slabs with this interesting spoor are now in the American Museum of Natural History in New York.

Warmblooded or Not?

Some specialists believe that the upright posture of sauropods is an indication that these dinosaurs were also warmblooded and must have been very much more active than generally supposed so far. It is postulated that the upright gait required a fairly high rate of metabolism. Indeed, there is no evidence from modern fauna proving the contrary but this alone does not constitute any proof. What constitutes the basic link between the two phenomena?

There are two aspects to warmbloodedness which should not be confused: the internal production of heat (endothermy) and the constant body-temperature (homoiothermy) through the regulation of temperature. The perfect thermoregulation of our modern warmblooded creatures emerged on two occasions under different conditions in the course of the evolution of vertebrate animals. We find both in the mammals and in the birds a complicated system of regulatory circuits for maintaining a constant body-temperature which is linked to a large number of anatomical, physiological and hormonal conditions.

With birds and mammals, the body-temperatures range between 35 and 43°C according to the species, the birds displaying the higher temperatures. This temperature range is optimal for life and metabolism since the ever-present proteins then have their greatest reaction-capability, especially the ferments which are necessary for the vital processes. At lower temperatures, the chemical processes take place more slowly while at higher temperatures the proteins break up, apart from a few exceptions. Consequently, the emergence of the regulatory system of warmblooded creatures in the history of development must be understood as an optimization process.

Certain skeletal features indicate that it is

likely that the first steps towards warmbloodedness for the development of mammals from the mammal-like reptiles of the Permian and the Triassic were already taken by their ancestors. The only question is whether it was not a similar state of affairs in the development of the birds from the dinosaurs and whether some or all of the dinosaurs were already warmblooded as well. A high regulatory capability along the lines of the perfect thermoregulation of the present day is inconceivable without a highly developed central nervous system but this is what the saurians did not possess, as shown by the casts of their brain-cases. The examination of bone tissue in a very good state of preservation has revealed that it must have been characterized by a very good blood-flow, like the bones of mammals. A good blood-flow would be a precondition for a high level of metabolism. Thus the production and transportation of heat in the sauropods could have attained high levels and the risk of overheating may have even been greater than that of undercooling. Body-temperature could only have been regulated by the dissipation of surplus heat.

The heat-exchange between a body and its environment depends on the nature and relative size of its surface. In relation to their volume, large creatures have a smaller surface than small animals. A small animal therefore loses heat faster than a larger one but, on the other hand, absorbs heat more quickly. A large body, in contrast, tends to suffer from a build-up of heat, at least under tropical conditions. With the giant saurians, therefore, it is to be expected that there would have been adaptations enabling the dissipation of heat to be increased whilst with the small dinosaurs and pterodactyls there would have been measures to prevent this. These flying reptiles possessed fur to keep them warm. However, the proof of original feathers in small dinosaurs has unfortunately not yet been demonstrated.

Predatory Saurians

Those who are familiar with the great saurian collections or with the popular literature on

the subject will, at first sight, miss the mighty predatory saurians in the Berlin collection. They will not be entirely satisfied either when their attention is drawn to the theropod skeleton on show there since *Elaphrosaurus* with its relatively small head does not give the impression of being a dangerous character. However, if we take a look at the big cats of today, it will be realized that these include not only lions and tigers but also jaguars who take their prey by speed of movement. Like all predatory saurians (theropods), *Elaphrosaurus* ran only on its powerful hind legs, the short front limbs having only a prehensile and supporting function. The mighty tail acted as a counterweight for the front part of the body. It was indispensable for the balance of the animal when it was running in particular.

The anatomy of the pelvis and of the first tail vertebrae of *Elaphrosaurus bambergi* reveal that the tail could be swung powerfully from side to side. The slim saurian, almost six metres long, was a specialist in speed and manoeuvrability. One can imagine how it hunted down the dysalotosaur, another fast-moving creature, or easily escaped from even larger saurians.

The incompleteness of the skeletal elements excavated meant that a great deal of supplementary material had to be included in the reconstruction. Thus the parts missing on one side were modelled on those present on the other or missing vertebrae were replaced on the model of adjacent ones. To some extent, use had to be made of the anatomy of related forms such as *Ornithomimus* and *Ornitholestes*. For instance, of the bones in the skull only the teeth were found. *Elaphrosaurus* would probably have taken care not to come too close to the great sauropods but the latter would nevertheless not have remained unscathed. In the excavations at Tendaguru, a certain kind of isolated teeth attracted particular attention because they were repeatedly found in the vicinity of the neck vertebrae of sauropods. These were the dagger-like teeth of predatory saurians and especially of *Megalosaurus* with its great head. The greedy giant had broken them off while feeding on its prey since the teeth found were all old and worn. In contrast to their teeth, bones from predatory saurians were a very rare find at Tendaguru. Nevertheless, the remains found indicate that there were several species of carnivorous theropods. They devoured the flesh of dead sauropods but probably killed sick animals as well.

Ornithischians

As was subsequently the case with the mammals, too, a natural balance between specialized herbivores and carnivores had developed also among the dinosaurs. The threat represented by the predatory animals had to lead to protective adaptations on the part of the herbivorous saurians. These include both the appropriate behavioral norms, such as living in herds, and also certain physical features. By their size alone, the sauropods were difficult to attack but, if only for rest, they were obliged to seek the protection and buoyancy of the water. The two-footed ornithopods found their salvation in rapid flight. A third possibility was protection by defence, actively with horns or spiny tails and passively by the armouring of the body.

One of most popular saurians specializing in defence was *Triceratops*, the triple-horned skeleton which is on show at the British Museum. No less popular are the medium-sized stegosaurs, also quadrupeds, which carried a double row of large, triangular bony plates on their backs. Doubt has recently been raised as to the authenticity of the picture which has far been imagined of them. In the skeletal reconstructions, these comb-plates have always been shown at a steep angle, as in the natural history museums of New York, Washington and Denver, for example. But could an upright row of plates have offered effective protection against a predatory saurian attacking from the flank? New illustrations therefore show *Stegosaurus* with plates which hang down sideways from the ridge of the back. Other authorities doubt the defensive function and see the plates as a cooling-surface system. It is obvious that the bony plates had a particularly good blood-flow. Through the extension in the surface area of the body and through a turbulence effect on the flow of air, an enhanced exchange of heat could have been effected.

In the very small skulls of the stegosaurs, there was only room enough for a brain the size of a walnut but the passage of the spinal cord in the area of the sacrum was of several times this volume. This is the same kind of disproportion as with the sauropods and for a long time speculations about the second brain of these saurians was a favourite subject of discussion. Today, it is suspected that this space might have been filled by a glycogen gland, as is known in birds. It could have played an important role as an energy reservoir for the activation of the mighty muscle system.

The Spiny-Tailed Saurian

A small relative of the three North American species of *Stegosaurus* was to be found at the same period in East Africa. Since it was only at the very front of the curved back that it had small, upright plates but powerful spines towards the rear, Hennig gave it the name of *Kentrurosaurus* which means spiny-tailed lizard. However, in the first brief communication of the find at Tendaguru prior to this the designation *Kentrosaurus* had been used and nowadays this is the name to which priority is usually given.

The Berlin saurian hall also has the only reconstructed skeleton of the genus *Kentrosaurus*. Unfortunately, it is not based on a single, complete find. Nevertheless, numerous groups of bones, clearly recognizable as skeletal remains and a great number of single bones were recovered—most of them from a single excavation site of barely a thousand square metres in area. Bones from at least forty animals, i.e., from an entire herd, were excavated from this restricted area. The reconstruction of the skeleton, dating from 1925, was based on the skeletons of the American stegosaurs which had already become known by this time. The small pointed head with the horny beak could thus be reconstructed from the *Stegosaurus* head since comparable individual skull-bones had been discovered. As regards the position of the spines on the back, the circumstances under which they were found only indicated that they had probably been

arranged in pairs. From the shape of the spines found, it was also possible to arrange them in an obviously natural row. The order of the spines is thus relatively certain but their distribution along the skeleton can only be regarded as a scientifically founded surmise.

This example will perhaps convey an idea of the degree of theoretical knowledge necessary to compensate for the lack of completeness of the finds, to gain an idea of the unity of the skeleton and to give tangible shape to this idea in the form of the skeletal reconstruction. A saurian skeleton in an exhibition is the result of many years of research work. But it is only the reconstructions of skeletons which can provide the basis for the imaginative depictions.

Kentrosaurus was a highly specialized dinosaur. It lived on soft plants which it plucked with its horny beak and chewed up with its molar teeth. Its compact shape was adapted to defence. In the form of life it represents, this saurian recalls the giant armadillo of the South American Ice Age.

The stegosaurs (*Stegosaurus* and *Kentrosaurus*) must have descended from twofooted creatures of considerably greater mobility. Their ornithischian pelvis is an indication of this. The short front legs and the three-toed hind legs also represent hereditary features, however. It was towards the end of the Jurassic that the family of the stegosaurs experienced their heyday. Already during the Cretaceous period, they were increasingly being displaced by the iguanodonts and the ankylosaurs. The latter, as close relations, were very similar to the stegosaurs but were more effectively armoured. Remnants of their principal armoured parts have repeatedly been found in fossilized form.

The Bird-Footed Saurians

Together with the ankylosaurs, other races of ornithischians flourished during the Upper Cretaceous period. The flowering plants which now began to spread increased supply of food available for herbivores. From two-footed ornithischians, there developed the horned ceratopsids, four-footed creatures resembling a rhinoceros. But also long-tailed bipeds, of the type only really represented by the kangaroo nowadays, continued to flourish and one family of the ornithopods even attained the highest degree of differentiation known for saurians. These are the duck-billed saurians (hadrosaurs) of which a large number of intact skeletons has been found in North America and in the Gobi Desert. Even mummies of this peaceful herbivore have been discovered. In museums, hadrosaurs are often exhibited in the position in which they were found, for example *Anatosaurus* in the Beaked Dragon Basement of the Senckenberg Museum in Frankfort-on-Main (Federal Republic of Germany) or *Lambeosaurus* lying as its prey under a predatory saurian *(Gorgosaurus)* in the Field Museum of Chicago.

Strangely enough, the new diversity of the saurians in the Upper Cretaceous is found only on the northern continents. On the African continent, following its isolation in the Cretaceous period, it was the old saurian fauna of the late Jurassic which survived. Of the herbivores, the sauropods still continued to play the principal role there. Even before this, the bird-footed saurians had only been represented by a few species of small stature. In the excavation material of Tendaguru from the Upper Jurassic, a single species predominates: *Dysalotosaurus lettow-vorbecki*. The bones of this fleet-footed saurian were found in such masses that it can only be concluded that entire herds of these creatures were killed at the same time. Since a more or less intact skeleton could not be found, only a reconstruction from individual bones was possible in this case, too. *Dysalotosaurus* most closely resembles *Hypsilophodon* from England, once the historical model of a bird-hipped dinosaur (p. 85). In habit, there is also striking agreement with the fleet-footed theropods but this is probably a case of convergent adaptation to running. Anatomical examination reveals the different origin, especially in the construction of the pelvis.

The End of the Saurians

More than ever before, the disappearance of the saurians remains a particularly spectacu-

lar event in the history of life. This is not surprising in view of our present-day environmental problems. Mankind is confronted with the need to identify the ecological systems in nature and to control them. The rapidly increasing destruction in our biological environment is a potentially dangerous matter. This is why crises far back in the history of life are attracting more and more attention. The races of the saurians dominated the seas, the land and the air for 130 million years before they quietly vanished from the stage of life.

There are many speculative opinions about the end of the giant dinosaurs, most of which explain a special aspect but leave other questions associated with the event unsolved. Up to now, it is still only possible to give a very general account of what happened. The biosystem species/environment was irreparably disturbed for some orders of reptiles at the end of the Cretaceous period. In such cases, the constant decline in the numbers of young animals and ultimately their non-appearance led to the death of the species. In the history of life, this was a constantly recurrent happening, paralleled by the emergence of new species. The death of a species always occurred when species adapted in too one-sided a manner to a complex environment so that in the end they became the victim of apparently only slight changes in the environment.

In general, the coming and going of species in the history of life leaves us unmoved. The news of the extinction of entire families and orders, however, has a more momentous impact on us. If, from the fossils, we follow the history of life, a series of significant breaks will be noticed. On repeated occasions within a geologically short period, not only innumerable species but even large groups of related creatures vanish from the scene. These breaks have permitted the classification of the periods of the geological past. The disappearance of old groups of organisms, like the first occurrence and, sooner or later, the subsequent flourishing of new and more efficient groups, is a sign of a more advanced development. The new displaces the old by virtue of its superiority or it takes over the place that the latter has vacated without coming into direct competition with it.

The particularly clear-cut breaks include that between the Mesozoic and the Cenozoic eras which has been defined as the dividing line between the Cretaceous and the Tertiary periods. The revolution of that time in the animal world took place on a worldwide scale in all the areas of life of land, sea and air. Only certain groups of organisms failed to survive while others came through more or less unscathed. Of the molluscs, it was the ammonites, belemnites, rudista and inocerami which vanished but the principal loss was the saurians.

To us, 65 million years after the event, the happenings in the history of life at the end of the Cretaceous and the beginning of the Tertiary period appear as a sharp dividing line. But just how sharp was this division in the fauna in actual fact? Did creatures suddenly become extinct? Probably not since it was unlikely that one catastrophe alone could mark the end for so many species. In all likelihood, it was the cumulative effect of a series of catastrophes over a fairly long period. Life on Earth passed through a period of crisis. If it is assumed, for example, that the crucial events took place in only a few stages in the geologically short period of 500,000 years, a length of time which nevertheless appears inconceivably long to us, we would not be able to draw a distinction between these events from the fossils left behind. Seen from a distance of 65 million years, these events fuse into a single one. Our accuracy of measurement is still incapable of dividing a great break into many individual ones or of reliably establishing a true relationship between the individual events documented here and there on the Earth.

When we are able to consider, with a high degree of probability, that those happenings of long ago were differentiated in time, then there is no reason either why we should seek a single cause to explain everything in an all-in manner. Whenever only one possible cause with a global effect is imagined, the question arises as to why it affected this and not that species; why did the dinosaurs die out while the closely related crocodiles survived? The succession of many causes may indicate that long before animals became finally extinct a decline in the groups in question had already begun. Ammonites and belemnites, pterodactyls and dinosaurs still existed in large numbers and were still in the process of evolution. Towards the end of the Cretaceous period, there was a steady decline in the number of species, this taking place later in the case of the land saurians than with the creatures of the sea. It was only after the number of species had been greatly reduced that the lines of descent ultimately came to a complete stop. Thus the decline of the dinosaurs took place over a period of millions of years.

The causes of their extinction must have been worldwide in their effect since it is not known that they retreated to any specific areas. One can imagine cosmic events which might have caused a change in radiation and thus had a direct or indirect influence on the biosphere. However, hypotheses of this kind cannot explain the selection of the creatures affected. This also applies to the assumed consequences of the many proven changes in polarity of the Earth's magnetic field. On the other hand, there were certainly the effects of terrestrial happenings, even though their extent and the links between them are still obscure. Also of a global nature in their effect were the biotic conditions: the interrelations between organsims and their hereditary mass.

Terrestrial causes result from the movements of the Earth's crust, from continental drift, the forming of mountains, volcanic activity and the fluctuations in the level of the sea. These factors can totally change habitats and climate. The drift of continents and the appearance of new straits can even transform the climate of the Earth. Fluctuations in the level of the sea as a consequence of changes in deepsea regions enlarge or reduce the habitats of land and water. Smaller areas of land mean a reduced supply of food from the land and thus a lower productivity of phytoplankton and, ultimately, a disturbance in marine food-chains. Such processes could have played a part in the end of the ammonites, belemnites and marine saurians.

The death of the dinosaurs is most frequently associated with changes in climate. The stable, warm climate of the Mesozoic came to an end. Seasonal fluctuations in tempera-

ture increased and ultimately there were fluctuations in climate. While the responsibility is most often attributed to a sudden and protracted drop in temperature, other authors are of the opinion that it was an undue rise in temperature that marked the end of the saurians. Another theory is that the herbivorous saurians died out as a result of richets since the soil at the end of the Cretaceous period is said to have been totally decalcified by a high level of precipitation. Another writer takes the view that exceptionally large quantities of the element selenium were released by the weather conditions of the time and thus had a negative effect on the saurians via their herbivorous feeding habits.

Many other authorities continue to put forward hypotheses with a biological orientation. The flowering plants developed on an increasing scale from the Lower Cretaceous period onwards, as documented by fossils. It is postulated that the herbivorous saurians had difficulties with the new diet, especially with the alkaloids which were frequently a part of it. But it was precisely in the Upper Cretaceous period that new groups of herbivorous saurians flourished. Not very convincing either is the view that the early mammals, hard-pressed by the saurians in restricted areas, had specialized in robbing eggs and had thus decimated the new generations of saurians. Finally, the possibility of large-scale plagues has been raised but up till now no case has ever been known of a species being demonstrably eradicated by a plague.

There is no doubt that the great transgressions of the oceans in the Upper Cretaceous Period led to the habitats of the dinosaurs becoming smaller in area. Living in a restricted space, the saurians are supposed to have been killed off by stress. In this case, observations made from domestic animals kept in large-scale units have been applied to saurians. Hormonal disturbances could have led to the eggs of the saurians becoming infertile but such manifestations would have only been of local significance and could scarcely have played a worldwide role. Masses of broken shells from saurian eggs have been found in the South of France and these might be a pointer to such stress-defects.

In an attempt to establish an ecological grouping of the animals involved at the time, D. A. Russel (1977) considers that fresh-water animals were not involved. Land creatures were not affected to any great extent, apart from the saurians. Nevertheless, it is asserted that no land creature of more than 25 kg in weight survived the end of the Cretaceous period. The crisis was most evident among the inhabitants of the sea but, as fossils, these are overrepresented of course and cannot be placed in any real relationship with the other groups. Towards the end of the Cretaceous period, there were also signs of a crisis among those groups of organisms which survived with a sufficient number of species. In critical times, however, even very slight causes are capable of having major effects. We can already say quite a lot about the situation at that time and we have many illuminating explanations for the individual phenomena but nobody can yet say much about the specific causal structure and it still remains a riddle.

Plateosaurus

The first appearance of the dinosaurs is scarcely less mysterious than their disappearance, even though it is mysterious in a different way. Their evolutionary origin is still unclear since various interpretations are possible of the fossils found. The various lines of development of the archosaurians still cannot be traced back to a single point. The crocodile-like *Ticinosuchus* is regarded on the one hand as a representative of the ancestral group of the dinosaurs but, on the other, this is disputed by virtue of its specialized foot-joint. *Ticinosuchus* and its relatives are thought to have been responsible for the *Chirotherium* footprints often found in Triassic red beds (Bunter Sandstone). (page 173)

What we know of the history of the dinosaurs begins in the Triassic. The first skeletal remains were found in deposits of the uppermost Middle Triassic but trackways of dinosaurs have been discovered in strata five to six million years older. The largest dinosaurs of that time were the plateosauri which attained more than six metres in length. Their close relative *Melanosaurus* in Southern Africa was even 12 metres long. The first remains of *Plateosaurus* were described in 1837 by H. von Meyer and came from the Nuremberg area. At the time, *Plateosaurus* was the fifth genus of dinosaurs to be identified, the first four having been found in England between 1832 and 1836. Numerous complete skeletons of *Plateosaurus* have been discovered in particular in the Middle Keuper (red marl) of Trossingen in Württemberg (Federal Republic of Germany) and of Halberstadt (German Democratic Republic). At the time, plateosaurs were regarded as the German dinosaurs as such.

Since then, related forms have been identified throughout the world. *Plateosaurus* was chosen as the heraldic animal of the State Museum for Natural History in Stuttgart (Federal Republic of Germany).

Plateosaurus is one of the ancestors of the later sauropods. The prolongation of the neck by the extension of the vertebrae had already begun in this creature. The large number of uniform teeth is a pointer to the vegetable diet of the creature which it obtained by reaching up to high-growing plants. *Plateosaurus* was one of the first herbivorous saurischians. In opposition to this, there is the view that the sharply pointed teeth, flattened at the sides and with good cutting characteristics, show that it consumed the flesh of other creatures.

There have likewise been various interpretations of the posture and gait of these great animals. Experts now tend to take the view that *Plateosaurus* could run on two or all four feet as it wanted.

The front extremities are relatively short but well developed and strong. They look more like arms with prehensile hands than front legs. From the local accumulations of skeletons and from trackways, it was realized at an early stage that the plateosaurs must have lived in herds. By virtue of their great weight, they are also now considered to have been warmblooded creatures.

Saurians are to be understood, in the widest sense, as the fossil amphibians and reptiles. The present-day range of these two groups of creatures conveys no idea at all of the diversity that once existed. To examine them in more detail would be to go beyond the scope of this book. Nevertheless, in addition to the dinosaurs already considered, a few examples of fossil reptiles will be illustrated here so that an impression may be obtained of the reptiles from which they descended, the mammal-like reptiles, of the flying saurians and the marine saurians. Their dissemination in time and their place in the line of evolution can easily be found from the evolutionary diagram.

Gondwana

"A sensational find . . .", this was the sort of headline to be read in the newspapers a few years ago. In the Antarctic in 1969 only 640 km from the South Pole the discovery was made of remains of *Lystrosaurus murrayi*, a saurian which had long been known as a particularly common fossil in South Africa. These creatures had lived 220 million years ago at the time of the Lower Triassic near lakes and rivers. This spectacular find demonstrates once again and without the slightest doubt that there really have been radical changes in climate on the present-day Antarctic continent. Even the Antarctic must once have been closely linked with Africa at the place where there is now a wide and deep area of water separating them.

This find is a major contribution to the evidence documenting the history of the Earth but it did not come as such a surprise as might be supposed. Palaeontologists had long been searching systematically for the remains of saurians in the Antarctic. A North American expedition was the first to achieve success. Why were these palaeontologists so confident of finding fossil reptiles in the Antarctic of all places? An international programme of Antarctic research had produced numerous results concerning the development of the geological formations of the Antarctic as early as the 1950's. Many a geological secret had already

The Many Different Forms of the Saurians

Development is the magic word by which we can solve all riddles surrounding us or at least move towards their solution.

E. Haeckel

been wrested from some of the smaller ice-free areas. For the saurian hunters, however, it was the discovery of Gondwana layers which was especially important, as described already in the previous century at the Indian coalfield of Gondwana and then in Australia, South Africa and South America. Since that time, characteristics of this sequence of rock formations are known as traces of glaciation at the base, followed by strata with coal seams and *Glossopteris* flora and finally mighty marl and sandstone strata with saurian remains.

The Gondwana strata are considered to be the deposits of a once intact southern continent. The climatic history reflected in them ranging from glaciation in the Upper Carboniferous to the desert climate of the Upper Triassic was first satisfactorily explained by the Drift Theory of Alfred Wegener (1912). When originally postulated, Wegener's concept of the mechanism of the drift was not accepted and the entire theory thus dismissed but in the last twenty years the facts of the drift have been given a new geophysical foundation by the theory of plate tectonics. For the last 300 million years of the history of the Earth, the continental drift theory presents the picture of a super-continent, Pangaea, which has been disintegrating since the Triassic period. Such an event, extending over such a length of time, is of great importance for the history of the development and dissemination of all land plants and animals. Isolation and the passage of different climatic zones must have played a role here. Familiar manifestations of the history of life such as directional adaptation, immigration, endemic variation and extinction appear in a new light.

The recent geological history of Australia is an interesting example. Deep-sea drillings indicate that the belt of deep sea separating Australia and the Antarctic was formed by drift only in the course of the Tertiary period. The Antarctic came into its present position at the Pole and glaciated while Australia drifted into the southern dry belt, even penetrating in the north as far as the tropics of South-East Asia. This provided the opportunity for Eurasian plants and animal tribes to migrate to the continent which had been isolated for such a long time. The only refuge which remained for the old fauna and flora elements from the wet temperate climatic situation which had previously existed was in the oceanic climate of the South-East, insofar as endemic tribes of the dry areas had not developed from them. The glaciation of the Antarctic led to harsher climatic conditions throughout the world. The west wind drift also increased as a consequence of the straits which had now emerged around the Pole. New current conditions appeared in the southern seas, leading to changes in climate. The significance of this hypothesis for Australia is a stimulus for the examination of other areas and earlier times where the lack of information still makes it very difficult to formulate an interpretation.

How does the history of the saurians fit into the geological frame of a divided supercontinent? Does a study of the saurians enable any relations to be identified here? Up to quite recently, there was hardly any reason for saurian specialists to pay any attention to the drift concept. The only exception was *Mesosaurus*, a small freshwater reptile of the Lower Permian which had been found on both sides of the South Atlantic in Angola and South-Eastern Brazil and was certainly never able to cross such a large area of water. The dissemination of *Lystrosaurus*, the genus mentioned at the beginning, in South Africa, the Antarctic, Bengal, Laos, China and along the upper reaches of the Volga then presented a second and highly significant example.

Here, however, it is not just a question of Gondwana contacts but also of the possibility of spread to the northern continent.

North/South relations for saurians are so general that they can certainly be interpreted in the sense of a modern continental division. The uniformity of saurian development on all the continents is a striking circumstance which is not to be overlooked, especially when account is taken of the close faunal relations between the Permian saurians from the North-East of the Russian Platform and those of the Karroo Formation in Southern Africa and between the Upper Triassic saurians of Central Europe and those of South America. Up to now, the points of agreement between the southern continents were primarily attributed to corresponding immigrations from the

Skull of a large Lystrosaurus andersoni *Broom From an original. Height of skull 30 cm. Karroo formation, Lower Triassic, Bergville, Natal*

northern continents and not to exchange on one and the same continent. It was only in the last few years that clear Gondwanaland relations have been found after all. Precise faunal analyses of the Triassic saurians of South America and South Africa indicate that certain highly differentiated forms are found on both sides of the south Atlantic. This fact can scarcely be explained by a spread via Asia and North America. The reptiles in question are the mammal-like *Cynognathus* and *Kannemyeria* from the Lower Triassic and the primarily Middle Triassic traversodonts.

Such highly specialized genera from different family circles certainly shared no common worldwide dissemination. In the case of the somewhat older fauna of the *Lystrosaurus* strata, a clear transformation of the forms is apparent even over the distance China—South Africa.

Early Reptiles in Time and Space

The transformation from the lobe-fin to the four-footed amphibian took place towards the end of the Devonian but the first steps on dry land do not mean at all the conquest of the mainland as a habitat. The amphibians remained largely dependent on water. It was the reptiles which were the first to establish themselves in the new habitat, primarily by reason of new achievements such as the amniotic egg with its high yolk content. The oldest fossil eggs found date from the Permian but they cannot be identified as belonging to any particular group of saurians. To judge by the skeletal features, the transition from amphibians to reptiles took place in a continuous manner. The first reptiles still retained close links with water and like modern crocodiles, had an amphibian way of life.

The cotylosaurs (type reptiles) of the Upper Carboniferous are regarded as the oldest reptiles. The pelycosaurs emerged from one of their base-groups, thus constituting that tribe which ultimately led to the mammals. The pelycosaurs overtook the cotylosaurs even during the Lower Permian. The reptiles experienced their first golden age in the tropical areas of the climatically differentiated super-

Preceding page:

The head of the giant

Tendaguru beds of the Upper Jurassic, Tanzania.
Length : 75 cm.

The skull of Brachiosaurus brancai *Janensch, is one of the best sauropod skulls known. Striking features include the downward slope of the mighty snout part and the division of the cranium into narrow strips of bone.*

Brachiosaurus brancai *Janensch*

The Saurian Hall of the Museum of Natural History of Berlin's Humboldt University is dominated by the only complete skeleton on show of the largest saurian species of all time. With its height of 12 metres, the skeleton can only just be accommodated in this great hall. Four mighty, column-like legs once supported the massive body of this animal which

weighed about 80 tons, fed on plants and certainly reached an age of more than 120 years. The skeleton was excavated 70 years ago at Tendaguru in the south of Tanzania after surviving for about 140 million years in the saurian marl. The cast of the American Diplodocus *can be seen at the back of the hall.*

The dinosaurian trackways of Barkhausen

During the excavation of Upper Jurassic sandstone (Kimmeridge) the tracks of dinosaurs were discovered on the ridge of the Wiehengebirge hills at Barkhausen (Federal Republic of Germany). Orogenic forces during the Upper Cretaceous period had tilted the sandstone strata at a steep angle so that the exposed spoor layer now appears as a great mural of the history of life. The exposure, which is unique in Europe and is protected as a natural monument, is evidence that the giant dinosaurs, whose skeletons are known from Africa and North America, were also to be found on the great islands which then existed in the area of present-day Europe. The elephant-like sauropods footprints lead towards the observer whereas the tracks of a gigantic predatory biped saurian go in the opposite direction. Its three-toed prints are 60 cm long. In a remote past, saurians trod out this path on a flat and sandy coast and the ripple marks indicate that it was covered by shallow water.

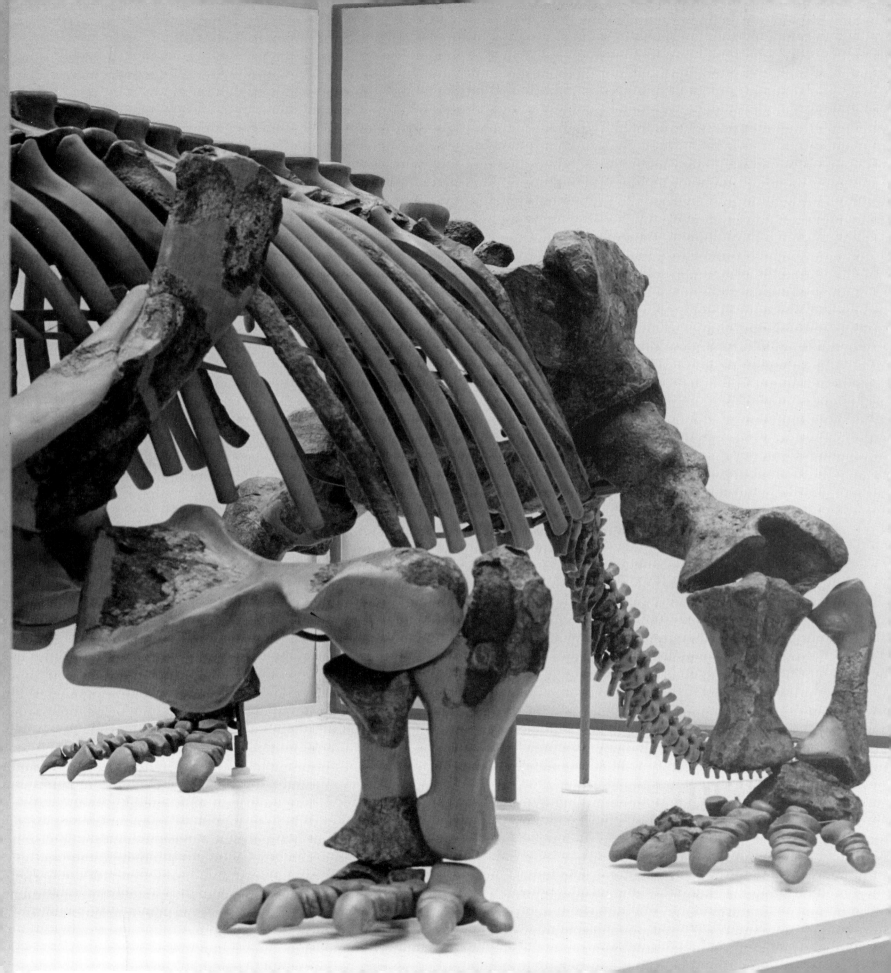

Preceding page:

An ancestral reptile

Letjesbosch in Cape Province (South Africa). Middle Permian. Length: 3 metres

Bradysaurus baini *(Seeley) is a typical representative of the Pareiasaurs, that group of Permian ancestral reptiles which were distinguished by large, plump, turtle-like forms. They had an armoured skin and their massive skulls were crowned with growths of various shapes. Their legs were set at an angle in relation to their body. Numerous complete skeletons of pareiasaurs have been excavated in Northern Europe and Southern Africa. Our skeleton was found by Professor Janensch in 1929.*

Skull of a mammal-like reptile

Lower Triassic, Cynognathus *zone; Cape Province (South Africa). Length 22 cm.*

Diademodon mastacus *(Seeley). The designation mammal-like reptile is easily understood when one sees this skull which is in a unique state of preservation. This is the jaw of a herbivore, differentiated into incisors, canine teeth and molars. A bony secondary upper palate and a lower jaw which almost entirely consists of a single bone, all identifiable as mammal characteristics.*

The cranium, however, is of a simple reptilian type. Diademodon *belongs to a vegetarian side-line of the otherwise carnivorous Karroo dog* (Cynodontia). *The skull was excavated by Reck in 1932.*

Plateosaurus quenstedti *(von Huene)*

The plateosaurs of the Upper Triassic were the forerunners of the great sauropods and were some of the largest herbivores of their time. A famous site was the former Baerecke brickworks at Halberstadt (German Democratic Republic) where marl of the middle Keuper was excavated. Several skeletons were discovered and recovered there at one horizon between 1909 and 1911. The complete skeleton XXV, a detail of which is shown here, and the fine skull of skeleton XXIV, which was described by Otto Jaeckel in 1914 as Plateosaurus longiceps *n.sp., come from Jaeckel's excavation material. The skull (top) has been somewhat crushed at the side by the burden of sediment and therefore looks higher than it really is. The section of the skeleton (bottom) shows the lizard-like pelvis and the rear extremities. As is apparent, Jaeckel regarded* Plateosaurus *as a plantigrade. Other reconstructions show it as a digitigrade (cf. page 162).*

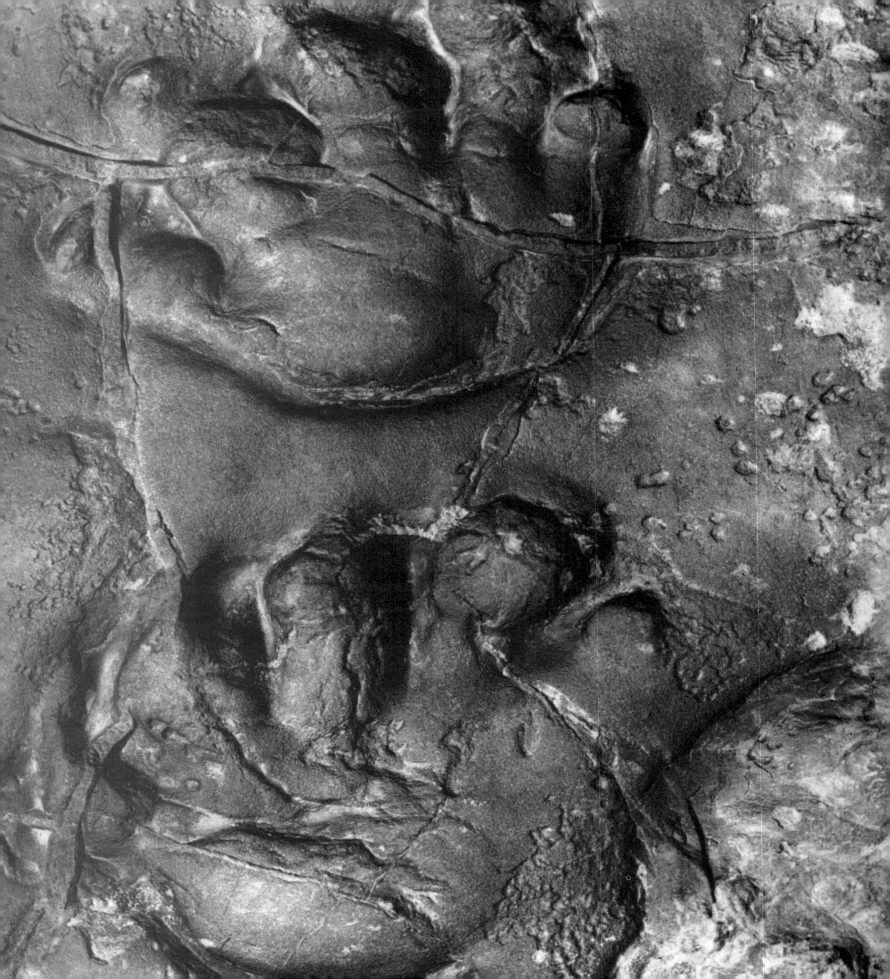

Tambach track

Ichniotherium cottae *(Pohlig, 1885) is one of the frequent fossil tracks in the upper Permian red beds of the Thuringian Forest. The spoors there constitute the only remaining trace of an early saurian society. The two prints (hand and foot, right) are on the lower side of a sandstone slab of Tambach sandstone and are part of the trackway of a mammal-like pelycosaur. The ancient 2-3-3-3-3 pattern of the finger and toe bones still survives in our own hands and feet.*

Trackway of footprints

Chirotherium barthi. *Thuringian Chirotherian beds of the Bunter Sandstone of the type-locality of Hessberg near Hildburghausen (German Democratic Republic). Lower Triassic.*

The spoor of the hand creature—the footprint is like a reflection of the human hand—has been the subject of controversy since 1834. Amphibian, marsupial and monkey have been suggested as the possible cause. Chirotherium *became a problem. Soergel endeavoured to establish the proportions of the creature from the spoor. Large rear feet, carrying a heavy load contrasted with small, lightly laden fore-limbs. At the present time, pseudosuchians are being considered as the possible originators, e.g.,* Ticinosuchus *from Tessin or, on account of the great age of the spoors, representatives of another ancestral group of the archosaurs, as yet unknown.*

Nothosaur

Single bones of nothosaurs which every collector of Triassic fossils probably has in his collection. They belong to the most common vertebrate remains of the Muschelkalk of the German Triassic, but joint remains of skeletons are rare. The majority of the famous Nothosaurus species was described on the basis of skull finds. The most complete remains of a Northosaurus is a find from Rüdersdorf near Berlin (see p. 18). The anatomical proof of this and other finds made it possible to reconstruct a complete skeleton from the numerous isolated bones of the same locality, the so-called Orbicularis strata at the basis of the Middle Muschelkalk. Because of the somehow artificial character of this assembled and partly reconstructed skeleton, it was only referred to as Nothosaurus sp. The length of the skeleton is 1.30 m, but obviously nothosaurs could reach a length of up to 3 m.

The choice of the generic name Nothosaurus (bastard saurian) was made in 1834 by Count Münster because of the strange mixture of features. The nothosaurs were obviously fish-hunters as can be seen by the fang and adaptations to the life in water. But these adaptations are not so great as to exclude a former relatively good movability on land. The nothosaurs thus lived amphibically. They were inhabitants of the coast and also caught their bag far away in the flat peripheral seas.

The nasal orifices were already situated further back, but still not as far back as on the Plesiosaurs. The limbs too, along with the appertaining middle section were already adapted to life in water, but did not as yet have the extreme paddle shape as on the snake-necked saurian.

Preceding page:

Triassic turtle

Proganochelys (Triassochelys) dux *Jaekel. The oldest remains of turtles found so far date from the Middle Keuper in Württemberg (Federal Republic of Germany) and Halberstadt (German Democratic Republic)—from the same strata in which the plateosaurs were found. The type of the Halberstadt species shown here is the most complete specimen of a Triassic turtle. The photographs show it from above and from the side. It is 85 cm long. The flat, broad, armoured shell is similar to that of a turtle but at the same time there were also species with a domed shell of the tortoise type. Turtles (and tortoises) are a very conservative group of animals which have not really changed since the Triassic period. In contrast to other animals their neck has consisted of a constant number of cervical vertebrae (8) since that time. Nevertheless, there were some differences, some features which recent turtles do not possess. The free neck-section had bony neck spines because it was as yet unable to draw its head back fully under the shield. The eating habits of the Triassic turtles already corresponded with that of turtles today. They too had a horny bill and small teeth in their gums. Unfortunately, the extremities of Triassochelys have not been passed down to us but they were probably typical turtle legs even at this time. First turtle spoors are even to be found in the strata of the upper Bunter Sandstone.*

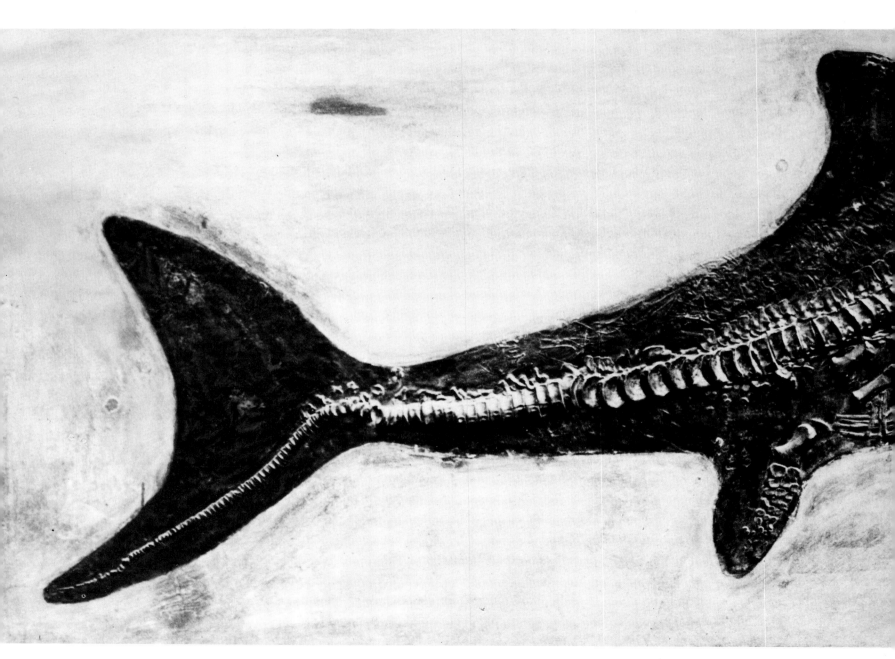

Ichthyosaurus

Jurassic, Lias Epsilon, Holzmaden (Federal Republic of Germany). Length: 1.7 metres.
Stenopterygius quadriscissus (Quenstedt). The majority of all known ichthyosaurs come from the bituminous Posidonian shale of Württemberg and especially from Holzmaden. More than a thousand finds of varying value have been made. Rarities include ichthyosaurs with remains of the rough skin giving an idea of the dolphin-like outline of these creatures.

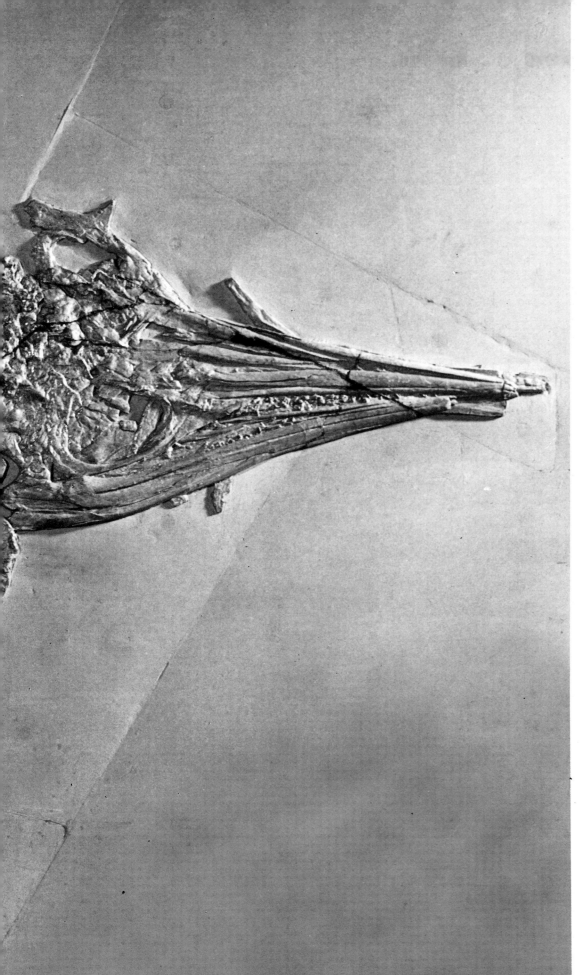

Portrait of an ichthyosaurus

Lias Epsilon, Holzmaden (Federal Republic of Germany). Length of head: 75 cm.

Up to now it has been possible to recover about 300 excellently preserved skeletons of ichthyosaurs from the Posidonian shale of Württemberg, an extraordinarily high number for vertebrate fossils. The quantity of this fossil material is statistically representative. It shows the variability of species, makes it possible to pursue the genesis of a species and also gives impressive evidence of the ontogeny.

Stenopterygius uniter von Huene, a rather plump kind of ichthyosaurus. The existing skeleton clearly shows the dark spot of a stomach filling. The indigestible food remains consist of many thousands of ceratocephali of octopus arms, but significantly enough do not contain belemnite shells.

As deep-sea creatures, the young of the ichthyosaurs were born alive. Many embryos have been found, both within the body of the mother and outside. It may have been that the gas produced by decaying matter and muscle contractions led to a postmortal birth. The fossil evidence of such processes shows that the young animals were born tail-first.

Snake-necked saurians

Plesiosaurus brachypterygius *von Huene*. *These long-necked, paddle-limbed reptiles were the successors of the Triassic nothosaurs but not their direct descendants. They were even better adapted to life in the open sea. A strange feature are the long paddles which were used like oars for propelling the creatures—as with turtles. Unlike the ichthyosaurs, only a few specimens of plesiosaurs were found at Holzmaden but these include some of the best ever discovered. They are usually found lying on their back but the skeleton illustrated is lying on its side. Plesiosaur skeletons in an excellent state of preservation from the English Liassic were described by Conybeare as long ago as 1821.*

continent Pangaea. The so-called Four Corners (Utah, Colorado, Arizona and New Mexico) and the Midcontinent (Oklahoma and parts of Texas) now form the best sites for finding the quadrupeds of the Lower Permian. It is possible to distinguish delta fauna, living near the coast on either side of the Midcontinent Seaway of that time, from the fauna living in more elevated areas further from the coast. However, the plants and animals of the real highlands are not found here since their buried remains sooner or later had to fall victim to erosion, together with the sediments. This is one of the unavoidable features of the history of the Earth.

Apart from skeletal remains, trackways also bear witness to the animal world of far-distant days. Extensive spoor-finds from the Lower Permian have long been known in the lower New Red Sandstone of Thuringia, too. In the alternating fine and mostly red sandstones and clays of intramontane basins, they are often the only fossils. In the past, practical geologists did not consider them suitable for the classification of strata but this view has changed in recent years. Tracks associated with groups of saurians which developed rapidly have become increasingly important for the clarification of stratigraphic questions particularly in the Red Beds. There is a comprehensive local collection of saurian tracks in the Museum of Nature at Gotha (German Democratic Republic), totalling more than 30 square metres of slabs. The pelycosaurian track *Ichniotherium cottae* (p. 172) is one of the most numerous from the Tambach sandstone of the Permian red beds. The Geological Institute of the University of Birmingham possesses a large collection of tracks from the Stephanian B of England. In the USA, most of the spoor-finds from the Lower Permian of the Grand Canyon are kept in the US National Museum at Washington.

While tropical coal-swamps continued to extend across the Northern half of the supercontinent in the vicinity of the Equator during the later Carboniferous and the early Permian, extensive areas of the South of the Pangaea were glaciated. When, at a later date in the Upper Permian, Gondwanaland was no longer in the polar area, a temperate cool and

The supercontinent of Pangaea 230 million years ago with the sites of the twin-tusked saurian Lystrosaurus. *For orientation, the present coastlines are drawn in on the continental shelf.*

moist climate with moor formation developed which gradually became warmer and drier. As the temperature rose, the reptiles, coming from the North, also appeared on the Gondwana continent. The most extensive finds of Upper Permian and Lower Triassic saurians are in the strata of the Karroo Formation in the South of Africa. They document the golden age of the therapsids, that group of mammal-like reptiles which, in comparison with the preceding pelycosaurs, already displayed a noticeably higher level of development. Of the individual and relatively isolated lines of descent of the cotylosaurs, the pareiasaurs were some of the few to survive. They were herbivorous, straddle-legged reptiles, often quite fat, with spines and humps on the skull and with an armoured trunk, causing them to bear a resemblance to turtles. Their size clearly distinguishes them from the lizard-like forms of the central line of descent of the cotylosaurs. A typical representative of the pareiasaurs is *Bradysaurus baini* from South Africa (p. 168).

Also large and plump were the cotylosaurs from the group of the diadectes, dating from an even earlier stage of the Lower Permian of North America. They were the first reptiles to feed on land plants. Otherwise, the early tetrapods were obviously flesh-eating animals which lived on worms, insects and fish or hunted each other.

Mammal-like Reptiles

Time and again, the progressive evolution of land vertebrates began with relatively small and not unduly specialized forms which usually fed on insects. Through differentiated adaptation and in the course of time, their new constructional elements became component-parts of a new diversity. In this, the evolution of the various groups of reptiles did not differ from that of the mammals. Only relatively small animals can live by catching insects while hunting involves too much effort for larger ones. This is why many animals then specialize in larger prey (carnivores) and some feed on plants (herbivores). Other remain relatively non-specialized omnivores.

In the Upper Permian Karroo fauna of Gondwana, an equilibrium of herbivores and predatory animals had already emerged under the mammal-like reptiles, corresponding to the present-day situation among the mammals. When the plant world changed, just before the Triassic, this resulted in serious consequences. The replacement of the *Glossopteris* flora by the *Dicroidium* flora brought about the end of almost all the saurians having only a pair of large canines (dicynodonts). Only one group was able to change over to the new plant diet or had already made the change prior to this date: the Kannemeyeriae. Together with the newly emerged herbivores from groups which had previously been exclusively predatory, they took possession of the vacated habitats. The new vegetarians included *Diademodon*, the vegetarian Karroo dog of which a particular fine skull is illustrated here (p. 170). The real Cynodonts, however, developed into carnivores but some remained insect-eaters and this line subsequently led to the mammals. The balance which emerged between the herbivores and the predatory animals was again disturbed as early as the Upper Triassic by the appearance of the dinosaurs but was soon restored again from the latter's own ranks.

In their exceptional variety, the mammal-like reptiles represent the most important group of saurians of Gondwana. They developed often in parallel branches at a varying rate of progress and in a multiplicity of combinations, those features which, in their totality, ultimately established the pattern of features characterizing the mammals known to us today. In the course of the millennia, the skeleton became lighter and the body was carried further and further away from the ground. The jaws acquired the additional function of chewing. In this connection, a differentiation took place in the jaw area with the teeth aquiring a stronger foundation (roots) and the lower jaw becoming more powerful. The latter now consisted only of one pair of bones and a new jaw-joint appeared on the scene, in many species functioning in parallel with the old one for a long time. The joint-bones of the head region also acquired a new function (directional hearing) as stapes. The emergence of a

Skeleton of Lycaenops; *lightly built early predatory animal. Upper Permian (according to Broom)*

Skeleton of Kannemeyeria; *a ponderous herbivorous twin-tusked saurian. Lower Triassic (according to Broom)*

second palate permitted chewing and respiration at the same time. Finally, there was the development of warmbloodedness, resulting in a considerable increase in energy and food requirements. The growing independence of climate and the consequent expansion in habitats was paralleled by an increasing dependence on food. Creatures dependent on a specialized source of food were particularly at risk, however.

These dialectics provide the most convincing explanation of the rise and fall of the mammal reptiles. The decline in the sharp climatic variations and a general rise in temperature as the possible consequences of the drift promoted the emergence of competitive cold-blooded reptiles. There was no longer selection on the basis of independence of climate. Only the most highly developed warmblooded creatures, who may have already become specialized as small nocturnal omnivores and insect eaters, still had the chance of furhter development.

The Reptile Breakthrough

In the Permian, the mammal-like reptiles and the armoured amphibians had still been the most numerous quadrupeds but a complete change in this picture occurred in the course of the Triassic. This was the beginning of the golden age of the real reptiles. Mention has already been made of the dinosaurs dominating the mainland. It was during the Triassic, however, that reptiles moved into areas which had not previously been inhabited. In particular, they now made use of the supply of food available in the sea. Various groups of marine reptiles developed: ichthyosaurs, sauropterygians, placondonts. From now on even branches of primarily terrestrial groups turned towards the sea, as exemplified by the turtles, lizards and crocodiles.

Gliding is repeatedly achieved, especially by small, lizard-like forms. The oldest creature capable of gliding dates from the Upper Permian of Madagascar (*Daedalosaurus*). It was the flying saurians which first achieved active flight. The vertebrates thus succeeded in emulating that which had already been

Skull of Cynognathus; *highly developed predatory animal. Lower Triassic (according to Romer)*

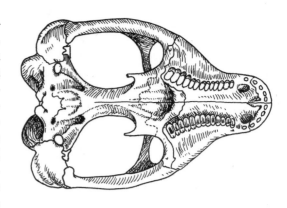

Underside of the skull of a traversodont closely related to Cynognathus. *Highly specialized herbivore jaw; secondary gum. Middle Triassic (according to Romer)*

achieved insects in the Devonian—the utilization of air space as an area in which to live. The oldest known remains of a flying saurian were found as recently as 1973 and date from the Upper Triassic. It is only in the Lower Jurassic that complete skeletons have been discovered. By this time, the new design had already been implemented. The connecting links between these creatures and the original archosaurs are still missing. Similarly, the ichthyosaurs emerged in the Triassic as reptiles fully adapted to the new way of life from the obscurity of their early history. It was the same story at a later date when the similarly adapted bats and the whale appeared on the scene when the mammals occupied the vacated habitats in the Tertiary.

Of the marine saurians, there are two groups which are limited entirely to the Triassic and are especially characteristic for the German Triassic: the nothosaurs (bastard saurians) and the placodonts. The jaws of the placodonts with their powerful broad flat teeth indicate that they preyed on hard-shelled food such as, molluscs, brachiopods and crabs and perhaps echinoderms as well. On the other hand, the long-necked nothosaurs, which as powerful swimmers could seize their agile prey with lightning speed, possessed jaws and teeth perfectly adapted to catching fish. These creatures were obviously still able to move around adequately on dry land.

Individual bones and teeth from placodonts and nothosaurs are no rare occurrence in the shallow sea deposits of the Muschelkalk. Interesting skeletal finds in the lowlands of Northern Germany have been supplied by the small Muschelkalk deposit bound to a salt mass at Rüdersdorf to the east of Berlin. The plesiosaurs of the Jurassic and Cretaceous periods were relatives of the nothosaurs. Famous Liassic sites are Lyme Regis on the English Channel coast (Dorset) and Holzmaden in Württemberg (Federal Republic of Germany). The extremities of the plesiosaurs had changed to paddle-shaped fins. Like the neck, their length was greatly increased by additional bone elements—vertebrae or tarsi.

Without doubt, the optimum adaptation to rapid and protracted swimming among the reptiles was displayed by the ichthyosaurs (fish-saurians). Like present-day whales, they assumed the streamlined shape of the fishes but had not reduced their rear extremities on the same scale, developing a vertical tail-fin instead of a horizontal one. In the tail-fin, the supporting spinal column was bent downwards in a remarkable manner. The action of the tail-fin thus counteracted the buoyancy of the lungs. As deep-sea creatures, the young of the ichthyosaurs were born alive. There is fossil evidence of embryos in the body of the mother and even of the birth process. Even today, it is frequently possible to identify food remains in the contents of the stomach. Indigestible fish-remains have been found and also masses of horny hooks from squid tentacles. The largest complete skeletons of ichthyosaurs are eight to ten metres in length. Large bones indicate that a length of 17 metres was possible.

The flying saurians also made use of the great supply of food in the seas and inland waters. Their pointed, rake-like teeth were adapted to catching fish and their small feet, in a variety of shapes were provided with webs for swimming. Whether small or gigantic with wing spreads of up to 15 metres, the flying saurians were expert fliers and gliders. Like bats, they spread out a flight membrane but not all their fingers were used to span it like struts and in fact only the fourth, greatly lengthened finger was used for this purpose. A hairy fur helped the creatures avoid heat-losses. They were certainly warmblooded. The strikingly well-developed brain is to be seen in association with their flight capability.

Turtles

Turtles are some of the most frequently found fossils of land vertebrates. Their rigid armour is the obvious explanation for this. What is astonishing here, however, is that they appeared relatively suddenly on the fossil scene when they were already fully developed as a type. Their evolutionary origin is still obscure. In their skeletal features, the turtles remind us of the cotylosaurs. They, too, lack the temporal apertures in the roof of the skull. The Triassic turtles had already developed a beak with a horny sheath but still had teeth on the palate. The neck part of the spinal column already consisted of eight vertebrae but still carried powerful spines at the back of the neck. These creatures could not retract their neck under the armour.

The finest and most complete example of a Triassic turtle was excavated by O. Jaeckel in 1912 in the Baerecke brickyard pit at Halberstadt and was described in 1918 as *Triassochelys dux*.

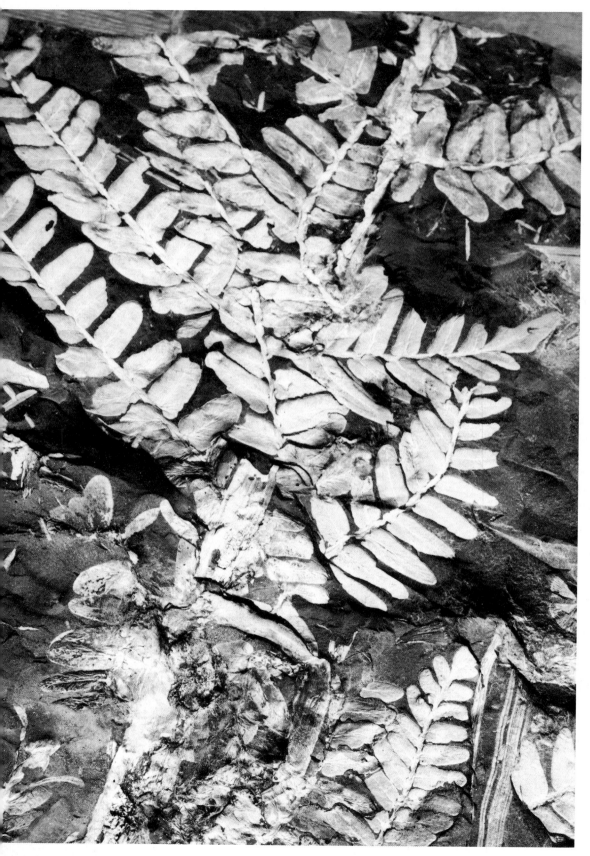

Preceding page:

Neuropteris subauriculata

A species which clearly demonstrates the leaf vein systems to be observed in many finds. The pinna vein systems from a basal corner-point. Similar patterns have been observed in Odontopteris *species. Magnification: 4×.*

Neuropteris attenuata

Site: Piesberg near Osnabrück (Federal Republic of Germany).

It is normal to find black, carbonized leaf remains in the shale of coal heaps but what has happened when the leaf remains are white or silvery-white? Such white leaf remains are known from the heaps of Coal Measures in Switzerland, Austria and Southern France (Central Plateau). Another well-known deposit is at Piesberg (not far from Osnabrück, Federal Republik of Germany). Wherever, the protracted development of heat by pluton caused the rock to reach a temperature of 150 to 250°C, carbonization or the formation of pit-coal reached a maximum, producing semi-bituminous coals up to anthracite. Transformation of clay minerals obviously took place in the course of this and the plant remains received a covering of gümbelite or were completely transformed into the silvery-white clay mineral.

Linopteris brongniarti

Site: Zwickau coalfield (German Democratic Republic).

An old original. August von Gutbier published a picture of this specimen for the first time in 1836 and named the plant as a new species: Linopteris brongniarti. *The naming of the species was a scientific tribute to the French palaeobotanist Adolphe Brongniart of Paris. Magnification: 6×*

Pecopteris pluckeneti

Site: Zwickau coalfield (Westphalian D) (German Democratic Republic).

A bifurcated seed-fern of the Upper Carboniferous (Westphalian D and Stephanian) and the lowest New Red Sandstone (Permian). The leaf frond, in a few examples, shows a bud or a continuation of an axial piece at the point of bifurcation. It is assumed that in such fronds the entire programme of growth was repeated once more in the interior of the fork. Clearly recognizable is the beginning of the zigzag axes of the last order to which the small leaflets were attached. Did the frond parts to which seeds were attached grow in the inside of such bifurcated fronds?

Pecopteris pluckeneti

Site: Zwickau coalfield (Westphalian D) (German Democratic Republic).

A small piece of the leaf frond of Pecopteris pluckeneti *with seeds still attached tò it! Years ago, Sterzel at Chemnitz (now Karl-Marx-Stadt) and Kidston in Edinburgh had already interpreted small round scars on the leaflets ot this plant as development points for seeds. The piece illustrated here confirms this supposition. The seeds were located individually on a vein at the base of the leaflet. Similar forms are known from some other Pteridosperms of the Late Carboniferous, e.g., from an* Odontopteris *species in France.*

Magnification: 3×

Sphenopteris nummularia

One of the species with round leaflet shape described for the first time by A. von Gutbier in 1835/36. It is not yet clear where the little seeds were attached. Magnification: 2×

Odontopteris reichiana

Also a species described for the first time by A. von Gutbier in 1835/36 with dentate leaflets and a wedge-shaped basal leaflet.

Alethopteris subdavreuxi

A genus widely distributed in Europe, North America and China but with species which were restricted to smaller areas. Some of the basal leaflets appear to have slipped down the main axis. Is this a transition to genera of the Stephanian and Permian periods with characteristic intercalated pinnae?

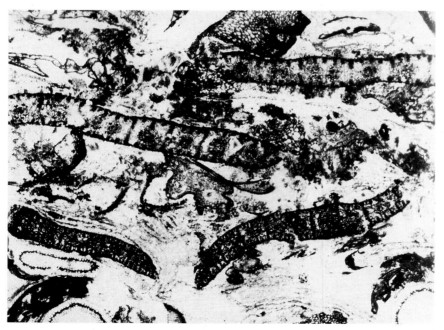

Cordaites principalis

Site: Wettin, near Halle/Saale (German Democratic Republic).

The leaf-top of a cordaitean tree, which was found in strata of the Uppermost Carboniferous (Stephanian), shows about 50 individual leaves. This specimen indicates that the cordaitean trees had dense foliage at the ends of their axes.

Cordaites principalis

Site: Bochum, Westphalia (Federal Republic of Germany).

This dolomite nodule concretion permits a glimpse of the interior of the Cordaitean leaf. The cordaitean leaves are tightly packed, one above the other. The longitudinal section shows the side-by-side arrangement of the longitudinal veins and the hard-tissue strands (sclerenchyma strands) supporting them above and below.

Pseudocycas roemeri

Palaeobotany owes a debt to Friedrich Schulze, a Berlin botanist. It was he who pioneered the art of preparing leaf cuticles, millions of years old, when he invented the Schulze reagent for the maceration of leaves and wood (1855). These bennettite leaf remains, which are about 130 million years old and come from the Lower Cretaceous period (Wealden) have been transformed into microscopic slides by this maceration method.

It is a long time since science was content with merely seeing the outer appearance of these fossil leaf remains. It is almost as if the evolution of these palm-like leaf remains came to a halt 200 to 100 million years ago since leaf forms of almost the same appearance can still be seen today in the form of the Cycas leaf-frond. When it became possible to identify the cell outlines of the epidermis cells complicated stomata were rendered visible. The picture shows such a stoma of a bennettite, magnified 1,000 times. The slide is taken from Schenk's original specimen. This is known as a Syndetocheilic type of stoma, resulting from a triple division of an epidermal cell.

Up to now, this species has been found only in North-West Germany in the standstone of the Osterwald forest. Finds in other areas such as Sussex (England) and Greenland still have to be confirmed.

Zamites buchianus

Site: Kefr Seluan (Lebanon).

There were probably not yet any palms at the time of the Lower Cretaceous. The leaf frond of a bennettite shown here preceded this type of leaf-fronds far as the outer appearance is concerned. Zamites fronds were found on Cycadeoidea stems. This was observed by Tatsuaki Kimura in Japan in the Tetori formation of the island of Honshu (1967). The example illustrated here comes from the Lower Cretaceous of Lebanon. In addition to Japan and Lebanon such finds are known from the North-West of the Federal Republic of Germany, England and the USA.

Microscopic examination of tiny leaf-fragments

When the degree of carbonization is high it is worthwhile simply dissolving a rock sample such as a drilling core.

When the rocky material—sand or clay—has been washed away, the tiny leaf-fragments are collected on a wire-mesh screen, washed and then placed in a porcelain dish with the preservation fluid.

Preparation of a Ptilophyllum species

This cuticle preparation from a leaf of Lower Cretaceous age (Wealden, about 180 million years) shows both top and undersides. After maceration, the cuticle of the top side of the leaf is scored longitudinally with a thin glass needle and opened out to the right and left. The 20× magnification shows how the stomata, arranged in lines—recognizable as dark points—meet the edge at a sharp angle. The top side of the leaf did not have any stomata.

A 250× magnification shows the epidermal cells of the underside of the leaf and the complicated stomata. The cell walls are sinuous and each cell displays a wart-like light-spot.

The arrangement of the stomata in lines also caused the division of the middle part of the leaf tissue (mesophyll) into thin longitudinal segments. These natural longitudinal sections were revealed by maceration. The long palisade cells can be easily identified. They were formerly used, 180 million years ago, for assimilation. At that time, they were filled with chlorophyll grains. It is thought that remains of these, or their products of transformation, can still be seen in the picture.
Magnification: 250×

Pseudocycas acifolia

In another case, the stomata can be recognized in random order in a furrow on the underside of the leaf. This is a third bennettite genus and species.
Magnification: 40×

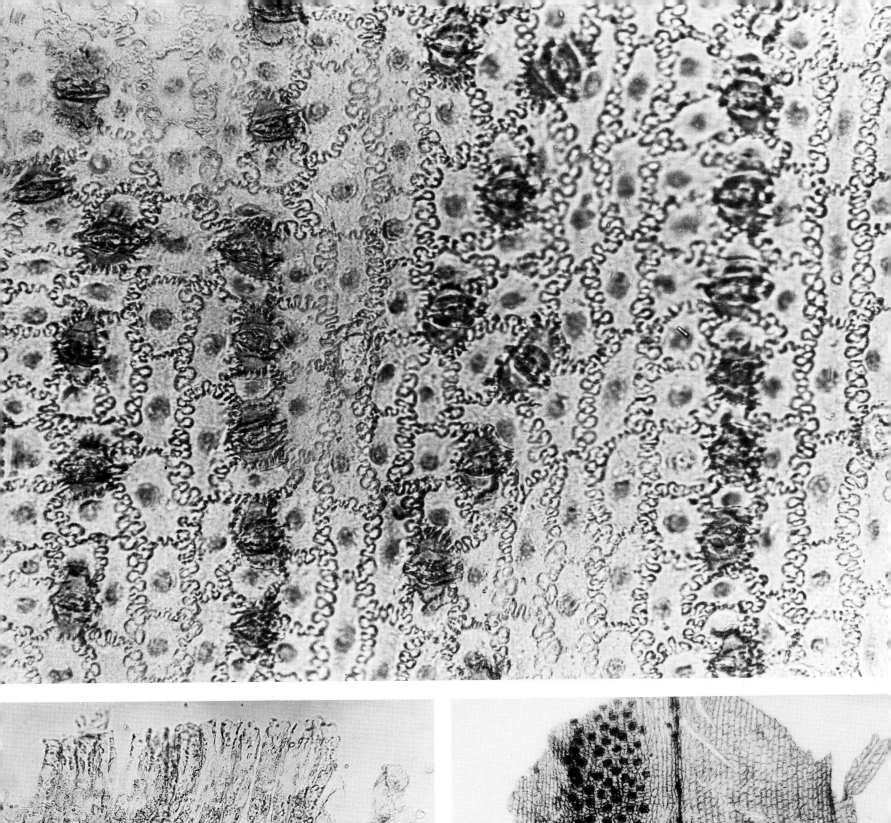
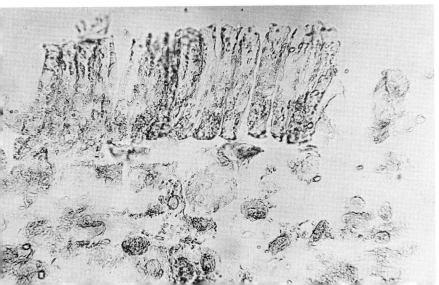
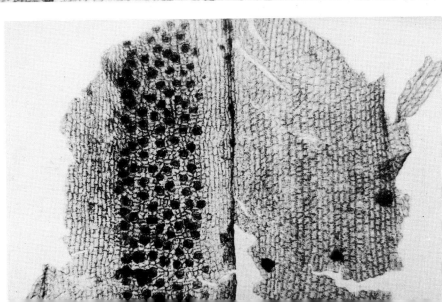

Cycadeoidea reichenbachiana

Bennettite stems of the Cretaceous period concealed their flowers between the innumerable leaf-frond scars on stems. The stem-fragments collected in North America are famous but exceptionally well-preserved specimens have also been found in Central Europe, as, for instance, thousands of years ago in Italy (cf. p. 33) and this specimen two centuries ago in Poland, in the vicinity of Wieliczka. The specimen is now in the Museum for Mineralogy and Geology in Dresden.

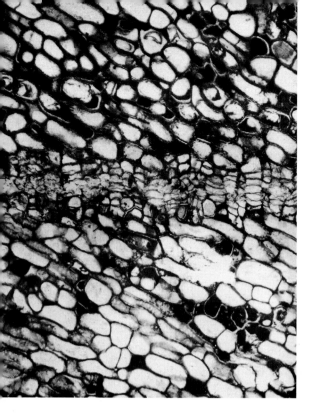

Cycadeoidea reichenbachiana

A thin section shows the cell structure of the stem (100× magnification), including a narrow zone in the process of cell-division. The plant structure was preserved by silicification.

Cycadeoidea reichenbachiana

A glimpse inside the Cycadeoidea *flower of Dresden, 130 million years old. This longitudinal section shows seed-bearing structure (gynoecium) in the flower which is still closed like a bud and recessed. The small ovules were located between interseminal scales. Stamens, which should be located below the gynoecium here, are lacking. It can therefore be assumed that these were exclusively female or that at another point on the* Cycadeoidea *stem hermaphrodite flowers were formed, the latter presumably having the function of producing pollen.*

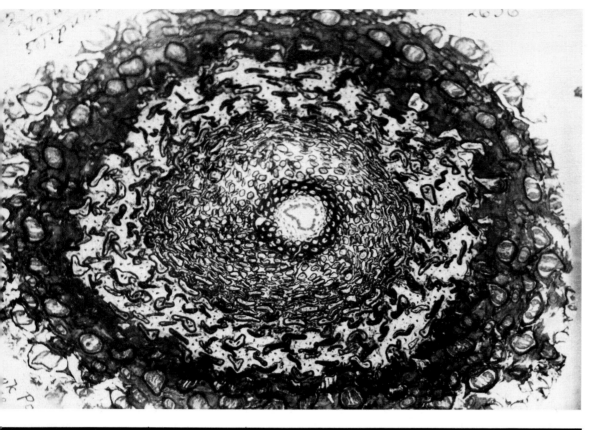

Osmundites dunlopi

Site Isle of Wight (Great Britain).

Whether the underground fern-stems of the Osmunda-ceae *really come from certain fern-stems, found in sili-cified form, from Karl-Marx-Stadt (German Demo-cratic Republic) and Orenburg (USSR) from the Permian period is disputed but possible. We would know more if we also had the leaf fronds for these stems. However, the stem cross-sections are so charac-teristic that the name* Osmundites *is applied to all of them.*

On the inside, they display a woody cylinder (siphono-stele) filled with parenchymatic pith. From here, the leaf shoots branch outwards, leaving behind a net-work of leaf-gaps on the woody cylinder. These leaf-shoots then show their horse-shoe-shaped cross-section in the cortex.

This picture shows a cross-section of Osmundites dunlopi *from the Wealden period (the lowest divi-sion of the Creataceous period), found at Brook Point on the Isle of Wight in Southern England. Cretaceous* Osmundites *stems display an exceptionally large number of individual frond elements, almost like the petals of a* Magnolia *blossom.* Osmundites *stems of the Permian period have developed a central stele on the inside of the woody cylinder and centrally situated woody cells also occur lately, even in the young* Osmunda *stems of the present day.*

Magnification: 5×

Stromatolite

Site: Northern foreland of the Harz Mountains (German Democratic Republic).

It looks like the convolutions of a brain but it is only a calcareous concretion, produced by primitive blue algae.
A stromatolite from the Lower Triassic Oölitic lime-stone between Benzingerode and Heimburg, northern foreland of the Harz Mountains.
The oldest stromatolites of the Earth are 3,5 million years old.
The most splendid forms, however, as shown here, were probably formed in the Triassic period.

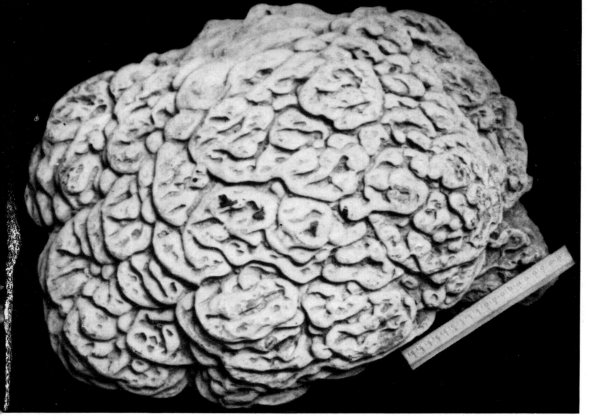

Weichselia reticulata

Much patience is needed for the recovery of the fossil frond, preserved in sandstone, of Weichselia reti-culata, *which is still a mystery for botanists, and a sure hand is needed for the removal of the material around it. Since sandstone is lacking a natural binding agent, a liquid adhesive (such as latex) must be applied immediately after the recovery of the find and the removal of the material around it. The Lower Creta-ceous sandstone (Hauterive-Barreme level) of Qued-linburg (German Democratic Republic) has supplied the largest* Weichselia *remains so far. Other sites, as in Belgium and Southern England, have supplied small fragments which nevertheless can still be subjected to microscopic examination. It is the sum total of the results obtained from all the sites which then constitutes the state of knowledge.* Weichselia *was obviously a widespread riverbank plant of the Lower Cretaceous period which, through the inclined mounting of its leaflets was also capable of adapting to very dry condi-tions for a time.*

Page 200:
Fresh find of Weichselia reticulata; *in hand. Before the find is reinforced the leaflets have to be prepared.*

It would be enough, of course, just to follow the chronological succession of the occurrence and disappearance of the individual species and thus of the genera, families, orders, classes and divisions of the animal and plant world. The result would be and is a flood of biostratigraphic data. For the classification of this material, systems would have to be created. As always, there would be the urge to identify common features and then to collect the feature-bearers in columns. This would have and has the advantage that generalizing concepts can be allocated to the columns. Columns can then be reassembled in columns and corresponding abstract concepts can be allocated to these once more. Systems of classification of this kind have already been introduced in the history of botany and they fulfilled a very important function: they gave the many known and unknown species of plants short and unmistakable names which therefore contributed to the understanding of them.

The Influence of Linné

It is well known that Carolus Linnaeus (1707 to 1778), who called himself Carl von Linné for the last 20 years of his life, was one of the great men of the systems of classification. With his perceptive eye, he not only produced his "Systema naturae" (Leiden, 1735) while still a young man of 28 but also endeavoured to apply this system of knowledge as a systematic tool for the further investigation of plants, animals and minerals. Reference has already been made to a trilobite namend by him (page 36).

When the fossil plants were recognized as largely unknown species which no longer existed (Schlotheim 1804, 1820; Brongniart 1822, 1828), efforts were made to compile a similarly satisfying system for these as well. Many of the species and generic names still valid today date from this initial period of palaeobotany. Accordingly, in the International Rules of Botanical Nomenclature, the year 1820 is fixed as the date back to which the search for the legitimately published name has to take place. At an International Botani-

Great Ideas of the Laws of Development

Nature obscures everywhere the real boundaries by average and poor forms which always produce instances in opposition to every firm distinction, even within certain genera . . . In order to be able to discern the same forms as imperfect, poor, misshaped, a definite type is assumed but it would not be possible to define this by experience . . . it rather presupposes the independence and dignity of definition . . . Nature, as such, is a living whole

G. W. F. Hegel

cal Congress (Montreal 1959), the competent nomenclature commission specified this date as 31 December 1820 and thus expressly excluded Schlotheim's principal work *Die Petrefactenkunde* (but not the *Nachträge zur Petrefactenkunde* of 1822).

This was a decision which was not observed by many palaeobotanists and will be cancelled again at a subsequent Congress. There is no reason to ignore the scientific founder of palaeobotany and his work which set high standards for the time, quite apart from the fact that for palaeontologists there is not the slightest doubt about the validity of the animal fossils published by Schlotheim in the same work.

The collection of original fossil plants appertaining to the work is in the Museum of Natural Science of the Humboldt University, Berlin (German Democratic Republic) and, in recent years, has been recognized and catalogued in a clear manner.

It was evident, of course, to the palaeobotanists of the 1820's that they could not use Linné's system of the stamens for classifying fossil leaves. Consequently, the French palaeobotanist Adolphe Brongniart (1801–1876) produced between 1828 and 1830 his great standard work of palaeobotany with splendid illustrations of fossil plants, especially of the Carboniferous period.

On the basis of the classification of the pinna forms of Carboniferous, fern-like plants, he formed new and comprehensible generic namens:

Pecopteris   leaf of comb-like appearance
Alethopteris leaf resembling a true fern
Sphenopteris leaf displaying a wedge-shaped lamella
Neuropteris leaf displaying characteristic veins and heart-shaped
Odontopteris leaf with numerous veins ending in the lamella and tooth-shaped

In the decades which followed, the plant world of the Carboniferous period, the Permian, the Mesozoic and the Tertiary were documented by splendid illustrated volumes and the results of anatomical investigations were also published. Nevertheless, the decisive morphological and theoretical trains of thought failed to materialize. It is hard to say whether the theoretical discussion of botany first had to reach a certain state or whether it was first necessary to make the find which would stimulate a new theory. At any rate, it was only in the first half of our century that the time became ripe for the experts to accept a theory. The previous century had still managed in some way to see fossil remains classified in the present-day plant system. The bennettites, for example, were known and investigated in detail at a very early date in the last century— the best-known bennettite genus *Cycadeoidea* was described by W. Buckland (Oxford, 1784–1856) as early as 1829 and presented as a new family of plants.

Development or Only Transformation?

Longitudinal sections through bennettite flowers were produced in 1867 and 1868 by W. Carruthers (England). Nevertheless, these bennettites were still regarded as cycads which had somehow changed. The attempt to see them as transitional to the magnolias failed to prove very convincing and was seriously supported only by a few botanists.

The discussion of the seed-ferns took a different course. It was asserted in 1899 in Berlin by H. Potonié who discussed the theory in a series of examples that this could be a transitional group leading from ferns to cycads. Finally, however, the English palaeobotanists Oliver and Scott were able to demonstrate in 1904 the probability of a relationship between certain bifurcated frond types with fine lamellae of the Upper Carboniferous, certain stems with a distinctive cortical layer and certain seeds, presenting a strange plant of prehistory. There was still no drawing of it—it was only decades later that this appeared— and the experts contented themselves with drawing up a list of technical names and with regarding the relationship as probable on the basis of one piece of evidence—the possession of glandular hair.

Stem:	*Lyginopteris oldhamia*
Cortex:	*Dictyoxylon oldhamium*
Frond:	*Sphenopteris hoeninghausi*
Frond-stem:	*Rhachiopteris aspera*

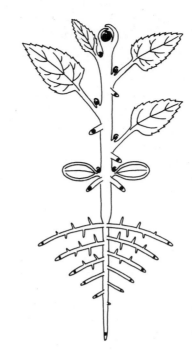

An angiosperm, dicotyledonous seed-plant can be imagined without having to characterize a special genus or species. Shown here is the general seed-plant of W. Troll (1954) as representative of Goethe's ancestral plant.

Roots:	*Kaloxylon hockeri*
Seeds:	*Lagenostoma lomaxi*
Seed cupules:	*Calymmatotheca*
Pollen organs:	*Crossotheca* or *Telangium?*

The last assumed relationship in the list (pollen organs) has remained an open question up to the present time.

Stem were imagined on which there were sterile and fertile fronds and indeed this hypothesis stimulated the investigation of many similar organs of fossil plants and produced new results concerning knowledge of the diversity of the types of seeds and stems of these pteridosperms (fern seeds). However, a convincing theory postulating the history of evolution was not yet adequately nurtured by these types of plants, at the beginning of the century. Support of such a kind came only with the Lower or Middle Devonian psilophyte finds of Rhynie in Scotland between 1916 and 1920.

Even at Goethe's time, persons with an abstract turn of mind in search of general concepts had endeavoured to match the general concept, in the case of botany, with a corresponding picture. The profusion of higher plants (angiosperms) was a direct incentive to this. Various botanists published their vision of this while Johann Wolfgang von Goethe (1749–1832) only wrote about it. In his Italian Journey, he calls it the "Ancient Plant" (1787) and four years afterwards he had a discussion with Schiller about it. It is said that he sketched it with a few strokes of the pen in Schiller's house, causing the latter to shake his head and remark that "... that is not experience, that is an idea". It is reported that Goethe peevishly replied: "That can be very welcome to me, that I have ideas ... and even see them with my eyes."

The Influence of a Site on the Information Obtained

Of the Scottish Devonian plants, one was found in 1917 which was of such a simple form that it practically demanded the formulation of a new land-plant theory: *Rhynia*. The type species *Rhynia gwynne-vaughani* was described by Kidston and Lang as an early land plant characterized by warty surface-structures and strange, separate shoots; it was only the second species *Rhynia major* which seemed more like a believable early land plant.

To remove all doubt, the author of the Telome theory, W. Zimmermann, drew a simplified picture (1938) of what he had in mind. This had not been included in his original book (1930). In actual fact, both species of *Rhynia* have round terminal shoots which either taper off or have swollen sporangia. All subsequent plant forms could indeed be imagined as consisting of such ends (Gr. telom = the end). Zimmermann also sketched this concept in the form of five possible variations.

In the case of *Rhynia*, the simple outer form is also matched by the very simple xylem situated in the centre of the stem with its protoxylem in the middle (see also p. 101). From this state of the inner tissue, it is possible, in turn, to imagine a series of stem types (steles). It is now up to scientific experience to confirm the value of this idea of the logical pattern of the course of development as essentially correct by fossil or to refute it in a well-reasoned manner.

As is so often the case, many fossil examples correspond to Zimmermann's theoretical sketch of the course of development but, at the same time, it is of most interest for research on those points where additional or contradictory possibilities emerge which were also part of the overall development.

Thus, for example, *Rhynia* is indeed not the oldest land plant; there were other land plants at the same time and before. Particular attention should therefore be paid to *Zosterophyllum myretonianum*, known from the Scottish Lower Devonian, since it shows in the form of a close succession of dichotomies that such division must have been a basic characteristic of the oldest land plants already at an early stage and that the *Rhynia* form was only one of many. If the study of other land plants is continued, it will then be discovered, in the case of *Taeniocrada*, for example, that the bifurcation of the central stele does not necessarily have to coincide exactly with the subsequent bifurcation of the stem.

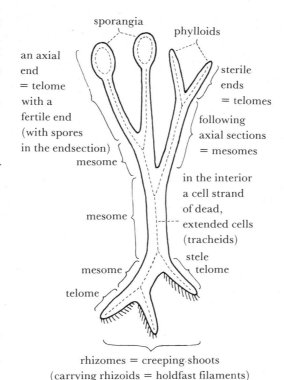

Another imaginary ancestral plant? W. Zimmermann (1938) combined in a drawing the simplest axial forms of the first land plants of the Lower and Middle Devonian which really existed 370 to 400 million years ago. His Telome theory asserts that all subsequent land plants must have originated from such a form.

The early lycopod *Asteroxylon* (see Fig. on p. 104/105) found at the *Rhynia* site consequently presents us with a riddle which has still not been solved: conducting strands come off from the star-shaped, centrally located steles and move outwards through the cortical tissue. On the outside, the stem has small leaflike emergences (seen here in cross-section) but the vascular strands end in the cortex and do not extend into the leaves. Are they preliminary stages of leaf strands or are they veins which have been reduced at an early stage? In the sense of the Telome theory, it is theoretically that they should be interpreted as reduced but it is attractive to see them as a preliminary stage, as a half-step which may be completed later and this latter Eration theory of Bower finds favour with many botanists. In actual fact, such land plants have been shown to be older than *Rhynia* and are found in the Lower Devonian of many sites on almost all the continents (e. g., *Drepanophycus* species).

In the Middle Devonian, thicker stems appeared with dichotomizing branches and with appendages. These included the first fern-like plants (*Cladoxylon scoparium*) which in the curvature of their sporangia show a horsetail feature (*Hyenia, Calamophyton*), regular small trees, divided into trunk and branches (*Pseudosporochnus*) and reduced forms (*Duisbergia*), resembling cacti. These stems and the nature of their xylem supply have been the subject of much intensive research in recent years.

The Complicated Beginning

The stem structure of *Pietzschia schülleri*, described in 1927 by W. Gothan, from the lowest part of the Upper Devonian of Wildenfels (German Democratic Republic) was also discussed by Leclercq and Lele (1968) when investigating some *Pseudosprochnus* stems. These well-preserved anatomical structures have again been investigated and illustrated here. For a long time it was thought that the primitive sections figured in the treatise by Gothan had been lost but they have since been found. The preservation is an exceptionally good calcite petrifaction (see Fig. on p. 135). The interior of the stem is occupied by individual protosteles, as already seen in *Rhynia* and *Psilophyton* (see Fig. on p. 112). In some cases, two protosteles are so close to each other that a division into two in the stem can be assumed as probable. A very characteristic feature, however, are the radial bands of xylem in the outer layer of the stem which are separated by wedges of hardened cells (sclerenchyma). Up to now, it has been assumed that these radial wood strands were formed from their corner-points outwards. The present photo micrographs show, however, that they are a chain-like succesion of such protoxylems. It is as if an intensive branch-strand separation took place in the stem without these branches emerging at the side or with this only taking place at the top of the stem. This is thus one of the stem structures which cannot be classified in the simple logic of the course of development as outlined by the Telome theory. It is likely that in the course of development complex and simple structures alternated with each other, were a reciprocal condition for each other and even produced each other. It must have been possible for simple and just as highly developed forms to emerge again from the complicated forms of a more advanced development.

At the time of the Lower and Middle Devonian, it seems that as yet there were scarcely any land plants with leaves, roots and branches in the present sense. All these now familiar parts of plants are the product of subsequent development not yet seen in those stem plants.

The way out of the form of existence of this group of plants is demonstrated by a plant of the late Lower Carboniferous period which was found a few years ago in Mongolia. It seems likely that several developments in the Upper Devonian took place in a similar manner. The Mongolian finds are used here since they appear convincing to us in the logic of the course of development and permit comparisons with other plants of a much higher level of development. Without doubt, however, our example is representative of a whole series of ancient ferns (known as Primofilices) which existed from the time of the Upper Middle Devonian, during the Upper Devonian and, in subsequent forms, even in the Lower Car-

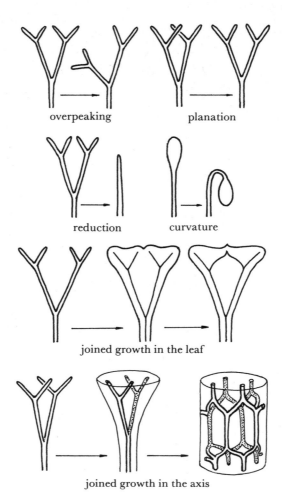

In the further development of the Devonian land plants, five morphological and anatomical possibilities of development emerged. In Zimmermann's Telome theory they are known as elementary processes.

boniferous, i.e., for about 50 million years. Similarly, our example is representative of the initial situation of the seed-ferns which at the time of the Upper Devonian displayed a strangely contradictory mosaic of some highly developed features on the one hand and not at all highly developed features on the other. Thus the genus *Archaeopteris* had compact woody stems in which, mainly towards the outside, a ring of initial xylems formed secondary wood, consisting of tracheids in the manner of coniferous wood, so that a modern tree-trunk resulted. At the same time, however, *Archaeopteris* had fern-like leaf-fronds with wedge-shaped leaves which in some species had not yet even grown together to form a leaf-area while in others they display a most primitive vein-pattern, an uneven fan-like system formed from the dichotomies of veins. Furthermore, this tree-growth, quite unlike a fern in appearance and consequently classified with the group of the progymnosperms, had leaflets with sporangia like a fern but these were highly developed and contained large female and small male spores. Like *Archaeopteryx*, *Archaeopteris* is a mosaic picture of primitive and highly developed parts but the decisive feature has emerged here somehow unexpectedly in the growth form and stem anatomy and not in the production of ovules which subsequently became a major feature. Can such a plant, without doubt a missing link, be designated as the first seed-plant when it is precisely these seeds which it does not posses? Is it conceivable that a great new development begins not so much with what subsequently becomes the key feature but rather with a development which is not unimportant but nevertheless not in the direct line of advance, that the aspect of major importance in the history of development is added later, after various detours of the development thus set in motion?

All these questions result when the term progymnosperms is applied to plants from the Upper Devonian period.

The Mysterious Leaf-Bifurcation

When we consider the Middle Devonian *Cladoxylon*, the Upper Devonian *Rhacophyton* or the *Chacassopteris* from the Mongolian Lower Carboniferous, our special interest is caught by a phenomenon of great importance for all subsequent plants of a higher stage of development, ferns and seed-ferns: the forked leaf.

It is somehow strange and, seen from a modern standpoint, unnatural that at the time of the Carboniferous and Lower Permian periods so many ferns and seed-ferns had a frond which was divided like a fork. Our pictures of seed-ferns of the Carboniferous period show this in convincing manner: the base of a plant which is either bare or with small and large pinnules, quite different in shape from those on the two halves of the frond above the dichotomy. A completely analogous (or even homologous) phenomenon may be observed in ferns of the Carboniferous and Lower Permian periods. The two halves of the frond emerge from the stem in a V-shape, usually with a pair of aphlebiae (i.e., basal pinnae). Occasionally, these aphlebiae are not at all so unimportant and carry the sporangia.

On the one hand, the Telome theory, which stresses the significance and mosaic-like nature of the ends and centre-pieces (telomes and mesomes), provides a good basis of terms for the phenomenon but, on the other, the V-shaped frond of the forked frond represents something so basic—a form of existence of the leaf feature—for a hundred million years that an additional and timely point of departure for this point of departure must be sought. The *Chacassopteris* leaf, as if it were a model, shows us such a possiblity.

As in the ginkgo leaf and also completely identical with this, the *Chacassopteris* pinna had two identical sides which in some way come from dichotomous division. The pinnae are located as appendages to the stem, as in many cases of Devonian land plants. In the centre part of the *Chacassopteris* pinna, a bifurcation can be seen which is repeated a number of times in exactly the same shape. At the side, however, there is a succession of bifurcations arranged like roof-tiles.

Zimmermann incorporated the type of branching called overtopping in his Telome theory. The leaf forms characterizing the ferns and seed-ferns of the Carboniferous period

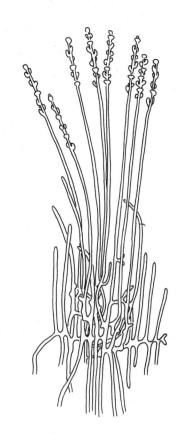

With the spike of sporangia at the upper end of the axis and the multiple bifurcation of basal axes, the Lower Devonian Zosterophyllum myretonianum *plant appears more complicated than Zimmermann's telome plant or* Rhynia.

obviously grew in this manner. Let us assume that they grew at the top until their programme was completed. Such fronds, already finished at the bottom but still growing at the top, have indeed been found.

It is necessary to emphasize this growth process because the modern leaf-growth process is different. The conifer needle grows at the base (basiplast), like banana and palm leaves while the leaf-area of the beech, the lime and rhubarb subsequently grows wider (intercalary) and bigger. The Permo-Carboniferous period was thus a transitional time and the leaf forms of 300 million years ago were transitional forms.

Intermediate Forms, Transitional Stage or Important Rudiments for Later?

It is legitimate to compare the *Chacassopteris* leaf with later leaf forms in order to see certain parts and forms reappear. It would be wrong to draw a connecting line directly from a *Rhynia*-like telome plant to the modern plants of a higher stage of development. Natural history takes account of the total reality of intermediate forms, especially as even obvious detours in the course of development of nature must have had a logical basis.

Chacassopteris was discovered in 1960 in the USSR at Kuznetsk, Minusinsk and Tomsk. A new species reconstructed and called *Chacassopteris mongolica* in 1972 was brought back from Mongolia by an expedition from the German Democratic Republic. A brilliant reconstruction of a similar but already more advanced Upper Devonian plant *Rhacophyton* was published by H. N. Andrews of the University of Connecticut, USA, in 1968. The basis of this idea, however, is a reconstruction of the Upper Devonian *Cladoxylon scoparium* plant, made known by R. Kräusel and H. Weyland in 1926. At that time, only a fairly large fragment of this interesting species existed and this was lost during the Second World War. However, a piece of the counterpart still survives in the Museum for Natural History of the Humboldt University, Berlin. *Cladoxylon* and *Rhacophyton* had spores of one size (isospores), *Chacassopteris mongolica* had large and small sporangia and

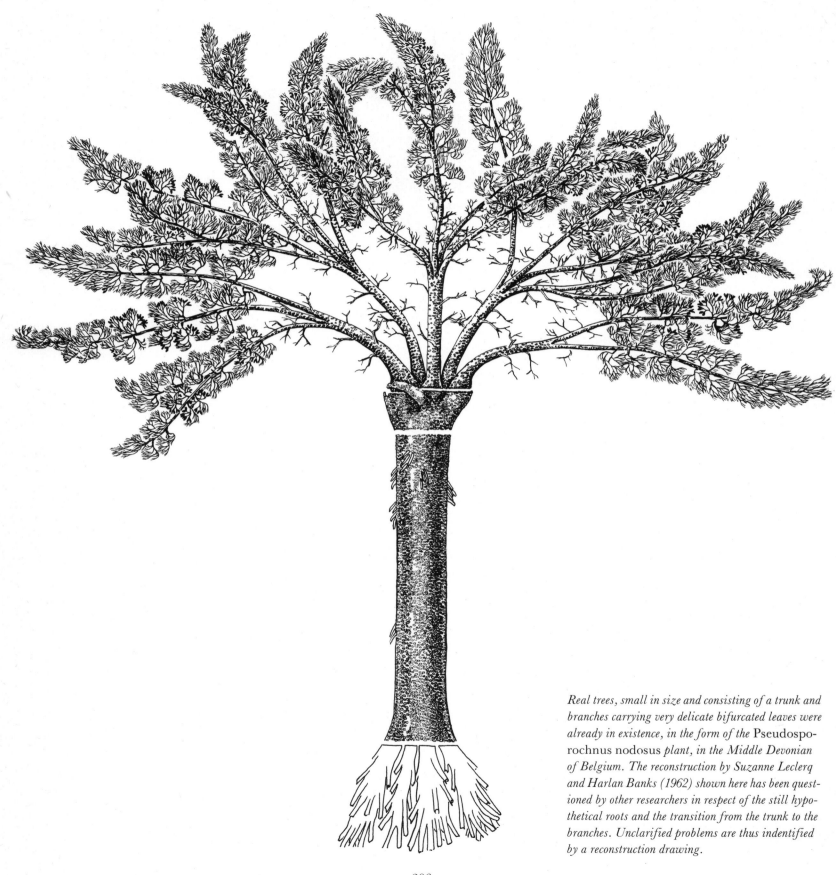

Real trees, small in size and consisting of a trunk and branches carrying very delicate bifurcated leaves were already in existence, in the form of the Pseudosporochnus nodosus *plant, in the Middle Devonian of Belgium. The reconstruction by Suzanne Leclerq and Harlan Banks (1962) shown here has been questioned by other researchers in respect of the still hypothetical roots and the transition from the trunk to the branches. Unclarified problems are thus indentified by a reconstruction drawing.*

probably large and small spores (micro- and megaspores).

When we examine a plant from earlier times such as *Chacassopteris* or *Cladoxylon*, it is clear that our attention is concentrated only on certain specific aspects which appear important to us. This is reasonable enough since we are always seeking an answer to a very specific question: in this case that of the origin of the leaf in the Devonian and Carboniferous periods. In the quest for knowledge, human understanding seeks possible generalizations and establishes a link between very many individual phenomena by stripping them of the coincidences which obscure it. As a result, abstract concepts are formed and accordingly also stripped mental images. The disadvantage of this method is that it creates imaginable but at the same time historically unreal zero-value ancestors. Many primitive plant or primitive animal concepts have this failing.

Simply by the mental omission of structures and forms which once existed in then highly developed plants during the course of natural history, I do not automatically obtain the theoretically logical form, I do to automatically eliminate troublesome coincidences but presumably visualize an oversimplified mental model, of which Zimmermann's telome concept may possibly be an example.

To be sure, initial forms conceived in such a simple manner have the advantage that I can imagine their successors by the mere addition of developments. This manner of imagining basic models along the lines of Zimmermann's elementary process which in a few intermediate stages can be modified to models of later leaf, blossom, cone and stem structures, illustrate the historical course of development in a greatly simplified form of perception. However, this requires corrections by those which are known to have really existed. Examples such as *Chacassopteris* and *Cladoxylon* are fixed points by which such corrections can be made. In this respect, plants such as these really are missing links which we need for an understanding of nature, realities from which we can progress to further knowledge. Thus our train of thought and its correctness will be confirmed in proportion to the number of convincing examples of fossil plants.

The highest level of development at the time of the Upper Devonian was attained by the genus Archaeopteris. *Although its organs of assimilation (pinnae) were still very primitive and although it was reproduced by micro- and megaspores*, Archaeopteris *was a tall tree with a conifer-like wood (sketch reconstruction after C. B. Beck 1962).*

A Deviation from the Established Path of Development

It is now apparent that the course of natural history led, on a path marked by antitheses, from an ancient plant-axis to a less ancient and therefore more highly developed plant-axis and we could also speak of experiment and error in this connection. Whereas the simple and rapid historical path would certainly proceed from a round protestele (as *Rhynia, Psilophyton*) to the eustele (as *Archaeopteris* and later trunks of conifers and angiosperms), the Devonian and Lower Carboniferous plant axes found frequently contain parts and segments of hard tissue in the outer cortex. Perhaps this strengthening tissue (sclerenchyma) in the stem and axes of the plants of that time was a necessary concomitant phenomenon for the growth in circumference.

Asteroxylon displays a star-shaped cross-section of the central strand starting at outer corner-points (protoxylems). What was outside in the cortex remained outside—separate black points—not leaf-conducting strands in the present sense!

Pietzschia displays radii of water-conducting cells (xylems) with wedges of strengthening tissue between them. Protosteles are separated towards the inside, towards the pith and not to the outside. It is as if the course of development had first taken a completely opposite direction: no strands leading to the outside, only branch bifurcations separated towards the inside and thus leading upwards. The original picture of the stem cross-section does not apparently correspond to the subsequent result.

Thus the descendants of the early land plants were initially condemned to bearing no leaves but only weak appendanges, the hairs and the spines which looked more like outgrowths of the epidermis than the later leaves.

It was only when the determination of the axis correlated with the determination of such originally algae-like thalloid outgrowths that a new form emerged—such as the *Chacassopteris* leaf. When the never-ending potency of axial growth was united with this form, the leaf-frond grew and an overtopping programme reproduced the initial small bifurcation as a geometrical form.

The real message is that for 50 million years (Middle Devonian, Upper Devonian, Lower Carboniferous) there was no question of a leaf in the later sense and in particular no possibility of a leaf with a network vein system. Indeed, it was a long path in the history of nature, a path beset with many detours, without which a vein network would never have materialized.

To begin with, the most highly developed forms in the Lower and Upper Carboniferous periods were the seed-ferns. Fern-like in external appearance but neither fern-like nor phanerogam-like in their stem-anatomy, these plants of the Carboniferous period had seeds on their leaves! But these leaves were bifurcated fronds and thus, once again, were not really what we think of as leaves and the seeds were really only ovules in which the female large spore developed the prothallus and waited for fertilization by sperms or the pollen tube of the small male spore (pollen). And these ovules did not generally grow directly on the leaf either: the bifurcated frond had a small axial system in its fork with numerous ovules or cupules on which these were located. Once again, therefore, everything was quite different and, above all, of a much more complicated arrangement to that which came later.

Was such a complicated mosaic really the predecessor of such simple things as the leaves and blossoms of the present day?

A cross-section is shown here (s. Fig. on p. 140) of the stem of the best-known seed-fern *Lyginopteris oldhamia* from the Upper Carboniferous (Westphalian A) of Rhineland-Westphalia (Federal Republic of Germany). The exceptionally fine state of preservation of a thin section from a calcareous nodule now proves valuable. On the outside, there is a series of strips of cortical tissue, seen as an anatomizing mesh in tangential longitudinal section. On the inside, there is a wood body and a very much larger area of pith which, in its dark colouration, shows the thick-walled cell-groups of nests of sclerotic cells. It is as if the thick radial plates of the *Pietzschia* had now been banned to the inner part of the stem

An Archaeopteris *species* (A. halliana) *with pinnae forming a surface and with fertile forked leaves (according to Phillips, Andrews and Gensel 1972).*

where they no longer have any apparent function. Was this not the location of the protostele cross-sections at an earlier date? At any rate, the wood (xylem) in cross-section presents a modern appearance and is formed from the inside outwards (centrifugally and only to a very slight extent still in a centripetal manner) as is appropriate for a stem growing in thickness.

However, this is not the only cross-section of the stem of a seed-fern. The illustration on p. 23 shows a lower Permian silicified seed-fern cross-section from Karl-Marx-Stadt: *Medullosa stellata*. In the large area of pith, there are still real steles of water-bearing cells instead of the dark strands mentioned in *Lyginopteris*. The starting points of the fronds are also known from these stems. The fronds are fed by a large number of individual strands, recognizable as concentric conducting bundles in basic cell tissue. In the stem, these xylem strands still display growth, as if they were subject to different laws in the stem than on the outside.

Strange Fruits

In comparison with the present day, the pollen organs of the Carboniferous seed-ferns also seem as strange and alien as the stem-structures. At first sight, the Telome theory, which emphasizes the basic importance of simple but fertile axial ends, appears to be correct in respect of these organs. In the Upper Carboniferous, there are essentially two types of pollen organs: a beaker-like assembly of fertile telomes, known as *Whittleseya* and consisting of long, pollen-filled tubes, and a brush-shaped assembly, known as *Potoniea*.

The beaker-shaped *Whittleseya* pollen organs grew to several centimetres in size and have always been found with a certain type of *Neuropteris* leaf, regarded as the progressive ones, and nowhere else. It is a different matter with the brush-shaped *Potoniea* pollen organs, which are also measured in centimetres; these belong to the Pteridosperms which had almost the same pinnae as *Neuropteris* but are said to have a series of backward features. Perhaps the mere fact of the possession of *Potoniea* brush-

Baragwanathia longifolia

The long, thin leaves can be clearly seen with round sporangia near the bases. Were these located on the upper side of the leaf in the manner of the later club-moss plants (lycopods) or were there also other possibilities? At any event, this plant from the Australian Lower Devonian is one of the most ancient of land plants and yet its form is not of primitive simplicity. H. Jaeger found this specimen in 1967 at Wilson's Creek shale (Victoria) in the Monograptus thomasi *Zone which, according to his investigations, belongs to the lowest Lower Devonian but not to the Upper Silurian, as assumed by several workers in the past. Magnification: 2×*

Calathiops bernhardti

Calathiops bernhardti *from the lower Upper Carboniferous (Namurian B) of Vorhalle near Hagen (Federal Republic of Germany) is a supposed fruit of the seed-fern* Mariopteris acuta *and consists of leaf-tips, drawn together and concealing ovules on the inside. Magnification: 2×*

Credneria triacuminata

Leaves of the platanoid type dominate in Upper Cretaceous sandstone of Quedlinburg (German Democratic Republic).

Weichselia reticulata

The ochre-coloured pinna-impressions of the Lower Cretaceous Weichselia reticulata *stand out against the light sandstone of an Ice Age erratic found near Rostock (German Democratic Republic). The pinnae point diagonally upwards in the butterfly position. Of even greater interest, however, is the other side of the rock. Parallel axes are marked with tubercles in a net-work pattern. These are sporocarps, aggregations of sporangia in spheroid clumps, something like the stamens in a yew-tree blossom or the sporangiophores in a horsetail. This find was studied and described by A. G. Nathorst in 1890.*

Metasequoia occidentalis

Metasequoia *was a fossil conifer genus discovered for the first time in 1941 by S. Miki in Japan. A few years later, this fossil conifer genus was discovered still alive in Szechuan in Southern China. The modern* Metasequoia glyptostroboides *illustrated here was described in 1948 and has subsequently become established in the parks and gardens of Europe, too. Fossil cones with their characteristically long stalks are known from Canada and the Western USA, from Japan and the USSR. No fossil evidence has been found in Europe so far. It is probable that it was in the Upper Cretaceous and Tertiary periods that Meta-sequoia colonized the coastal area of the North Pacific in particular.*

The fossil cone shown was found in the course of the palaeobotanical excursion through British Columbia (Canada) of the 9th International Botanical Congress (1959) in the Oligocene of Lamont Creek near Princeton. The remains of fossil needles come from the top layer of the Cretaceous period (Maastricht) and were found near the mouth of the Amur in the USSR.

Acer tricuspidatum

Upper Miocene of Salzhausen near Nidda at the Vogelsberg (Federal Republic of Germany).
This Tertiary maple species described by Bronn in 1838 is found in the foliated coal (Dysodil) of Salzhausen, the type-locality, in unusual quantities and in a very good state of preservation. Finds such as this have to be compared with present-day species.

Cycadeoidea reichenbachiana

The surface of the totally silicified stem of the Lower Cretaceous bennettite displays a few large oval holes which were once the attachment points of fronds and between them, arranged in a circular pattern, numerous small oval holes or depressions—buds!

In a ground section taken from a few centimetres lower, these buds, consisting of individual leaves, can clearly be identified. This is original material used for a paper by G. R. Wieland (New Haven, USA), who studied the bennettite stem of Dresden between 1924 and 1934.

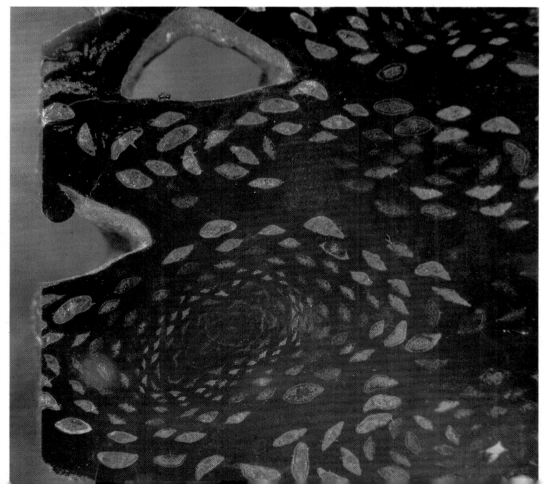

Cycadeoidea reichenbachiana

G.R. Wieland also produced longitudinal sections through the female central part of the flower. This is still protectively enclosed by the smaller leaves (bracts) around it but in this case the pollen-bearing organs cannot be identified. Did these flowers open for wind-pollination?

Other recessed flowers on the same bennettite stem certainly displayed pollen organs around the central part of the flower; in the picture—a thin section—the axes of the male sporophylls are cut longitudinally. Therefore this stem also produced hermaphrodites. Whether these opened or were self-fertilizing in the closed state is a subject which is once again being dicussed by North American researchers such as Dele-voryas (1968) and W.L. Crepet (1972). Our colour plate (bottom) shows a thin section which was studied by H.R. Goeppert (1853) and G.R. Wieland (1934) and has inspired flower reconstructions such as that shown in the illustration in the text on page 120. Wieland counted 9 of a total of 16 stamens in this thin section.

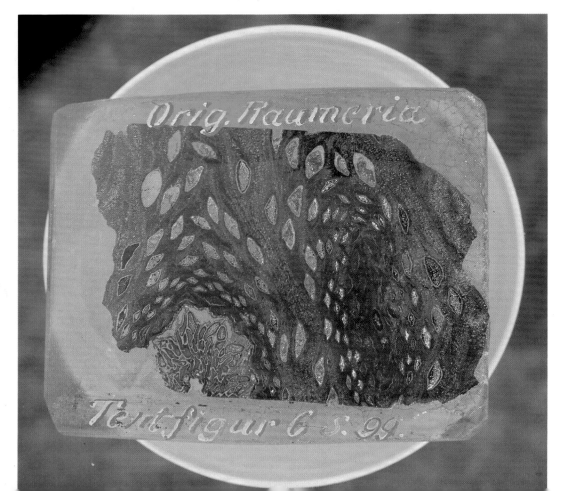

Cycadeoidea reichenbachiana

The multiplicity of buds on the Cycadeoidea *stem is an interesting problem. G. R. Wieland gave numbers to the many flowers between the few large frond cross-sections. The cauliflorous characteristic would now be interpreted as a feature of a very balanced and warm climate, the mass of flowers, however, as a specialization, a phylogenetic terminal development.*

Pietzschia schülleri

Thin section of the stem of this Upper Devonian missing-link plant (see pp. 136/137).

Page 216:

Neuropteris attenuata

Site: Piesberg near Osnabrück (Federal Republic of Germany).
Silvery-white leaf remains. The plant remains received a covering of gümbelite or were completely transformed into the silvery-white clay mineral.
Magnification: 2×

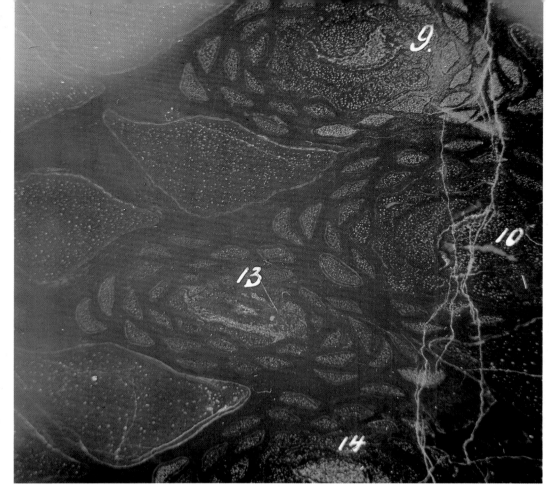

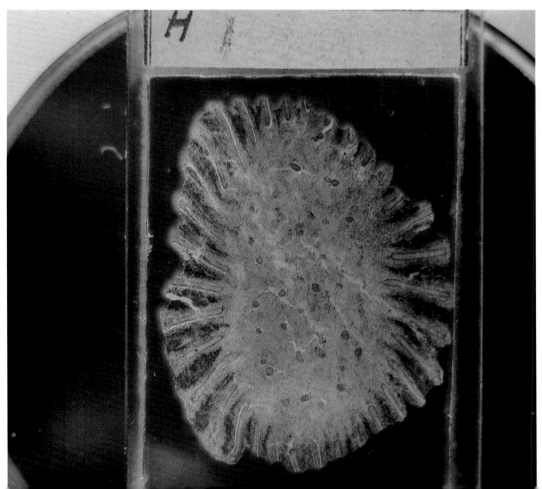

The transformation (higher development) of a certain leaf-form in the course of millions of years:

1 a—d *The varying axial appendages (forked leaf) of* Chacassopteris mongolica *from the Lower Carboniferous of East Asia. Similar leaf forms are displayed by* Cladoxylon *(Middle Devonian) and* Pseudosporochnus *(Middle Devonian).*

2 *During the Upper Devonian period, a strange forked leaf developed from the simple leaf form, here in* Rhacophyton zygopteroides *(according to S. Leclerq 1950), partly fertile, partly sterile.*

3 *The forked leaf shapes predominate in the ferns and seed-ferns of the Lower and Upper Carboniferous and appear with a notably high level of development.*

   a Anisopteris paniculata *(Lower Carboniferous) fern*
   b Odontopteris minor *(Upper Carboniferous and Lower Permian) seed-fern*
   c Diplopteridium affine *(Lower Carboniferous) seed-fern*

4 *The forked frond leaves have changed into the leaves and petals of the present day but sometimes the ancient and intrinsic forked leaf shape appears once again:*
   a Ginkgo *leaf of the present day, in this case abnormally developed with two ovules*
   b *the antler-shaped leaves of the* Platycerium *fern*
   c *the appendage on the front crown-leaf of* Polygala

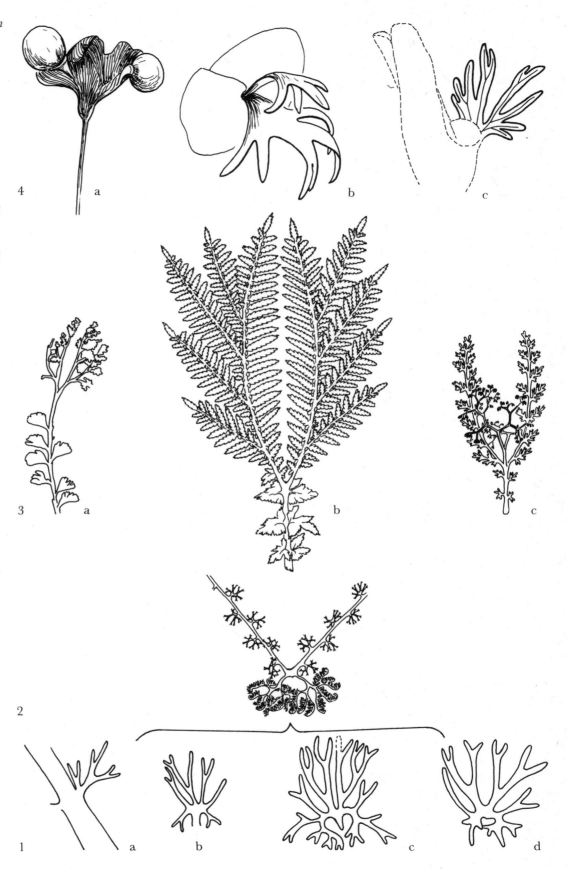

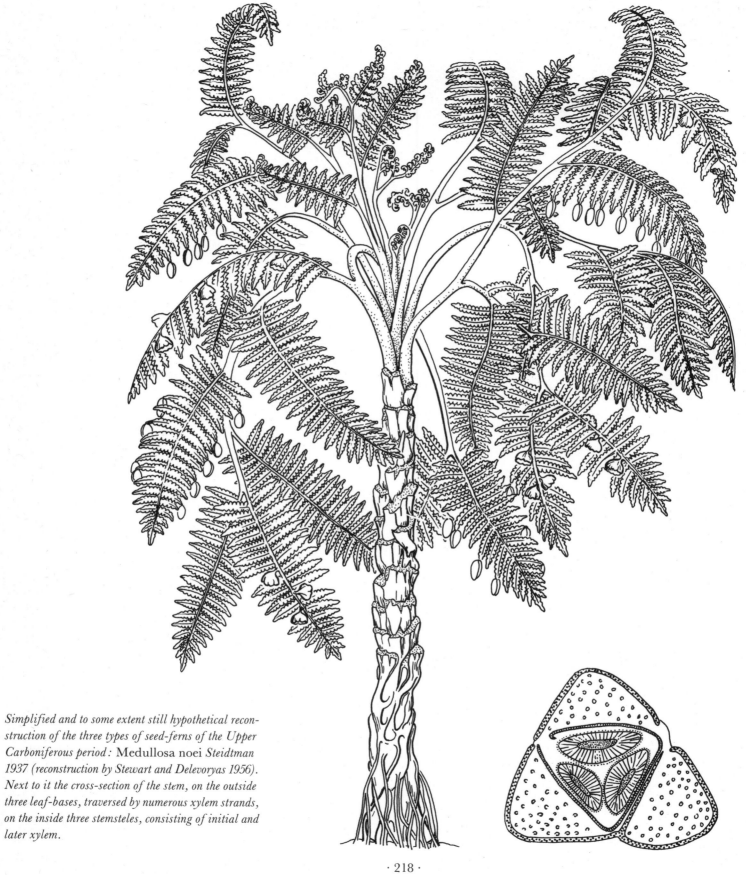

Simplified and to some extent still hypothetical reconstruction of the three types of seed-ferns of the Upper Carboniferous period: Medullosa noei Steidtman 1937 (reconstruction by Stewart and Delevoryas 1956). Next to it the cross-section of the stem, on the outside three leaf-bases, traversed by numerous xylem strands, on the inside three stemsteles, consisting of initial and later xylem.

organs is to be assessed as more primitive than that of the *Whittleseya* beaker. The same applies to the pollen contents: the pollen of the *Potoniea* is held to be more primitive and more fern-like while the *Whittleseya* is considered to be more differentiated.

The progressive features of the leaf-frond are considered to be its bifurcated form (typical of *Neuropteris*, *Odontopteris* and other genera), the large or small and always clearly defined end-pinnae, the central vein present in the pinna and in general the straightness of the frond axis (rachis). A whole series of previously unusual features now appear as backward in the other *Neuropteris* with *Potoniea*. Instead of a single leaflet at the end, there are two leaflets, like a swallowtail, at the end of each piece of frond. The rachis of the frond, especially at the tip, swings to and fro, as if it did not know whether it should be a principal axis or a side part. The axis of the frond finally forks towards the tip. The axial parts of the frond, which as the principal axis do not have any pinnae in the case of the former, are now suddenly covered with pinnae (leaflets) as if there are now equal rights also for the principal and secondary axes in the frond.

These additional pinnae have been called intercalated pinnae since otherwise they are seldom found and obviously represent a special problem, an additional interprosed programme at the frond.

The First Network Vein System

The paired end-leaflets and the intercalated pinnae were reason enough to give this genus the special name of *Paripteris*. Finally, there are two other features: the thinness or the total absence of the centre vein and a marked tendency for the individual leaflets to drop off. In almost all cases, the leaflets of the genus *Paripteris* and the genus *Linopteris* which succeeded it are found as individual examples in the Carboniferous strata (Namurian B–C and Westphalian A–D). Entire strata are often full of them.

It is not really suprising that the seed-ferns of the Upper Carboniferous period included one group with only progressive features and

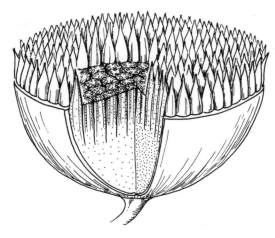

Strange microsporangia are a feature of the seed-ferns whose leaves are designated as Paripteris *and* Linopteris. *These brush-like forms, 1–2 cm in size, were once called* Potoniéa *after the Berlin palaeobotanist Prof. H. Pontonié (1857–1913) but 80 years after the bestowal of this name (1899) the reconstruction of the inner structure of this pollen-bearing organ is still disputed. Our illustration is based on the reconstruction by B. M. Stidd (1978).*

another with a host of non-progressive characteristics. At that time, 315 million years ago, with the beginning of the Westphalian-A stage, a significant advance took place in the plant world: the most highly developed plants, the seed-ferns, developed a network vein-system in the leaves. As a result, these leaves became stronger and less easily damaged and if a part of the leaflet dried out or was torn, the veins with the many connections between them still continued to feed the other parts of the leaflet. This was consequently an important development since nowadays all the leaves of advanced plants have a network vein-system, the few exceptions can be counted and include *Ginkgo*.

There seems to be a strange law in the course of the history of nature that assigns an advance in development not to the most highly differentiated examples but to a point of departure which is not so highly developed. It is known that Early Man is not descended from the highly developed anthropoid apes, that the primates are more likely to have come from the insect-eaters of the Old Tertiary than from highly developed mammals, and so on. In 1904, an American palaeontologist designated this as a law of development and since this time it has been known as Cope's Law. In our case, too, it is apparent that the network vein-system appeared in the genus which was less progressive at the time, as if its realization necessitated a detour.

What could have been the factors that enabled *Paripteris gigantea*, which was widespread at the time of the Upper Namurian and the Lower Westphalian, to achieve the transition to *Linopteris neuropteroides*, a plant of Westphalian A to D? At first we look at the sructural factors. The frond axis of *Paripteris* swings to and fro and ultimately forks at the end. We regarded this as a step backwards to the ancient, conventional transitional form. However, such a determination in the growth programme of the plant, when transferred to the course of the vein system as well, necessarily created a favourable preliminary condition for vein connections (anastomoses). In actual fact, it is known that *Neuropteris obliqua*, a widespread plant of the Upper Carboniferous period, has such adjacent leaf-veins. It

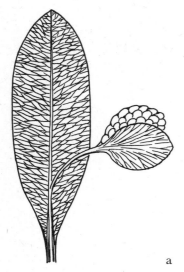

a

d

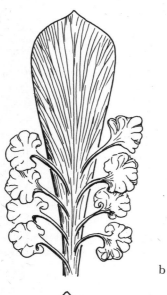

b

Original forms from the Permian period as petals of present-day angiosperms?

a *In 1952 Mrs E.P. Plumstead introduced the experts to Permian* Glossopteris leaves, *from the leaf stalk of which there sprouted a two-valve organ with ovules. K.R. Surange and Shaila Chandra (1974), whose reconstruction is shown here, demonstrated that this was not a question of a bisexual flower. The organ known as a scutum on the* Glossopteris *leaf consists of a round part with ovules and a sterile valve which for a long time covered the ovules.*

b *Known since 1958 and explained by K.R. Surange and Shaila Chandra in 1974,* Lidgettonia *is also a seed-bearing* Glossopteris *leaf; however, up to 8 special organs grew out of the base of the leaf and, in turn, carried the small seeds at the edge.*

c *In 1974, K.R. Surange and Shaila Chandra showed* Glossopteris *leaves from Orissa with a number of forked stamens:* Glossotheca orissiana.

d *Whorled* Glossopteris *leaves have already been found on several occasions. From* Glossopteris *finds in Australia, M.E. White considers that she has found transitional forms between bud-scales and* Glossopteris *petals (1978)—nevertheless it still took a hundred million years for the angiosperm flower to arrive.*

e

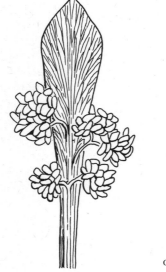

c

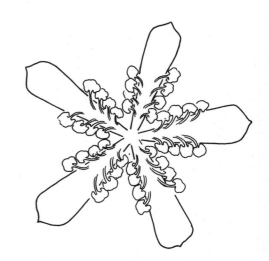

f

represents a transitional species, leading to a species with a network vein-system.

Thus the non-progressive features listed in connection with *Paripteris* could have been a concomitant factor, causing a feature which was quite certainly not progressive to develop in such a manner that it affected the leaflet vein system and produced something which was completely new and of a substantially higher level of development.

Now it may have been that these non-progressive features in *Paripteris* did not appear by chance at this time. There had been no intercalated leaflets since the time of the Upper Devonian, i. e., for about 30 million years. Perhaps the formation of the great Variscan mountain range and in its shadow the formation of the vast depressions, inland basins and wooded moor areas was another factor influencing the development of plant structure in a certain direction in the history of the Earth. The highly developed plants of that time had just grown out of an existence restricted to humid conditions. The Lower Carboniferous period had produced the first seed-ferns with fan-like and pinnate leaves. Entire areas of land together with their vegetation were now put back in the moor stage, geotectonically condemned in the history of the Earth to the formation of coal. Giant club moss trees *(Lepidodendron, Sigillaria)* and giant horsetails *(Calamites)* proliferated, spreading over wide areas, and developed into strange genera and species with a high level of development corresponding to their form of existence. In this environment, progress, which is probably always a mosaic of progressive and non-progressive characteristics, had to do without, for the time being, developments which would have led out of the moist world and perhaps even had to reactivate and utilize features from the past. This was the origin of this strange mosaic of features which was so favourable for the development of a highest stage as a point of departure: the zigzag vein system and the network vein system.

Once it had come into existence, it became a necessity for the other pteridosperms as well; the advantage of selection had an alagning influence and, after all, every frond had essentially resulted from overtopping.

This possibility was latent in every pteridosperm and indeed, in every fern. Other pteridosperm genera rapidly followed in the implementation of this network vein system: *Alethopteris* developed *Lonchopteris*, *Neuropteris* developed *Reticulopteris*. The ferns, however, as spore producers and possessors of complicated sporangia, were concerned with their existence as ferns: it was only 100 million years later that they developed vein networks in their leaves. Even the seed-ferns with network vein systems, which they had developed in a variety of forms in the course of 50 million years disappeared again in the Permian period. To be sure, they passed on the possibility but not the constant necessity of forming a vein network system.

In the Rhaeto-Liassic period, the *Sagenopteris* leaf with its worldwide distribution had a network vein system and continued this phenomenon up to the Cretaceous period. A few of the special bennettitalean genera form vein networks but the presentday *Cycas* species do not. For the angiosperms and their origin in the upper Lower Cretaceous period, however, the network vein system was an absolute necessity. What remains for us is the awareness of the complicated constellation attending the onset of this development.

A Great New Mystery—the *Glossopteris* Plant

From the great continent of Gondwanaland, comprising what are now Africa, India, Australia, Antarctica and South America, are known tongue-shaped leaves, initially still with a fan-type vein system and then with a central vein and a network vein system, characterized by a small shoot with male or female reproductive organs in the middle of the central vein. The leaves are common but their axes, roots and flowering shoots are rare. To find *Glossopteris* leaves with fructification attached has been the ambition of many palaeobotanists in South Africa, India, Australia and South America for two decades.

Once again, this is obviously a question of a missing link plant of the remote past. Whereas, in the case of the forked fronds of the Carboniferous period, the bud for a shoot with ovule

or pollen sacs was formed in the fork, it was formed here in the middle of the leaf, emerging at the principal vein. Sometimes there are also bifurcated shoots, recalling a forked frond form of the Carboniferous period. This still does not correspond to our idea of a modern leaf which is either a leaf with a bud in its axis or emerges from the axis bud as a shoot with flower or flowers. The axis cannot therefore be a leaf and, in particular, an axis cannot be situated on a leaf-form. In the past, however, 250 million years ago, this was obviously the case. Does this mean that our present views of the modern leaf are incorrect? The telome theory did not consider this question. Its point of departure was the demonstration of end-pieces and their connection and an answer was certainly obtained, but not to the question of the origin of the leaf and the flower.

This was why, in the 1950's, botanists and palaeobotanists began to compare the fertile *Glossopteris* leaf with certain modern leaf-forms. They thought of the leaf-like papery bract of the lime where the flower is located, but which can only be regarded as being leaf-like in form. Finally, attention turned to forms which were known in the poplar flower and in Australian Euphorbiaceae. In these examples, a flat form with an axis was always combined with an ovule or pollen threads. Could it be perhaps that the *Glossopteris* leaf of the Permian period could be identified once more in these forms?

In the early 1960's, R. Melville (Royal Botanic Gardens, Kew, England) evolved a new theory of the angiosperm flower on the basis of these thoughts, concept and fossil evidence and illustrated these ideas with schematic drawings. The basic hypothesis of this theory is that the angiosperms can be seen as originating directly from *Glossopteris* of the Permian period and that the original organ for the leaf of the higher plants is to be found in an organ which, at the time of the Permo–Carboniferous, was partly leaf and partly fertile axial organ. Such an organ could be called a gonophyll. In a certain sense, this theory assumes that the flowering organs and leaves of the higher plants (angiosperms) both originate from a hypothetical organ which was both assimilating and fertile at the same time. R. Melville sketched this organ in only a few strokes of the pen to avoid conveying too definite an impression of it. His diagrams are only intented to indicate that there were such mixed organs during the Devonian and Carboniferous periods and that the *Glossopteris* organ was a subsequent form from the Permian period which really existed. This evidence must be accepted from the viewpoint of Devonian-Carboniferous palaeobotany.

Of course, with this state of affairs, there is an obvious interest in taking a look at the club moss plants (Lycopods) in which there has always been, since their earliest existence in the Devonian, a combination of a leaf-like organ and a sporangium growing on it. The objection made to the gonophyll concept is that it sees angiosperms coming, as it were, from the club moss plants and does not represent the direct path from the psilophyte telome to the angiosperm ovaries. In our opinion, there is no objection to such logical reasons as the straight and direct path of development unless it is proved that it has not been taken.

It would have been logical for the psilophytes in the shape of *Rhynia* to have become heterosporous and ultimately angiospermous by the shortest route by the time of the Lower Carboniferous at the latest. Since this, in the course of the process of natural history in question, took place in a much more protracted and complicated manner, however, we must also take account of this in the elaboration of our theory. Thus the gonophyll is to be seen as an intermediate stage which can be proved to have actually existed after the time of the simple telomes and their connection potential. Both the leaf of the Cladoxyleae and the Pteridosperm leaf and, finally, the leaf of the *Glossopteris* plant are to be regarded as examples of the gonophyll.

The first finds of fertile *Glossopteris* leaves and the related statements by Mrs E. Plumstead, Johannesburg (Transvaal) in 1952, were the subject of lively discussion in which such well-known botanists and palaeobotanists as H. Thomas (Cambridge, England), T. M. Harris (Reading, England), J. Walton (Glasgow, Scotland), S. H. Mamay (Washington, USA), W. J. Jongmans (Heerlen, Holland) and Kräusel (Frankfort/Main, Federal Republic of Germany) took part. Further finds and statements by Plumstead soon followed (1965) relating to the considerably older *Gangamopteris* leaf displaying only a fan-like vein system and on which she had found a fructification known since 1902 by the name of *Ottokaria*. These finds demonstrated

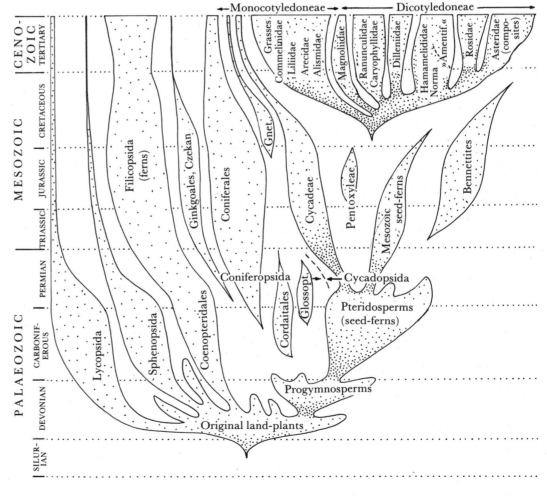

The advance in the development of the land plants in the course of the last four hundred million years appears as a differentiated process with contradictory currents, with rapid advances on the one hand (the early land plants, progymnosperms, seed-ferns, angiosperms) and conservative further development on the other (lycopods, sphenopsids (horsetails), ferns). (according to J. A. Doyle 1977)

the existence of a fairly large group of Permo-Carboniferous plants in the Southern Hemisphere which, by reason of their widespread dissemination there, their long life and their variety of forms, must have been of importance for the evolution of plants which subsequently took place. This work, too, was followed by an international discussion in which H.J.Lam (Ryksherbarium Leiden, Holland) described the Glossoperidales as a new order, put them as a whole on the same rank as the Pteridospermales and described them as an important transitional link in the line of descent to the angiosperms. He thus agreed with the views of Plumstead and confirmed them by the preparation of a diagrammatic phylum of his own.

Without doubt, however, it was only the finds of the following years, published between 1973 and 1975 by the Indian palaeobotanists K.R.Surange and S.Chandra (Birbal Sahni Institute, Lucknow, India) which rounded off these finds and discussions. Whereas Plumstead still assumed that the *Glossopteris* flower in the case of the *Scutum* genus had a flap with female seed-organs and a counter-flap with male (pollen) organs, the Indian palaeobotanists found only exclusively male or exclusively female leaves. In the leaf finds displaying an organ with ovules, it is possible to identify

two groups of these permogymnosperms of the Southern Hemisphere:

1. Cupule-bearers which should also be described as Permian pteridosperms of the Southern Hemisphere (with the genera *Lidgettonia*, *Denkania* and *Partha*).
2. Multi-ovulates which are so unlike known recent and fossil gymnosperms that they should be regarded as a separate order of plants (*Scutum*, *Dictyopteridium*, *Senotheca* and *Ottokaria*).

The Indian palaeobotanists took the view that although the first group should be regarded as pteridosperms they did not display any similarities with the Carboniferous Lyginopteridaceae and Medullosaceae of the Northern Hemisphere and were closer to the Mesozoic Corystospermaceae and Peltaspermaceae, which include genera such as *Dicroidum*, *Sagenopteris* and others.

They are of the opinion, however, that the second group, the multi-ovulates, cannot be compared at all with known fossil and recent gymnosperms. Naked ovules on this organ growing from the central vein of the *Glossopteris* signify naked seeds without a megasporophyll. They affirmed that such an arrangement was known only from a few isolated Indian plants of the Jurassic period—*Rajmahalia paradoxa* and *Carnoconites* (Pentoxylae).

Only this group should be designated as belonging to the order of Glossopteridales.

Thus some of the fundamental questions appear to have been clarified and, at the same time, other fundamental questions seem to be even less clear than before. Dr.Melville endeavoured to open up new possibilities of comparison between *Gangamopteris* and *Glossopteris* leaves and the present-day angiosperms by a classification of the types of vein and vein network systems. A whole series of possibilities for comparison did indeed result from this but a period of some 100 million years remains a definite gap if the last *Glossopteris* leaf remains are regarded as disappearing at the Permian/Triassic boundary and the first angiosperms as appearing in the uppermost layer of the Lower Cretaceous. Nevertheless, the attempt to derive recent angiosperm families in a morphological-anatomical manner from *Gangamopteris* and *Glossopteris* is a worthwhile exercise, resembling the actual course of events in nature but certainly not a reconstruction of every detail in reality. Dr.Melville, in a letter to the author, stated that, on the basis of morphological features, he sees about 46 angiosperm families as being derived from *Gangamopteris* and about the same number from *Glossopteris*. Why shouldn't it have happened in more or less this way?

Glossary

Abduction of the hand

The folding of the wings necessitates an extreme flexion of the wrist to the side which is characteristic only of birds (angling).

Angiosperms

The covering of the ovules, as in pteridosperms and Bennettitales has been implemented several times in the history of the Earth but the formation of ovaries, characteristic of angiosperms, in correlation with double fertilization and angiosperm wood (with vessels) only happened some 120 million years ago.

Biostratigraphy

Description and relative age comparison of sedimentary rocks from the fossils they contain, the index-fossils being especially important in this connection.

Butte

Elevation left behind like an island by erosion in a strata landscape.

Conducting tissue (xylem, phloem, protoxylem, metaxylem)

The water-conducting tissue (xylem) consists of woody, dead and accordingly empty, extended cells (tracheids, in angiosperms vessels) but the sap-conducting tissue (phloem), on the other hand, consists of large, extended living cells which are rich in sap (sieve-cells in the higher plants). Conducting tissue of this kind developed only after the earliest land-plants came into existence. The small, initial xylem cell groups are called protoxylem while the xylem cells of normal size which then follow are known as metaxylem.

Descendence theory

As elaborated by Charles Darwin in particular. Contrary to earlier theories of the constancy of the species, it states that all living creatures have evolved in a natural manner from common ancestral forms.

Emergences

This term is used for growths on the epidermis such as hairs, spines, etc.; in palaeobotany with the early land plants which were still leafless, these superficial growths, some of which are of a very strange shape and without a conducting strand to supply them, are also to be observed. Presumably these growths, as an extension of the surface area, were of importance for the exchange of air and moisture (assimilation).

Erratics

Pieces of rock carried along by inland ice or glaciers and, with the melting of the ice, deposited in moraines.

Eucaryotes

Organisms whose cells have a cell nucleus—in contrast to procaryotes (bacteria and blue algae).

Fauna provincialism

Marked hostility of fauna provinces at many times in the history of the Earth. It is the opposite of the fauna cosmopolitanism of other periods with an homogeneous sea or land fauna.

Fossils

The physical remains, imprints and traces of life of creatures of past times. Remains once embedded in sediment can be transformed into fossils of various different states of preservation.

Gonophyll

A term from the theory of R. Melville who assumes that the predecessors of the present-day angiosperm leaves and petal were double organs at the time of the late Palaeozoic, forms which possessed not only leaf-areas but also axes with ovules or pollen-members. He considers that it was only the reduction of these double organs which led to present-day leaves on the one hand and ovaries on the other.

Holotype

That specimen which, with the erection of a species, was declared to be the nomenclatural type or which was the only one at the disposal of the author.

Immuration (biomuration)

When walled in by calcareous deposits in the process of growth (from bryozoa, oyster shells, etc.), it is possible for plant and animal remains of a highly perishable nature to survive in a moulded fossil form (= immuration); when this occured with organisms which were still alive at the time, this is termed biomuration.

Index-fossils

Fossils which are typical for the sedimentary rocks from certain sections of geological time and thus possess the character of time-markers.

Intercalary growth

Plant tissue capable of division (meristem, residual meristem) forms axial parts which are interposed such as internodal extension, leafstems or conifer needles. This is a growth which, it is assumed here, did not occur before the late Palaeozoic.

Lectotype

Specimen subsequently declared to be the nomenclatural type of a species. Before the type procedure was adopted, it frequently happened that when the erection of a species was based on more than one specimen no holotype was selected. The lectotype is then selected from the original syntypes.

Maceration

Chemical process for treating recent or fossil tissue (with particular reference to plant tissue here) and hence isolating various parts (individual cells, detachment of the cuticule).

Missing link

Darwin's theory of evolution drew attention to the intermediate forms connecting the great animal and plant classes. These were sometimes called missing links since they had to be imagined as they had not yet been identified in a fossil or recent form. Sometimes called connecting links, especially when they were found as living (e.g., oviparous mammals) or fossil (e.g., seed-ferns of the Carboniferous period) specimens.

Mosaic mode of evolution

In the evolution of organisms, the individual complexes of features are transformed at different rates and are relatively independent of each other—like the stones of a mosaic.

Ontogeny

Development of an individual form from the embryo to old age.

Petrifaction (Intuscrustation)

Mineral solutions fill plant-tissue in such a manner that the organic structures in the interior of the cell and even in the cell-walls are replaced by mineral substance.

Phylogeny

Evolutionary development of related groups of organisms.

Progymnosperms

Gymnospermous seed-plants have been in existence since the Lower Carboniferous period, as can be demonstrated by their ovules (see Pteridosperms). In the Upper Devonian, however, there emerged heterosporous pteridophytes which were so highly developed in certain features (e.g., in the structure of the wood) that the term ferns can no longer be applied to them as they already possess certain features of the gymnosperms. The term progymnosperms is used to characterize this stage of development which still requires further investigation.

Pteridosperms

Seed-ferns, the group of plants which have fern-like foliage but are gymnospermous, bearing seeds.

Sclerenchyma

Tissue areas whose cells have died and whose cell-walls have become greatly thickened and hardened and were found to a remarkably frequent extent in the axes and cortices of palaeozoic land plants. Hard tissue of this kind found in higher plants of the present time can mostly by identified as serving a particular purpose.

Sporangium

Organ (receptacle) within which spores are formed. A complicated opening mechanism for the sporangium developed in the ferns in particular. In the early land plants, the thick multicellular sporangial wall still lacked an organized opening mechanism.

Stele (protostele, polystele, eustele)

Derived from the Greek word for column, stele stands for the conducting bundle of the plant in its totality. The very simple and initial protostele consists only of a central xylem strand, a polystele of more than one stele and a eustele, found in conifers and dicotyledons, of a ring of conducting bundles. The stelar theory attempts to derive the various types of steles from each other in the history of evolution.

Stomata

They have existed since the time when the first plants appeared on land. They are always in the form of multi-cellular (two guard-cells which may be surrounded by several subsidiary cells) organs of the epidermis. The waxy cuticle on the epidermis provides a surface replica of the always very characteristic stomata.

Telome (mesome)

Derived from the Greek word for end, an axial terminal piece. The Telome theory of Zimmermann is based on the fundamental importance of the successive attachment of such terminal pieces which were initially of the same kind but later became different in the course of development. Mesome denotes the axial section which follows in each case.

Transgression

The advance of the sea across the mainland with a rising sea-level or a sinking land area. The reverse process is designated as regression.

Type

The standard, defined by publications, to which the name of a species or genus is bound. In the case of a species, a single specimen is designated as the nomenclatural holotype; in the case of a genus, one of its species.

Bibliography

Alvin, K.L., P.D.W.Bernard, W.G.Chaloner (editors); *Studies on Fossil Plants*. Published for the Linnean Society of London by Academic Press, 1968.

Andrews, H.N.Jr.: *Studies in Paleobotany*. New York, 1961.

Andrews, H.N.Jr.: *Index of Generic Names of Fossil Plants, 1820–1965. Geological Survey Bulletin 1300*, United States Government Printing Office, Washington, 1970.

Augusta, J. and Z.Burian: *Flugsaurier und Urvögel*. Prague, 1961.

Bakker, R.T.: "Dinosaur physiology and the origin of mammals" In: *Evolution*, 25. Lawrence, 1971.

Bakker, R.T.: "Dinosaur Renaissance." In: *Scientific American*. San Francisco, 1975.

Banks, H.P., S.Leclerq and F.M.Hueber: *Anatomy and Morphology of Psilophyton Dawsonii sp. n. from the late Lower Devonian of Quebec (Gaspé) and Ontario, Canada. Palaeontograpica Americana VIII, No. 48*. Ithaca, New York, U.S.A., 1975.

Barthel, K.W.: *Solnhofen*. Thun, 1978.

Baxter, R.W. and G.A.Leisman: "A Pennsylvanian Calamittean Cone with Elaterites triferens Spores." In: *American Journal of Botany*, Vol. 54, No. 6, July 1967.

Beer, G.R. de: *Archaeopteryx lithographica*. London, 1954.

Boll, E.: "Die Beyrichien der norddeutschen silurischen Gerölle." In: *Arch. Ver. Freunde Naturgesch. Meckl. 11*. Güstrow, 1857.

Brack-Hanes, S.D. and J.C.Vaughn: *Evidence of Paleozoic Chromosomes from Lycopod Microgametophytes. Science*, Vol 200, 1383–1385, 23rd June, 1978.

Buch, L. von: "Über die Silicification organischer Körper nebst einigen anderen Bemerkungen über wenig bekannte Versteinerungen." In: *Abhandlungen der Königlichen Akademie der Wissenschaften zu Berlin*. Berlin, 1831.

Chaloner, W.G. and M.E.Collinson: *Application of SEM to a Sigillarian impression Fossil. Review of Paleobotany and Palynology, 20; 85–101*. Amsterdam, 1975.

Crepet, W.L.: *Investigations of North American Cycadeoids: The reproductive Biology of Cycadeoidae. Palaeontographica B 148, 144–169*. Stuttgart, 1974.

Daber, R.: *Chacassopteris—a fossil intermediate form. The Palaeobotanist* 21, 1, 52–58. Lucknow, 1974.

Daber, R. and J.Helms: *Das grosse Fossilienbuch*. Leipzig, Jena, Berlin, 1978. Melsungen, Berlin, Basel, Vienna, 1978.

Dalman, J.W.: *Uppställning och Beskrifning af de i Sverige funne Terebratuliter*. Stockholm, 1828.

Dames, W.: "Über Archaeopteryx." In: *Paläontologische Abhandlungen*, 2. Berlin, 1884.

Delevoryas, T.: *The Medullosae-Structure and Relationships. Palaeontographica* B 97, 114 to 167. Stuttgart, 1955.

Delevoryas, T.: *Investigations of North American Cycadeoids: Structure, Ontogeny and Phylogenetic Considerations of Cones of Cycadeoidea. Palaeontographica* B 121, 122–133. Stuttgart, 1968.

Eggert, D.A. and D.D.Gaunt: *Phloem of Sphenophyllum, American Journal of Botany*, Vol. 60, No. 8, 755–770. Sept. 1973.

Emmrich, H.: *De Trilobitis. Dissertatio Petrefactologica*. Berlin, 1839.

Foster, A.S. and E.M.Gifford Jr.: *Comparative Morphology of Vascular Plants*. W.M.Freeman and Company, San Francisco, 1959, 1974.

Fraas, E.: *Der Petrefaktensammler*. Reprint. Stuttgart, Thun, Munich, 1977.

Good, C.W. and T.N.Taylor: *The Ontogeny of Carboniferous Articulates: The Apex of Spenophyllum. American Journal of Botany*, Vol. 59, No. 6, 617–626. July, 1972.

Good, C.W. and T.N.Taylor: *The Morphology and Systematic Position of Calamitean Elater-Bearing Spores. Geoscience and Man*, Vol. XI, 133–139. April 25, 1975.

Gothan, W. and H.Weyland: *Lehrbuch der Paläobotanik*. Akademieverlag. Berlin, 1964.

Grzimek, B.: "Entwicklungsgeschichte der Lebewesen." In: *Grzimeks Tierleben*. Zurich, 1971.

Halstead, L.B.: *The evolution and ecology of the Dinosaurs*. London, 1975.

Hamilton, R. and A.N.Insole: *Finding Fossils—a guide to good collecting sites*. Penguin Book Ltd., Harmondsworth, Middlesex, England, 1977.

Haubold, H.: "Die fossilen Saurierfährten." In: *Die Neue Brehm-Bücherei*, 479. Wittenberg, 1974.

Haubold, H. and O. Kuhn: "Lebensbilder und Evolution fossiler Saurier." In: *Die Neue Brehm-Bücherei*, 509. Wittenberg, 1977.

Hauff, B.: *Das Holzmadenbuch*. Öhringen, 1953.

Heberer, G. (editor): *Die Evolution der Organismen—Ergebnisse und Probleme der Abstammungslehre*. Vol. I. Stuttgart, 1967.

Heinroth, O.: "Die Flügel von Archaeopteryx." In: *Journal für Ornithologie*. Kassel, Leipzig, Berlin, 1923.

Hölder, H.: *Naturgeschichte des Lebens*. Berlin, Heidelberg, New York, 1968.

Hölder, H. and H. Steinhorst: *Lebendige Urwelt*. Stuttgart, 1964.

Hucke, K. and E. Voigt: *Einführung in die Geschiebeforschung*. Oldenzaal, 1967.

Huxley, T. H.: "On Hypsilophodon foxii, a new Dinosaurian from the Wealden of the Isle of Wight." In: *Quarterly Journal of the Geological Society*. London, 1869.

Jaeger, H., J. Helms and H.-H. Krueger: "Geschiebeforschung—die wissenschaftliche Bedeutung der Geschiebe." In: *Wissenschaftliche Zeitschrift der Humboldt-Universität Berlin, Mathematisch-Naturwissenschaftliche Reihe*, XIX. Berlin, 1970.

Klöden, K. F.: *Die Versteinerungen der Mark Brandenburg*. Berlin, 1834.

Krause, A.: "Die Fauna der sog. Beyrichien- oder Choneten-Kalke des norddeutschen Diluviums." In: *Z. deutsch. geol. Ges.* 29. Berlin, 1877.

Kräusel, R.: *Die paläobotanischen Untersuchungsmethoden*. Jena, 1950.

Krebs, B.: "Die Archosaurier." In: *Die Naturwissenschaften*, 61. Berlin, Heidelberg, New York, 1974.

Krumbiegel, G.: "Tiere und Pflanzen der Vorzeit." In: *Akzent*, 24. Leipzig, Jena, Berlin, 1977.

Krumbiegel, G. and H. Walther: *Fossilien*. Leipzig, 1977.

Laveine, J. P.: *Sporomorphe in situ de quelques Parispermées (Neuroptéridées) du Carbonifère*. Annales de la Soc. Geologique de Nord, XCI, 2, 155–173. Lille, 1971.

Leclercq, S. and H. P. Banks: *Pseudosporochnus nodosus sp. nov., a Middle Devonian Plant with Cladoxylacean Affinities*. Palaeontographica, B 110, 1–34. Stuttgart, 1962.

Lehmann, U.: *Ammoniten*. Stuttgart, 1976.

Leich, H.: *Nach Millionen Jahren ans Licht*. Thun, 1968.

Lomax, J.: *Recent Investigations on Plants of the Coal Measures*. Transactions of the Manchester Geological Society, Vol. XXVI, Part IX, 237–262. 1898–99.

Macgregor, M. and J. Walton: *The Story of the Fossil Grove*. City of Glasgow Public Parks and Botany Gardens Department, City Chambers, Glasgow, 1948, 1955.

Mägdefrau, K.: *Paläobiologie der Pflanzen*, 4th edition. Jena, 1968.

Mägdefrau, K.: *Geschichte der Botanik—Leben und Leistung großer Forscher*. Stuttgart, 1973.

Martinsson, A.: "Palaeocope Ostracodes from the Well Leba I in Pomerania." In: *Geologiska Föreningen i Stockholm Förhandlingar*, 86. Stockholm, 1964.

Martinsson, A.: "Palaeocope Ostracodes." In: *The Silurian-Devonian Boundary*. Stuttgart, 1977.

Melville, R.: *Links between the Glossopteridae and the Angiosperms*. Second Gondwana Symposium South Africa 1970, 585–588. Pretoria, 1970.

Müller, A. H.: *Aus Jahrmillionen*. Jena, 1962.

Mundlos, R.: *Wunderwelt im Stein*. Gütersloh, Berlin, 1976.

Orlov, J. A.: *V mire drevnich životnich*. Moscow, 1968.

Ostrom, J. H.: "Archaeopteryx and the origin of birds." In: *Biological Journal of the Linnean Society*, 8. London, 1976.

Ostrom, J. H.: "The Osteology of Compsognathus longipes WAGNER." In: *Zitteliana*, 4. Munich, 1978.

Owen, E.: *Prehistoric Animals*. London, 1975.

Phillips, T. L., H. N. Andrews and P. G. Gensel: *Two heterosporous Species of Archaeopteris from the Upper Devonian of West Virginia*. Palaeontographica, B 139, 47–71. Stuttgart, 1972.

Phillips, T. L., M. J. Avcin and D. Berggren: *Fossil Peat of the Illinois Basin—A Guide to the Study of Coal Balls of Pennsylvanian Age*. Illinois State Geological Survey, Educational Series 11. Urbana, Illinois 61801, 1976.

Pinna, G.: *Fossilien in Farbe*. Munich, 1976.

Rast, H.: *Aus dem Tagebuch der Erde*. Leipzig, Jena, Berlin, 1978.

Rau, R.: "Über den Flügel von Archaeopteryx." In: *Natur und Museum*, 99. Frankfurt (Main), 1969.

Remy, W. and R. Remy: *Die Floren des Erdaltertums*. Essen, 1977.

Rietschel, S.: "Archaeopteryx—Tod und Einbettung." In: *Natur und Museum*, 106. Frankfurt (Main), 1976.

Rothwell, G. W.: *Evidence of Pollen Tubes in Paleozoic Pteridosperms*. Science 175, 772–774. 1972.

Rudwick, M. J. S.: *The Meaning of Fossils—Episodes in the History of Palaeontology*. London, New York, 1972.

Sakisaka, M: "On the Seed-bearing Leaves of Ginkgo." In: *Japanese Journal of Botany* IV, 3, 219–235. Tokyo, 1929.

Schlotheim, E. F. von: *Beschreibung merkwürdiger Kräuter-Abdrücke und Pflanzen-Versteinerungen—Ein Beitrag zur Flora der Vorwelt*. Gotha, 1804.

Schlotheim, E. F. von: "Beiträge zur Naturgeschichte der Versteinerungen." In: Leonhard, C. C.: *Taschenbuch für die gesamte Mineralogie*. Frankfurt (Main), 1813.

Schlotheim, E. F. von: *Die Petrefactenkunde*. Gotha, 1820.

Schopf, J. M.: *Modes of Fossil Preservation*. Review of Palaeobotany and Palynology, 20, 27 to 53. Amsterdam, 1975.

Schrank, E.: "Calymeniden (Trilobita) aus silurischen Geschieben." In: *Berichte der Deutschen Gesellschaft für Geologische Wissenschaften*, A 15. Berlin, 1970.

Spinar, Z. V. and Z. Burian: *Life before Man*. London, 1972.

Steel, R.: "Die Dinosaurier." In: *Die Neue Brehm-Bücherei*, 432, Wittenberg, 1970.

Stephan, B.: *Zeigt das Berliner Exemplar des Urvogels die Ventral- oder die Dorsalseite von Schwanz und Flügeln? Ornithologische Jahresberichte*. Halberstadt, 1976.

Stephan, B.: "Urvögel." In: *Die Neue Brehm-Bücherei*, 465. Wittenberg, 1978.

Stidd, B. M: *An anatomically preserverd Potoniea with in Situ Spores from the Pennsylvanian of Illinois*. Amer. J. Bot. 65 (6), 677–683. 1978.

Streel, M., P. M. Bonamo and M. Fairon-Demaret (editors): *Advances in Paleozoic Botany*. Amsterdam, London, New York, 1972.

Surange, K. R. and S. Chandra: *Fructifications of Glossopteridae from India*. The Palaeobotanist 21, 1, 1–17, Lucknow, 1974.

Surange, K. R. and S. Chandra: *Lidgettonia mucronata sp. nov. a female Fructification from the Lower Gondwana of India. The Palaeobotanist* 21, 1, 121–126. Lucknow, 1974.

Tarsitano, S. and M. K. Hecht. "A reconsideration of the reptilian relationships of Archaeopteryx." In: *Zoological Journal of the Linnean Society* 69, 2, 149–182, London, 1980.

Tasnádi-Kubacska, A.: *Bevor der Mensch kam.* Leipzig, Jena, Berlin, 1968.

Thenius, E.: *Versteinerte Urkunden.* Berlin, Heidelberg, New York, 1981.

Vogt, C.: "Reptilien und Vögel aus alter und neuer Zeit." In: *Illustrierte Deutsche Monatshefte* XLV., 265–266 (Berlin?), 1878.

Walton, J.: *On the Morphology of Zosterophyllum and some other early Devonian Plants. Phytomorphology* 14, 1, 155–160, India, 1964.

Wellnhofer, P.: "Das fünfte Skelettexemplar von Archaeopteryx." In: *Palaeontographica*, A 147. Stuttgart, 1974.

Wellnhofer, P.: "Das neue Eichstätter Archaeopteryx-Exemplar." In: *Natur und Museum*, 106. Frankfurt (Main), 1976.

White, M. E.: *Reproductive Structures of the Glossopteridales in the Plant Fossil Collection of the Australian Museum. Records of the Australian Museum* 31, 12, 473–505. Sydney, 1978.

Wieland, G. R.: *Fossil Cycads, with special Reference to Raumeria reichenbachiana Goeppert sp. of the Zwinger of Dresden. Palaeontographica* B 79, 85–130. Stuttgart, 1934.

Zagora, K.: "Über Tentaculites lebiensis n. sp." In *Geologie*, 21, Berlin, 1972.

Zimmermann, W.: *Evolution—Die Geschichte ihrer Probleme und Erkenntnisse.* Munich, 1953.

Zimmermann, W.: *Die Phylogenie der Pflanzen.* Stuttgart, 1959.

Zimmermann, W.: *Die Telomtherie.* Stuttgart, 1965.

Sources of Illustrations

Archive of Palaeontological Museum in the Museum of Natural Science Berlin: 48, 62, 67 below, 68, 71, 77–80, 114, 116, 125, 126, 129, top, 138–140, 165, 166, 168–172, 174–176, 180, 189, 192, 198.

Barthel, M.: 133 below.

Barthel, M. and Helms, J.: 13, 15–17, 81–83.

Bildstelle Universität Halle: 192 top.

The illustrated fossils predominantly are in the possession of the Museum of Natural Science of the Humboldt University Berlin (German Democratic Republic). Some fossils are kept in other museums: State Museum of Mineralogy and Geology Dresden: 213 below, 214, 215 top. Hunterian Museum Glasgow: 199 top. Joanneum Graz. Geiseltalmuseum of the Martin Luther University Halle: 192 top. Natural History Museum Vienna: 155 top.

Daber, R.: 21–28, 101, 102 middle right, 103, 104, 105 right, left, 106–113, 115, 127, 128, 129 below, 130–137, 185–188, 190, 191, 193–197, 199, 200, 210–215.

Helms, J.: 14, 18–20, 41–47, 57–61, 64–66, 67 top, 69, 70, 72, 84, 149–156, 171 top, 173, 178.

From: Kidston and Lang (1917): 103 left, 105 below.

Wedekind, U.-K.: 167.

Index